A History of St Kitts

A History of St Kitts

The Sweet Trade

Vincent K. Hubbard

Macmillan Education
Between Towns Road, Oxford OX4 3PP
A division of Macmillan Publishers Limited
Companies and representatives throughout the world

www.macmillan-caribbean.com

ISBN 0 333 74760 7

Text © Vincent K. Hubbard 2002
Design and illustration © Macmillan Publishers Limited 2002

First published 2002

All rights reserved; no part of this publication may be reproduced, stored in a retrival system, transmitted in any form or by any means, electronic, mechanical, photocopying, recording, or otherwise, without the prior written permission of the publishers.

Typeset by EXPO Holdings, Malaysia
Illustrated by Tek Art
Cover design by AC Design
Cover photograph courtesy of Museo del Prado, Madrid

Author's acknowledgements
Victoria O' Flaherty, St Kitts Archives; Jacqueline Armony, St Kitts Heritage Society, Bienecke Collection, Hamilton College, Clinton, New York; Dr Robert Paquette, History Department, Hamilton College, Dr Ralph Stenstrom, April Caprak, Hamilton College, Keithley Woolward, Conrad Smithen, Jérôme de Baecque, Images 4, Neuilly S/S, France

The author and publishers would like to thank the following for permission to reproduce their photographs:
9 Pam Berry, Golden Rock Hotel, Nevis; 11,12,13,14,15 Courtesy of St Kitts Archives.

Printed in Malaysia

2006 2005 2004 2003 2002
10 9 8 7 6 5 4 3 2 1

Contents

List of illustrations		vi
Acknowledgements		viii
Foreword		ix
1	Natural History	1
2	Indians	10
3	European Settlement	13
4	The Spanish Attack	19
5	The Coming of 'King Sugar'	24
6	The Birth of the French Caribbean Empire	32
7	The Birth of the British Caribbean Empire	38
8	Imperial Conflicts	41
9	Pirates and Privateers	64
10	The Eighteenth Century – the Best of Times and the Worst of Times	74
11	The Nineteenth Century – the Decline Sets In	109
12	The Twentieth Century	128
Notes		161
Bibliography		168
Index		173

List of Illustrations

1. 'The recapture of St Christopher' by Felix Castello. Painting shows Spanish Admiral Don Fadrique de Toledo directing his troops in the 1629 attack upon the French fort located where Fort Thomas Hotel and Ocean Terrace are presently. Courtesy of Museo del Prado, Madrid.
2. Governor de Poincy's Chateau La Fontaine. Built in 1649, it collapsed in the 1690 earthquake and was never rebuilt.
3. French map of St Kitts c. 1650 showing the French and English quarters and the silver mine.
4. The battle of Frigate Bay, 26 January 1782 with Nevis in the background. In the foreground a man pursues a horse terrified by the thunder of the cannon.
5. The Moravian church in Basseterre, c. 1795 from a German print of the time.
6. A receipt for 20 hogsheads of sugar shipped from St Kitts to London on the vessel *Britannia* 3 June 1809. The freight charge was 6 shillings per hundredweight.
7. Brimstone Hill 1812.
8. Basseterre c.1830.
9. The American fleet at anchor in Basseterre 1901. During the construction of the Panama Canal (1903–1914) the United States considered purchasing St Kitts and Nevis for use as a coaling station for its war fleet protecting the canal. Courtesy of Pam Berry, Golden Rock Hotel, Nevis.
10. An American Vought Kingfisher aircraft of the same squadron from St Thomas as the one which crashed in St Kitts in 1944.
11. Robert Llewellyn Bradshaw, first popularly elected leader of St Kitts and Nevis. He set in motion many improvements in living standards, education and local services which have made the life of the average person far better than it had ever been before. Courtesy of the St Kitts Archives.
12. Dr Kennedy A. Simmonds first elected Prime Minister after independence and leader of the People's Action Movement. Following the loss of his seat in the last election he has resigned as head of PAM.

13 C. A. Paul Southwell, successor of R. A. Bradshaw. In poor health when he took over the leadership of the nation, he died a year later while still in office. Courtesy of the St Kitts Archives.
14 The Hon. Lee Moore, QC, followed C. A. Paul Southwell as Prime Minister and Leader of the Labour Party. He lost to Dr Simmonds in the following election. He has since died. Here he is shown greeting the Ambassador of the People's Republic of China. Courtesy of the St Kitts Archives.
15 Dr Denzil Douglas current Prime Minister and Leader of the Labour Party. Courtesy of the St Kitts Archives.
16 Women washing clothes at Old Road c. 1890.

Acknowledgements

Any errors in this book are mine alone. I especially wish to thank Victoria O'Flaherty of the St Kitts Archives for her direction and assistance to records which I, and others, believed incorrectly had been destroyed in the 1982 court house fire. They were not lost for the most part, and she is actively copying those fragile ones which had been moved before the fire and working to preserve those that were damaged. She is doing an excellent job and I hope the government continues to support her efforts.

Jacqueline Armony at the St Kitts Heritage Society could not have been more helpful both in referring me to material in their archives and her personal observations and directions. It is people like Jackie who are working hard to bring the history of St Kitts to the public and the Heritage Society deserves full support from anyone the least bit interested in the history of the island.

The Bienecke Collection at Hamilton College in Clinton, New York, has what is undoubtedly the best collection of Lesser Antilles materials in the western hemisphere under one roof – perhaps in the world. Walter Bienecke collected them through his lifetime and generously donated them to the college and as the collection becomes better known, he deserves a vote of thanks for his generosity from all of us here who have used and will use it in the future. Dr Robert Paquette of the History Department at Hamilton College was instrumental in obtaining the collection and also deserves thanks.

Dr Ralph Stenstrom and April Caprak in the Hamilton Library cannot be thanked enough for their assistance in making the collection available to me and their generosity in allowing me to copy some materials for use in this book and for the St Kitts Heritage Society's Archives. Without their help this book could not have been written.

Keithley Woolward of Nevis, a student at Hamilton, assisted by sending me specific items from the library which were used in the book.

Lacking the support of Conrad Smithen of Nevis in helping me with the computer I would have had at least one mental breakdown when I suffered two crashes in the process of writing this book. His competence and calmness in the face of adversity were invaluable.

Last but not least, to Jérôme de Baecque of Images 4 in Neuilly S/S, France for allowing me to use the excellent photographs of St Kitts he took for use in his book *St Kitts – The Mother Colony*.

Foreword

I decided to call this book 'The Sweet Trade' because of the fact that the first mention of sugar being grown in the Caribbean was found in French records of St Kitts in 1643. More than anything else it dominated St Kitts to the present day and was responsible for the development, good and bad, of the island. Its influence caused both pain and profit and the horrors of slavery which, although long departed, linger on.

The sweet trade was what pirates in the seventeenth and eighteenth centuries called their avocation. Although legal, the sugar business caused much more difficulty and disruption in St Kitts than piracy ever did.

In writing this book I have become more and more impressed with the resilience of the people of the Leeward Islands in general and St Kitts in particular. From the arrival of Europeans in 1623 up to and including today, the population has had to endure every few years calamity after calamity resulting from wars, epidemics, earthquakes, hurricanes and the vagaries of the world economy. Yet in the face of these adversities they have always recovered and persevered to rebuild and repair and continue on with life, most often with little or no help from the outside world.

The History of the West Indies presents little more than a melancholy series of calamities and crimes.
Captain Thomas Southey, *Chronological History of the West Indies*, Vol. III, p. 616, London, 1827.

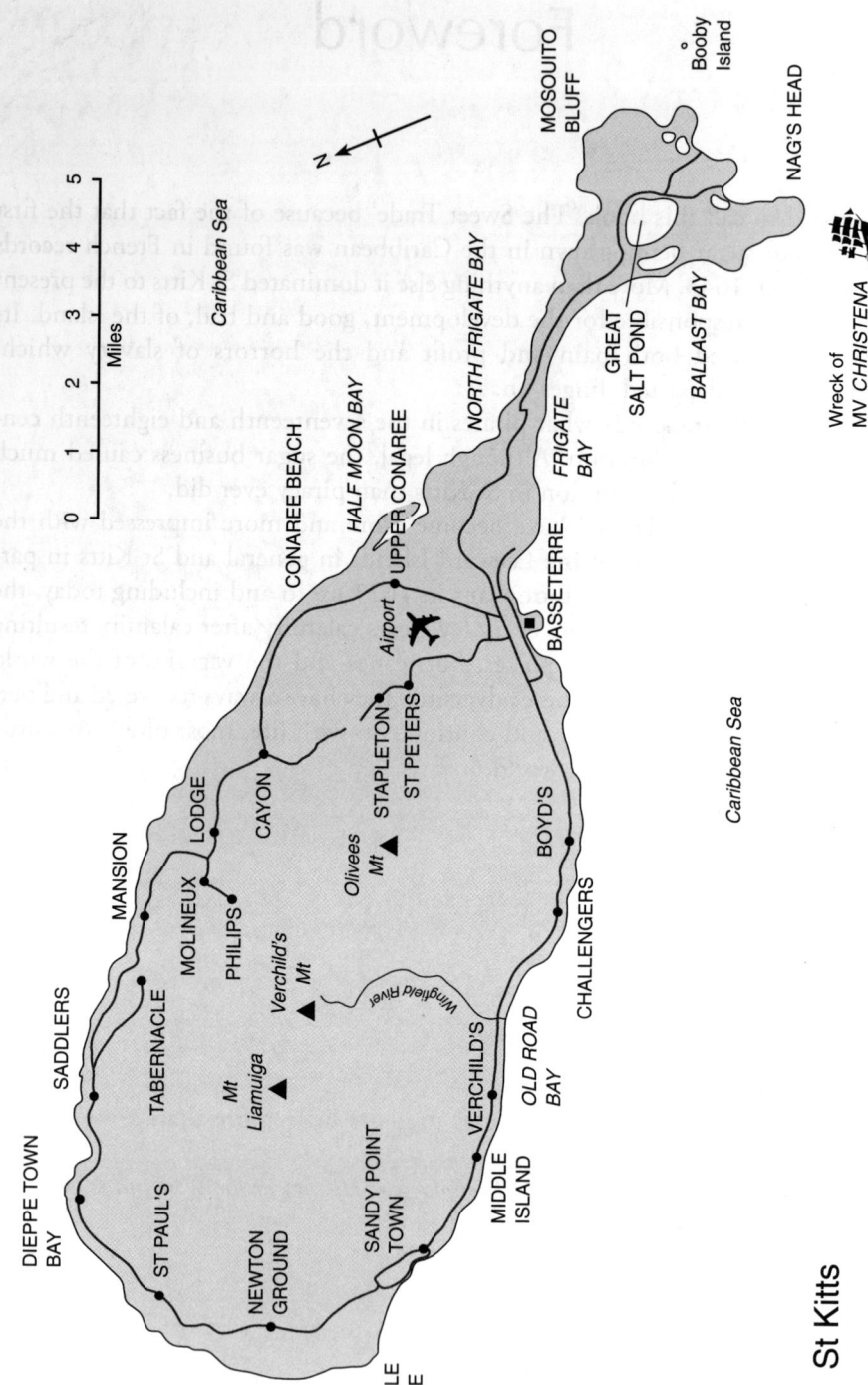

1
Natural History

In the seventeenth century an English visitor described St Christopher (vulgarly called St Kitts, according to another writer of that era), as follows:

This island is a place exceeding delightful, and of a most delectable Prospect to the Eye of the beholder.[1]

Not all aspects were as agreeable, however. The writer continued, 'Between the Mountains are dreadful Rocks, horrid Precipices, thick Woods and Hot, Sulphurous Springs at the foot of 'em'.[2]

The geological character of St Kitts developed as it did because of its volcanic origin. During the last ice age, the sea level was as much as 300 feet lower than today and the individual islands of St Kitts, Nevis, St Eustatius and Saba were one large island and looked considerably different from today. Some volcanic peaks have emerged and others eroded away. The Caribbean and Atlantic tectonic plates meet in an extended crescent beginning with Cuba in the north and sweep southeast down the islands to Trinidad and the South American mainland. That this activity continues to the present is witnessed by the ongoing volcanic eruptions on nearby Montserrat.

The volcanic nature of the soil gave it great richness, and when first Indians and then Europeans arrived their plants and trees thrived and to a certain extent overwhelmed the native growth. The plant life which had evolved here prior to their arrival was more an extension of South American flora north than that extending south from Florida and North America, but the two had intermixed to some degree. It was estimated informally by some botanists and geologists that as much as 80 per cent of existing plant life in St Kitts was originally brought from elsewhere. This may be an overestimate, but it indicates how much outside plant life has influenced the island.

Sugar cane apparently grew wild here and was utilized by the Indians, who used it to make an alcoholic drink called cane wine,[3] but other varieties were later imported by Europeans and planted for higher yields. Coconut palms were not native to the islands and were imported from India. Pineapple, guava, tannia, plantain and golden apple were growing here, but the Indians brought in cassava, or manioc, from South America and used it to make flour and cakes. It is still used for that purpose in the islands as wheat will not grow here and if it cannot be imported, as was the case during the two world wars in the last century, cassava may be substituted for it. The fluid in cassava must first be removed as it is poisonous. The root is squeezed dry and then ground to make flour and is baked as wheat flour would be.

Limes and oranges originally from Spain, mangoes from India, breadfruit from Tahiti, okra and pigeon peas from Africa were all brought in, as well as white potatoes, peas, tomatoes, beans, vanilla and Indian maize from elsewhere in the western hemisphere. Bananas came from the Canary Islands.

Nearly all ornamental trees and flowers were also imported. The flamboyant tree came from Madagascar, yellow allamanda (yellowbell) from Brazil, and hibiscus from the South Pacific.

Animal life differed as well and there were strange creatures present in St Kitts and surrounding islands which have since become locally extinct, but some survive elsewhere. A visit to St Kitts by a French naturalist and historian named Cesar Rochefort in 1649 has left us with detailed descriptions of unusual animals which he found here then.[4] Plantation agriculture had not fully taken hold that early, thus there remained large areas of the island which were uncleared and a refuge for indigenous animal life. Accounts from the eighteenth century declare that many of the 'curiosities' found here a century before had been 'eliminated by the industry of the inhabitants',[5] and that visitors should not assume they had never existed at all.

Chief among these oddities were what Rochefort called 'Land Pike' or what locals called 'squeakinge lisards'. He describes them as follows:

> ... creatures which have the perfect figure, skin, and head of the Fish we call a Pike ... but instead of Finns they have four feet which are so weak that they can onely crawl along the ground, and wind their bodies as Snakes ... The largest are not above fifteen inches in length, and proportionally big: their skin is cover'd with little scales which shine extremely, and are of a silver-grey colour ... In the night-time they make a hideous noise from under the rocks, and the bottom of hollow places where they are lodg'd: It is more sharp and grating to the ear than that of Frogs and Toads ... they are seldom seen but a little before night, and when any of them are met in the day time, their motion ... is apt to frighten the unwary beholder.[6]

Sir Henry Colt, visiting St Kitts and Nevis in 1631, complained that 'squeakinge lisards' annoyed him greatly when he was trying to sleep. They are now extinct.

Giant iguanas five feet long and one foot thick were common. Unfortunately for themselves, they were not afraid of humans and were thus easily killed by running a sharp stick through a nostril into the brain as the

Indians did, or captured by encircling their necks in a rope noose hung from the end of a pole. Europeans preferred the latter method as the creatures were difficult to kill with a gun and usually required at least three shots to dispatch them.

With typical French interest in cuisine, the visitor related that the meat of the giant iguana was overlaid with fat and many preferred its delicate flavour plain but others enjoyed it with spices or a piquant sauce. He cautioned that eating it too often tended to 'dry-out the body, and abates somewhat the good constitution thereof'.[7] Their eggs, he continued, were all yolk and used in the same way as hens' eggs. Giant iguanas are now extinct in all the Leeward Islands, but normal ones survive in some other islands.

Fallow deer, agouti and hutia were present as well. Hutia were called 'rats' by the earliest European settlers but they looked more like gerbils or hamsters, and were very tasty. Agouti were as well, but looked much more like rats. Both are extinct in St Kitts today but survive elsewhere on larger islands. A few fallow deer may still live on the southeast peninsula, but it is questionable. Some were reported seen a few years ago by naturalists.

Earthquakes and Hurricanes

As noted earlier, the Leeward and Windward Islands lie along a tectonic plate intersection and as a result volcanic activity is frequent. Earthquakes, usually of a minor nature, are commonplace. Larger ones seem to occur at intervals of about 150 years and they have been very destructive.

At 5 p.m. on 6 April 1690, a mighty earthquake devastated St Kitts and Nevis. Modern geologists have placed the epicentre of the quake in Nevis, where the original capital of Jamestown is reputed to have sunk beneath the sea. An anonymous tract published in London that year declared that all brick and stone buildings in both islands '... collapsed of a sudden from top to bottom in perfect ruines'.[8] A tidal wave came up on land as high as a third of a mile, followed by two smaller ones brought on days later by aftershocks.

Fortunately at that time many buildings were wooden and withstood the shaking, but at that time St Kitts (and perhaps the entire Caribbean) lost its most notable structure, the palace of the French Governor Philippe de Lonvilliers de Poincy which he called 'La Fontaine'. Some antique prints show what the building looked like; three storeys of brick and stone with turrets and formal gardens. A visitor in 1687 described it as follows:

> Here is also a stately Castle, being the residence of the Governour, most pleasantly seated, at the foot of a high mountain, not far from the Sea,

having spacious Courts, delightful Walks, and Gardens, and enjoyeth a curious prospect.[9]

It was never rebuilt as the seat of the French Caribbean Empire had moved from St Kitts to Martinique in 1669, and a modern house called Fountain Estate is today built upon the same spot. Few people are aware of its location and only the cellars which are reputed to have extended up to a mile underground and the walls of its garden terraces remain. De Poincy's name continues in botanical history, however. The royal poinciana (also called the flame or flamboyant tree) was named for him.

In 1843 another earthquake struck with near equal intensity and similar results. Masonry buildings were so heavily damaged that many of those not destroyed were badly damaged and pulled down and rebuilt. The number of casualties in these events are unrecorded but it is likely many perished.

Hurricanes appear to run in lengthy natural cycles. Named after the Carib Indian God Hunrakan, they were supposed to come when the god grew angry. As early as Columbus's time, European navigators were made aware of them by Indians and even so they were unprepared for the accompanying fierce winds and mountainous seas. Hundreds of ships have been lost in St Christopher in hurricanes and property damage on land has amounted to millions of dollars since European settlement.

It would appear that we may be heading today into a new hurricane cycle. Counting the total number which have hit St Kitts is difficult because of gaps in the records, but beginning in 1623, at least 17 hurricanes struck St Kitts during the seventeenth century. In the eighteenth century there were 26, in the nineteenth, seven, and the twentieth, as of 1999, seven. Of those in the century just gone by, five have come since 1989. The greatest frequency and intensity of storms occurred between 1770 and 1795.[10]

From books and records follow some descriptions of the most devastating of these storms to affect St Kitts:

On 29 September 1623, a hurricane destroyed the first tobacco crop planted in St Kitts by the English settlers who had arrived only in January of that year, and caused great hardship.

Three hurricanes struck in 1642. During the second one, a very powerful storm which blew for 24 hours, merchant ships loaded with tobacco from both St Kitts and Nevis were blown ashore between Basseterre and Old Road in St Kitts. They broke up and the tobacco poisoned the water, killing thousands of fish. These vessels were almost all of a convoy of 23 ships under the control of the famous Dutch Admiral Michiel de Ruyter, riding off Basseterre ready to sail to Europe. All but one vessel, including de Ruyter's flagship, were driven ashore and wrecked. 'Along the coast of Basseterre, one did see nothing but the dead bodies the tempest had thrown on the sand ...'.[11] The one vessel which escaped destruction was commanded by a Captain Volery, who cut his anchor cables and ran helpless before the storm for a distance of 600 miles to the south of St Kitts.

In 1666, during the second Anglo-Dutch War, the French had captured St Kitts and all the Leewards except Nevis. The English were seeking to reinforce their garrison in Nevis in order to protect it and ultimately to retake St Kitts. The Governor of the West Indies, located in Barbados, Francis, Lord Willoughby, organized a fleet of 17 men of war, 1500 militiamen and 2000 stand of muskets and set out from there for Nevis. After engaging a French fleet near Guadeloupe in which he sank or captured many of the enemy, on 15 August a powerful hurricane struck his fleet and every ship was lost. Willoughby and 2000 men were drowned and the wreckage of his vessels and bodies of his men were strewn across the beaches of the Leeward Islands. It was one of the worst maritime disasters in history.

HMS *Coventry*, which had blown ashore in the Islands of the Saintes, would be repaired, renamed and used the following year in St Kitts against the English. The French considered this catastrophe as an act of God which saved St Kitts from the English. 'A good hurricane which ruined the Milord and all his fleet ...'.[12] In Guadeloupe, the destruction of Willoughby's fleet is celebrated as a national holiday on 15 August to this day.

On 1 September 1667, the French Governor of St Kitts, Saint-Laurent, wrote in a letter to Colbert, Minister of Defence of France:

> There has blown here the most violent hurricane ever known; and I hold myself obliged to inform you that this island is in the most deplorable state that can be imagined, and that the inhabitants could not have suffered a greater loss or been more unfortunate, except they had been taken by the English [the war was still on and the French held the English part of St Kitts]. There is not a house or sugar-work standing, and they cannot hope to make any sugar for 15 months to come. As for the manioc [cassava] which is the bread of the country, there is not one root left, and is more than a year in growing. I cannot describe to you, Sir, the misery of this poor island, without wounding my heart. It is as a place over which a fire has passed.[13]

In 1681 three hurricanes struck within 37 days. Christopher Jeaffreson, owner of Wingfield Manor, described the first on 6 September as having blown down his house, sugar works and a stone wall, and caused the sheltered hut in which he had taken refuge 'to rock like a cradle'.[14] On 14 October the third hurricane took the roof off of the new house Jeaffreson had constructed after the first hurricane. It was noted by another writer that casks of rum from a vessel cast onto the shore and broken up in the 6 September storm were blown up to half a mile inland and gratefully salvaged by the surviving populace.

A fierce hurricane struck St Kitts and Nevis on 2 September 1707. Among the ships lost was HMS *Child's Play*, a 24-gun frigate which was broken to pieces off Palmetto Point. This English man of war was the pay ship for British forces in the West Indies during Queen Anne's War and some of the bullion it carried has never been recovered, but her cannon and those of HMS *Winchester*, lost at Sandy Point at the same time, were later salvaged.[15]

The Reverend Robert Robertson of Nevis described this miraculous escape on a ship driven aground in St Kitts during a storm on 30 June 1733:

> At Sandy-point in the same Island, a ship from Philadelphia, Captain Wright, was drove upon the rocks off Bel-tache, where she was beat to Pieces, and all the crew lost, except one man, and a Boy of about Ten Years old, the manner of whose Escape is thus related to me. You see, said the Man to him, they are all drowned; can you swim? No, answered the Boy. Then you must drown too, said the man; and with that flung himself from the Wreck into the Sea. The boy leaped after him, and a Dog which the Boy used to feed and play with, instantly follow'd. The Dog made up first to the Man, but finding his Mistake, fell a whining dolefully, when looking about, he saw the Boy and made up to him. The Boy too eagerly laid hold on the Dog, and hung so heavy, that the Dog with much ado got clear of him, but so as to swim close by, and the Boy, grown wiser, was content to lay his hand now and then on the Dog's Head or Neck, by which means he got safe to Land. The man, being a good Swimmer, and robust, sav'd himself.[16]

1772 was a very active year with three hurricanes. On 31 August the worst one struck and according to an English writer, 'Almost every house, sugar-mill, tree and plant at Basse Terre, Sandy Point and Old Road was blown down or very much damaged ... several persons were killed, and a great number dangerously wounded. The damage was estimated at 500,000 pounds sterling'.[17]

The last quarter of the eighteenth century was the worst season for hurricanes ever recorded in the islands. It included the most destructive one recorded in human history; the Great Hurricane of 10–15 October 1780.[18]

Beginning in Barbados, where 6000 perished and virtually all trees and buildings were flattened, it moved northwest to St Lucia where a squadron of British warships was totally lost and 6000 people were killed on land. Between there and Martinique, a French troop-carrying fleet was hit with a loss of 40 ships and 4000 men. In Martinique, the city of St Pierre was completely destroyed and 9000 died. At St Kitts approximately 100 ships were anchored in the roadstead at sundown. The hurricane struck that night. By morning, no vessels were visible except for those wrecked on shore and thousands were killed in the ships and on land. In Dutch St Eustatius, seven miles north of St Kitts, 5000 were estimated killed including ships lost with their crews.

The storm roared northward up the islands to Puerto Rico and then veered off into the Atlantic, where several British men of war were lost on the way to England from America. The total number of deaths in the Caribbean was estimated to be around 22,000. Of stumps of trees left standing in the islands directly hit, no bark remained. Such a thing has never happened before or since. The sustained wind speed of that killer hurricane is estimated to have exceeded 200 miles per hour.

In the 1890s the United States Meteorological Bureau, with the agreement of the St Kitts government, established a monitoring station on the island which enabled wind speeds to be measured. The equipment was first put to use when the hurricane of 7 August 1899 passed through with a sustained wind speed of 120 miles per hour. Four people were killed in St Kitts but 27 died in Nevis. A telegraph warning alerted St Kitts but it did not extend to Nevis, which as a result received no warning.[19]

In 1924 a moderate hurricane hit and in 1928 a more serious storm did considerable damage. For the next 61 years none struck St Kitts. This is the longest period without hurricanes in the island's history. Hurricane Hugo broke the hiatus in 1989. Since then hurricanes Luis and Marilyn hit in 1995, Bertha in 1996, Georges in 1998 and José and Lenny in 1999.

From 17 to 19 November 1999, the freak hurricane Lenny which started in the western Caribbean moved east, travelling in a direction completely opposite from the normal. Damage from wind and rain was minimal, but the unusually high sea surge caused by Lenny's origin in the Caribbean Sea did considerable damage to low lying shore areas in both St Kitts and Nevis.

Of the islands in the immediate area, St Kitts has suffered from devastating floods and washouts more than any other. Sometimes extremely heavy rains occur high in the mountains and there will be little or no evidence of them lower down. The result is that the ghauts (ravines) will suddenly fill and walls of water sweep downwards to lower levels. College Street in Basseterre, today lined with concrete, is one of the main channels and has been the scene of several disasters.

On 11 January 1880, 231 were killed after a night of terrific rains in the mountains when a wall of water swept down College Street into Basseterre at night. Fifteen bodies from the disaster were washed ashore on St Eustatius seven miles away. A monument to the dead stands today in Springfield Cemetery on Cayon Street on the northern end of town. Accounts tell of so much water pouring down that wooden houses were swept out to sea with the occupants still inside. Many were rescued from their homes at sea by men in boats. Nearby graveyards were washed out and numerous bodies unearthed.

In order to contain such events in the future, one Captain Alexander of the Royal Engineers made a proposal in the 1890s to widen the street and line it with masonry walls to channel flood water into the sea. His plans were carried out in 1895 at a cost of £7400, and since then the effects of these events have been considerably moderated.

The first such recorded occurrence took place in the seventeenth century for which no records survive. A second happened on 11 April 1792. That calamity was described by a Moravian missionary named G. C. Schneller, who wrote that after several days of intermittent rainfall, a heavy storm hit and College Street flooded up to the new wall constructed near the Moravian church. By 8 p.m., the water had gone over the top of it and he heard the screams and cries of people being swept past the church in the flood but because of the force of the water he was unable to save any of them. He noted the slave quarters of a plantation above Basseterre had been suddenly washed out by a wall of water and the people were carried away by the torrent. By midnight 50 feet of the wall surrounding the burial ground of the church had collapsed and bodies were washed out and swept away.

The following day he learnt that many persons, both at Basseterre and Old Road, were taken by the flood into the sea, some still inside their houses. That day a service was held praying for the dead and giving thanks that the survivors and the church building had been spared. Bodies from this disaster were again washed ashore on St Eustatius. Another such flood occurred in 1813, which was not nearly as severe as the one in 1792.

All possible measures have been taken to prevent a recurrence, but the island remains ever alert to the danger. In December 1998, another sudden flood took place at night resulting in the death of one person and 82 vehicles being washed into central Basseterre or out to sea, many with their headlamps still burning. In the central cinema the lights went out while the film was being shown and in the darkness people felt water rushing in around their feet. Using electric torches, the patrons made their way to the exits only to find water was knee-deep in the street and flowing fast. The channelling done in 1895 held firm and certainly prevented additional casualties and damage from this storm over a century later.

Aside from sudden natural disasters, the creation of sugar plantations in the mid-seventeenth century had a profound effect on the ecology of St Kitts. Prior to that time most agriculture consisted of small farms and estates, the chief crops being tobacco, ginger and vegetables. When the vast profits from sugar production became evident the changeover came in a few short years.

Smallholdings were consolidated into larger ones and almost all arable land was cleared for cane planting.

This caused a population decline as well. The higher the altitude, the poorer the soil was and after clearing land native wildlife declined and erosion became the enemy. Sugar cane is a type of grass and does not deplete soil rapidly, as does tobacco and cotton. However, after centuries of cultivation erosion has carried off considerable topsoil and the richness of the earth has declined for that reason.

In the 1640s, neighbouring Nevis was the first of the Caribbean islands to go over fully to sugar cultivation and as a result it was for a time the richest not only of the Leewards but of any British colony in the western hemisphere. The value of its produce in the seventeenth century exceeded all the rest of the Leeward Islands combined. Nevis being steeper, erosion took a greater toll sooner and by the early eighteenth century, St Kitts had eclipsed Nevis to become the dominant and by far the most prosperous of the Leewards, although Antigua had a larger population.

2
Indians

Exactly when the Indians arrived in these islands is not known, but it could have been as early as 3000 years ago. The first group were pre-ceramic and called Siboney. Their origins are unknown. Based on evidence of pottery shards, it is almost certain that later arrivals worked their way up from the Orinoco River in Venezuela and their origins in South America could be as far west as Peru. However, some archaeologists believe that the Siboney may have originated in Mexico. Without pottery to provide evidence, it is possible only to speculate on that point.[1]

Arawaks and Caribs

There has been and continues to be disagreement by experts about these two supposedly different tribes or cultures. Some have gone so far as to say that women spoke Arawak and men Carib. Some would contend that even today the two sexes speak separate tongues. Then as now, that hypothesis is doubtful, although some early writers gave specific examples of different words used by males and females for the same objects.[2] If the wrong word was used by a male or female, it was reported that it was the occasion for great mirth. The explanation for the different languages was that the Caribs had attacked and killed all the Arawak males and taken their women as slaves and although the languages were similar, the Arawak women had retained some words in their original tongue.

Traditional theory holds that the peaceful Arawaks, or Tianos as they are called in Puerto Rico and the Dominican Republic, came first and were followed by the warlike Caribs. By the time of the Spanish conquest of the Caribbean the Caribs had worked their way up to and perhaps slightly northward of St Kitts.

From archaeological evidence it would seem that the high point of Indian culture in terms of population was between 500 and 600 AD. By the time Europeans settled in the Leewards, Indian numbers had drastically declined. At the time of the arrival of Columbus it was estimated by the Spanish priest

Bartolomé de las Casas that the Indian population of the Caribbean numbered in the millions. He was a contemporary of Columbus who became a passionate advocate of the Indians and castigated the Spanish for their brutal treatment of them and the resulting population decline. He declared that within half a century after Spanish arrival the Indian population had been reduced by 90 per cent. He was quietly sent back home to Spain and until recent archaeological work lent credence to his story, he was largely ignored. The Indians had little or no resistance to European diseases which was the dominant reason for their population decline, but enslavement and sometimes outright murder contributed as well.

Whatever the cause, by the time the English arrived in St Kitts in 1623 the only sizeable permanent Indian settlement in the Leewards was there. We do not know their total number but the best estimate would be under 1000. The neighbouring islands contained small numbers although there is clear evidence there were many more present at an earlier time. It would appear the Indians in St Kitts were Caribs as that is what they called themselves.

An early English historian[3] declared that the Indians of St Kitts would go naked and added, somewhat disdainfully, that when the French settlers of St Kitts, who arrived in 1625, ventured among them, they too would remove their clothing. This and other conduct of the French made them the most favoured of the Europeans with the Indians. The Dutch were considered acceptable, but the English and Spanish in that order were disliked and distrusted.

A French priest declared that the Caribs painted their bodies with 'rocou' juice or 'arnotto' to guard against insect bites, '… which gave them the appearance of a boiled lobster'. He continued to say that 'They spent the greater part of their lives sleeping and smoking'.[4]

According to another writer the Indians would sometimes make whistles out of the bones of their slain enemies and wear them on cords around their necks. They would pierce their lips and noses with small fish bones or rings and the nobles would sometimes wear copper jewellery. A Mr Brigs, an Englishman living in St Kitts around 1700, declared that he had explored the Spanish territory of Florida and the 'Apalachites' there spoke the same language as did the Indians of St Kitts.[5] The Indians of St Kitts believed that Brimstone Hill was the top of Mt Misery (renamed Mount Liamuiga) which had blown off in an ancient volcanic eruption – an interesting but incorrect theory, as the rock composition of the two is entirely different.

The Caribs were termed cannibals by the Europeans and it was probably true to a certain extent. During wars there is good evidence that parts of the enemies' bodies were eaten, the theory being that consuming these parts would impart the courage of the vanquished to the victors. There is no mention of cannibalism in early accounts of the Indians of St Kitts, however. They were described by European settlers as being well proportioned people, the women attractive and the men well built with both sexes going about naked or nearly so. Some men had '… big bellies, as evidence of the richness of the land'.[6]

The Caribs were fierce fighters and were feared by Europeans in the Leewards because of their sudden and unpredictable attacks against coastal European settlements and sometimes vessels. They would paddle their dugout war canoes from Dominica almost 200 miles distant for these purposes. Their weapon was the bow and arrow. The bows were about six feet in length and the arrows three-and-a half feet. It was said that a skilled Carib archer could shoot ten arrows in the time it took for a European to fire a single musket ball.[7]

In 1656 a small French merchant ship on its way to St Kitts was tacking around the tiny uninhabited island of Redonda when several large dugout canoes carrying between 30 and 40 warriors armed only with bows and arrows appeared from behind the island making for the ship at high speed. The French sailors packed a deck gun to the muzzle with two cannon balls, a length of chain and a bucket of metal scraps. When one canoe came within close range and arrows began to fly, the gun was fired and the charge hit the canoe dead centre, breaking it in two and killing most of the warriors. The sailors were amazed to see the surviving Caribs load and shoot arrows at their ship while swimming in the sea. Such was their excellence as fighters and swimmers.

King Philip II of Spain became concerned by Bartolomé de las Casas's accounts of cruelty to the indigenous population and in the sixteenth century forbade Spanish enslavement of the Arawaks. However, he allowed enslavement of the Caribs as he believed they were cannibals. It is more than likely numbers of Arawak Indians were reclassified as Caribs overnight after the king's proclamation was received in the Caribbean.

Classifying the Caribs as cannibals sometimes went to absurd lengths. A French priest in the seventeenth century claimed that a Carib chief had assured him that of the Europeans, Frenchmen tasted the best. The Spanish were oily and the English were stringy and tough. Evidently the chief had not consumed any Dutchmen as he had no comment as to their flavour.

3
European Settlement

Christopher Columbus sailed past St Kitts on his second voyage to the New World on 13 November 1493. Contrary to popular belief he named the island San Jorge, not St Christopher. Nevis was named San Martín by him at the same time. For some reason both names were later changed by Spanish sailors to what they are today and by the early sixteenth century the names San Cristóbal and Nieves were given for the islands on Spanish maps.

A writer in the seventeenth century declared that the island appeared to Colombus like St Christopher carrying the Christ Child on his back and that was the derivation of the name. Others declared Columbus found the island so pleasing in appearance that he named it after himself, but neither was correct.

The earliest European visitor after Columbus who left a record (yet discovered) of a visit to St Christopher was Sir Francis Drake in 1585, with 25 ships and 2300 men. In his journal he wrote:

> ... we went to another island westward of it [Dominica] called Saint Christophers Island, wherein wee spent some dayes at Christmas, to refresh our sicke people, and to cleanse and ayre our ships. In which Island were not any people at all that we could heare of.[1]

Indians were certainly present in St Kitts at the time but wisely kept out of sight of the foreign visitors.

English sailors began using the name St Kitts shortly after settlement of the island. Kit was a popular nickname for Christopher and it was faster to write and speak, but in the earliest days the official name was St Christopher. Today the constitution allows the use of either name interchangeably. The Carib Indians called the island Liamuiga, which meant 'fertile land'.

Spain claimed all of the Americas (except for Brazil, owned by Portugal) and the Caribbean as its own by Papal Decree until 1671. Other nations did not recognize the authority of the Pope to make such a proclamation and by the sixteenth century Holland, France and England were making regular incursions into the Caribbean for trade and piracy, although they settled no territory. Spain was the superpower of that time and all countries considered the Caribbean to be a 'Spanish Lake' and ventured into it at their peril, as Spain reserved all trade in the region for itself and its ships.

Spanish sailors explored St Kitts and neighbouring islands early on and they decided they were useless for settlement as no gold could be found. Spanish fleets coming to the new world would steer for Guadeloupe because it had the tallest mountains of any island and could be seen first. They would then divide the fleets up, with the 'New Spain' fleet (Flota Nueva España) going to Vera Cruz in Mexico and the Terra Firma fleet heading for Cartagena and Panama. Individual ships would sometimes travel alone or in smaller fleets to other destinations, but all would come into the Caribbean in the vicinity of the Leewards.

Spanish ships mounted murderous attacks into the Leewards against Indians from Puerto Rico in retaliation for Carib Indian raids from the islands. Records show that on St Croix in the Virgin Islands the Spanish rounded up and executed all the Indians in the mid-sixteenth century. It is quite possible the Spanish came as far south as St Kitts on those incursions, but no records have yet been discovered to verify it.

By the early seventeenth century, following the defeat of the four Armadas Spain sent against England from 1588 to 1604, it was perceived by her rivals that the Spanish Empire was overextended and not the invincible power it had been considered earlier. The poorer European nations wanted a piece of the action in the western hemisphere for themselves. The lure of Spanish treasure first attracted Dutch freebooters, French buccaneers, and finally English pirates. Before long their governments decided to get in on the act themselves. The Caribbean became more and more tempting to those nations as the best spot to harass the Spanish.

In 1620 Ralph Merifield and Thomas Warner applied for and received a Royal Patent to settle the Leeward Islands and begin a colony. King James I gave it, and the Earl of Carlisle was granted overall authority to develop the islands and enforce the interests of the Crown. For this Carlisle gave the king a white horse and £100 annually. The patent read as follows:

> Whereas Thomas Warner at the charge of Raphe Merifield haveing lately discovered towards the Continent of America fower Islands vizt St Christophers alias Merwarshope, Mevis, Barbador and Montserate inhabited by Savage people and not in the possession or government of a Christian Prince or State and haveing begune a Plantation, and Trade there. Hath been a humble Suitor to his majestie, to take the said Islands into his Royal Protection and grant Lycence to the said Raphe Merifield and his partners and Agents to Traffique to and from the said islands paying the Customs Due, and doe all such things as tends to settle a Colony and advance trade there.[2]

The name 'Merwars Hope' as noted above was given to a joint venture settlement company and came from an amalgamation of the names Merifield and

Warner. The company name was changed shortly afterwards to the Society of Adventurers, and then when the Crown took over direct administration of the islands in 1664 and the African slave trade was becoming very profitable, it merged into the Royal African Company. In 1730, the name was again changed to the Company of Merchants Trading with Africa. When the African slave trade was abolished in the British Empire in 1807, the company was dissolved.

Every European nation except Spain formed joint venture companies for settlement of new lands. The participants risked only the money they put into company shares and not their entire fortunes. Originating in England, these joint stock companies were crucial to private development of new colonies.

The name 'Barbador' in the Royal Patent caused some confusion. It almost certainly meant Barbuda, located in the same area as the other islands. The Earl of Carlisle, however, had determined that Barbados was a far more valuable island than Barbuda and determined to take control of it under the patent. One Captain Powell had beaten him to it and led a group of settlers to Barbados. Powell refused to acknowledge Carlisle's claim. As a result, Carlisle sent Captain Henry Hawley out from England to take over in the Earl's name.

Hawley was an unscrupulous tyrant who arrested Powell on a trumped-up charge of treason and had him shot. Some years later after becoming Governor of Barbados, Hawley fell down the steps of a tavern after a night of heavy drinking and broke his neck. Before his end, however, he was to pay an unexpected visit to St Kitts in 1629 with the Spanish following close behind.

Thomas Warner arrived in St Kitts 28 January 1623 with 15 settlers, arrived at terms with the local Carib Chief Tegremond, and established a colony. The names of his settlers were William Tasted, John Rhodes, Robert Binns, Mr Benefield, Sergeant Jones, Mr Ware, William Ryle, Rowland Grasscocke, Mr Bond, Mr Langley, Mr Weaver, Sergeant Aplon, and an unnamed sailor and a cook. When he reached the island he discovered three Frenchmen living there with the Indians. They were reported to have tried to persuade the Indians to kill the English intruders. It is not clear how the Frenchmen got there but very likely they were pirates, castaways from a shipwreck or were marooned by a passing vessel. It has been said by some historians that they were Protestant French Huguenot refugees who settled at Dieppe Bay in 1615, but there is no specific evidence for this conjecture.

Warner's settlers first planted tobacco as a cash crop and vegetables for food. Pigs and goats were later brought in. Their plantings would be destroyed by a hurricane in September 1623, but the continuing inflow of more settlers and supply ships prevented the failure of the colony.

Critically important was the arrival in 1624 of the ship *Hopewell*, which carried supplies and Warner's childhood friend Colonel John Jeaffreson. Jeaffreson received a grant of 1000 acres of land and the family would retain a presence in St Kitts until the mid-nineteenth century. The grant was called Wingfield Manor. It is believed that another member of that family changed the spelling of the name to Jefferson and emigrated to Virginia. That branch later produced President Thomas Jefferson.

According to Rowland Grasscocke, 'All this while we lived upon cassado bread, potatoes, plantanes, pines [pineapple], turtles, guanes [iguanas] and fish plenty: for drink we had nicknobby'.[3]

'Nicknobby' could have been a local island drink today called mauby made of tree bark and roots devised by the Indians, or possibly sarsparilla.

Within 20 years the diet had improved. A Frenchman named Maurice de St Michel wrote of St Kitts in the 1640s:

> Here, instead of bread made from wheat, we eat bread made from the cassava plant, which is very common and abundant. Instead of beef we eat lamentine [manatee] which is a sort of sea cow caught along the shore. Instead of chicken we eat lizards [iguana], from which a soup is made, and the meat of which is very delicate ... one of the principal articles of food is peas, which grow here in abundance ... the ordinary dinner of the average man consists of pea soup, cassava bread seasoned with red pepper, lemon juice and a small piece of bacon ... [4]

Another factor soon entered the settlement picture. A French brigantine of 14 guns and a crew of 40 put into St Kitts. It was commanded by Pierre Belain, Sieur d' Esnambuc, and had been heavily damaged in a three hour engagement with a 35-gun Spanish warship near the Cayman Islands. There is some disagreement among historians as to the exact year of his arrival, 1623 or 1625. Some have said he reached St Kitts the same day as Warner but it is almost certain that the correct arrival date was in 1625. What d'Esnambuc was doing in the Caribbean is not clear, but more than likely he was a privateer or pirate preying on Spanish shipping and was caught at his task by a more powerful Spanish ship and barely avoided capture.

At any rate he saw an opportunity and took it. In 1627 he and Warner divided St Kitts equally into four quarters with the English taking two in the centre part and the French two, each on opposite ends of the island. The land division was roughly equal in size.

At that early time England and France were not the bitter rivals they would later become. This unlikely joint occupation was prompted by fear of the Spanish, who were the enemy of both nations, and the Carib Indians. The 1627 agreement declared 'If the Spaniards shall at any time invade the Island he that first discovereth them shall send word of it presently to the other nation'. Another paragraph stated the same about the Indians.[5] France and more so England at that time were not rich and ranked as secondary powers in

Europe far behind Spain. At that time the population of England was only three million, but France's population was several times higher.

Relations of Europeans with the Indians were at first cordial and Warner himself took as a mistress a Carib woman who gave birth to a son. Warner acknowledged the boy who was nicknamed 'Indian' Warner – much to the disgust of his English wife and her son Philip. Both sons were to play a significant role in later Caribbean history with 'Indian' Warner becoming Governor of Dominica and dying there in an attack by the English led by his brother Philip, a colonel in the St Kitts militia and later a member of the Antigua Council. The English ambushed the Indians during supposed treaty discussions and killed as many as they could. The village in Dominica where the attack took place is today called Massacre because of this event.

As an example of how dangerous life in early St Kitts could be, in 1628 a French supply ship arrived with 200 of its 400 passengers having died and many of the remainder sick with scurvy. These helpless people were landed 'inhospitably' on the beach to fend for themselves and were attacked and devoured by land crabs. 'The crabs had come down from the mountains in such numbers that they were in high heaps over the carcasses, and did not leave the smallest morsel of flesh upon any of the bones!'[6]

In spite of a considerable amount of fraternization, Chief Tegremond became uneasy as more and more settlers, both English and French, poured into St Kitts and cleared land for farming. Confrontations occurred with increasing frequency between Europeans and Indians. Finally Tegremond came to a decision in 1626 that the Europeans would have to be eliminated or they would completely take over the island. He sent word secretly to Caribs in other islands to come to St Kitts by canoe at night and land in a designated remote area. When sufficient numbers had gathered, they would fall on the English and French and kill all of them. Warner and d'Esnambuc reputedly got word of this from an Indian woman named Barbe. Meeting secretly, they reached the decision that a joint pre-emptive strike against the Indians would be made to prevent Tegremond's plan from being executed.

One night in 1626, a party was given for the Indians at which large amounts of alcohol were served. After the intoxicated Indians had returned to their village, the Europeans attacked by night. Killing Chief Tegremond was the first objective. He slept in a royal hammock (a Carib invention) which was large and well decorated. English soldiers surrounded it and ran their rapiers through the hammock, and Tegremond was killed. However, he was not alone at the time. He had as a sleeping companion an English boy who miraculously escaped injury. According to an account written at the time, 'The little boy was one whome Capt. Warner had brought over with him, and ye King had taken a great affection to him & would have him lie in ye hammaccoe with him & he was saved by ye mercie of God, for they had forgot the boy'.[7] Tegremond's infant son would survive this attack and later would be taken to England and raised as an Englishman and never return to St Kitts.

The soldiers put all the Indians they could find in the village to the sword, amounting to about 120 persons, and together with the French on the following day drove from 2000 to 4000 Caribs (the numbers vary considerably depending on the writer) into a ravine through which a stream flowed. A bloody battle ensued and the Caribs fired arrows poisoned with manchineel at the Europeans and killed about 100 of them. A Frenchman named Fresnouvelle was slightly grazed by a poisoned arrow and died raving mad. The only antidote to poisoned arrows was salt and arrowroot administered to the wound, but this was not known to the Europeans at the time.

When the surviving Indians attempted to surrender they were systematically executed by the soldiers. An estimated 2000 were murdered and the rest escaped into the mountains. The waters of the river ran red with Indian blood for two days. The land area today carries the name Bloody Point and the stream Bloody River as a result of that tragic episode.

Sometime around 1640 all the remaining Indians except those enslaved were removed from St Kitts, Nevis and Antigua and sent to Dominica, where a handful of their descendants survive today. The only remaining evidence of the Indians' thousands of years of occupation of St Kitts are some petroglyphs carved into the rocks near Bloody River. It is an isolated spot even today and may have been sacred ground for the Caribs as it was the refuge to which they retreated when under attack. The truth will never be known.

4
The Spanish Attack

In 1628 a bold and daring Dutch privateer named Piet Heyn attacked the Spanish treasure fleet near Cuba with a fleet of 31 ships and took every vessel. He sailed the captured Spanish fleet to Holland and the influx of this vast amount of money into the Dutch economy catapulted it from a small but prosperous trading nation to a world power almost overnight and also resulted in the end of Holland as a Spanish colony.

The effect upon Spain was almost as dramatic. Upon being informed of the loss of his fleet at a grand ball on Christmas Eve, the 24-year-old King Philip IV fell to the floor babbling incoherently and foaming at the mouth. He was placed under sedation in his private apartments for four days.

With her immense empire in the western hemisphere, Europe and the Pacific, Spain was totally dependent on the treasure her galleons brought home once a year through the Caribbean to maintain her armies and navies. With the loss of that fleet Spain was bankrupted and had to turn to European bankers for loans in order to carry on.

Upon his recovery, King Philip was determined that this embarrassing event would not recur, and it never did. In 1629 he gathered a powerful fleet of 36 heavily armed galleons to carry that year's treasure back to Spain and placed it under the command of his best Admiral, Don Faderique de Toledo. De Toledo was the aristocratic son of a Viceroy of Peru and had recently defeated a large Dutch war fleet off Salvador in Brazil and recaptured it for Spain. His orders were not only to bring the gold and silver safely home but on the way to the new world to load it, drive the English and French from St Kitts and Nevis. The Spanish still claimed all the Caribbean and treated other Europeans as interlopers, sometimes none too gently.

De Toledo's armada sailed from Spain to Guadeloupe, and then turned northwards. He attacked Nevis first, approaching from the south and sailing around the west side of the island past Nevis's only fort at Pelican Point. Settled only the year before, Nevis had but one cannon in the fort and there was no guard posted. The English were taken completely by surprise.

That very morning Captain Henry Hawley, the Earl of Carlisle's representative in the West Indies, had arrived on Nevis on the vessel *Carlisle* from Barbados. Captain Hawley had finished a midday meal with Deputy Governor

William Vallett of Nevis and the two had just boarded *Carlisle* for an afternoon of drinking and talking when the boom of a cannon froze them in their tracks. They were appalled to see de Toledo's fleet rounding Pelican Point where the single cannon had opened fire on it and continued to fire until its ammunition was exhausted.

Hawley wasted no time in escaping. He ordered *Carlisle*'s cables to be cut and ran for St Kitts, where the ship was beached on the southeast peninsula. Hawley and Vallet escaped ashore in the French quarter of St Kitts. There were 15 English ships anchored in Nevis at the time and the four which could not escape through the Narrows between St Kitts and Nevis were captured by the Spanish. Nevis did not resist further than firing its cannon and surrendered to de Toledo the same day.

The indentured servants in Nevis, many of whom were Roman Catholic Irish, had refused to fight and some even swam to the Spanish ships where they informed the invaders of the condition of the island's defences and joined them. In those early years religious affiliation was often a more powerful force than nationalism.

After his forces mopped up Nevis, de Toledo turned to St Kitts. St Kitts had prepared itself as best it could in the face of overwhelming Spanish power. The Spanish ships anchored in what is now Basseterre harbour fired a five gun salute and sent in a longboat under a flag of truce. The French welcomed it by firing three cannon balls at the boat from their fort there but not hitting it. The French in the fort were commanded by Captain du Rossey and had been reinforced by 120 men from Capisterre under Captain du Parquet and 800 English under Thomas Warner.

That was enough for the Spanish. De Toledo attacked the small French fort at Basseterre with several galleons which fired into it from the sea and at the same time landed troops and moved them inland to attack the fort from the landward side. This fort was situated where the Ocean Terrace Inn and Fort Thomas's ruins are today. For a day the English and French fought the Spanish together, but the outcome was never in doubt. Both the French and English were short of powder and shot and unable to resist for long. The next day the English retreated to the mountains and the French evacuated their troops by ship to surrounding islands, primarily St Martin and Antigua.

St Kitts was surrendered under the same terms as Nevis had been. De Toledo declared that all settlements would be destroyed and that settlers had the choice of returning to their homes in England in the four ships de Toledo had taken in Nevis, swearing allegiance to the King of Spain and joining de Toledo's forces, or being put to the sword. No one, as one would expect, chose the latter.

Five hostages were taken from St Kitts by de Toledo to ensure the agreement was kept. The nine hostages from both Nevis and St Christopher were transported to Spain where they were held in prison for five years before being released. It is said that 600 men were taken by de Toledo to work the mines in Spanish America. It is not clear whether they were taken as captives or volunteers seeking to make their fortunes in the rich Spanish Empire. It is very possible the latter is correct, as many believed Spanish gold and silver was the ticket to personal wealth in the seventeenth century.

Most English settlers from both islands were packed into the captured vessels and dispatched to England. However, the ships supposedly going to England waited for a judicious time until the Spanish departed and then returned. Most French on nearby islands did the same. Others who did not come back went to the island of Tortuga (north of Hispaniola), becoming pirates and preying on Spanish shipping in the Caribbean.

Du Rossey, the French commander, departed from St Kitts for Antigua after the initial attack, where he remained briefly, and then journeyed on to St Martin. There was not an adequate water supply in St Martin, so du Rossey took passage on a ship bound for France and returned home. Cardinal Richelieu was very displeased that du Rossey had abandoned St Kitts and expressed his anger by locking him in the Bastille for a considerable time.

This event set back the colony, but only temporarily. As late as 1631 a visitor from England noted that not all the buildings there had been reconstructed and he had to sleep in a tent while on land. The settlers of both islands kept a wary eye out for the Spanish for many years afterwards, knowing that they were violating the terms of the agreement with de Toledo. However, in spite of several false alarms, the Spanish never returned to the Leewards with a military force.

Contemporary accounts of the Spanish invasion do not reveal the number of vessels in the harbours of St Kitts – Old Road for the English and Basseterre for the French. They had ample warning of the Spanish attack and no doubt ran for it or were prepared to do so when Spanish ships were sighted approaching St Kitts from Nevis. However, the presence of 15 merchant vessels in Nevis gives clear indication that trade in both islands was brisk that early on, given that Nevis had been settled for only a year. It contrasts favourably with English settlements in North America sometimes waiting months for a single ship to appear. Evidently Warner and Merifield were good promoters and organizers.

The French at the direction of Cardinal Richelieu formed the Compagnie de Saint-Christophe in 1626 to develop a commercial maritime fleet and trade with St Kitts. That same year arrangements were made by the company to purchase 40 slaves from Senegal in West Africa for use in St Kitts. That is the first written record of slaves taken from Africa to St Kitts, although it is quite possible small numbers of African slaves were brought in before that time by Dutch traders. In 1635 the number of slaves in St Kitts was between five and six hundred. By 1636 it was legal to trade for African slaves in St Kitts. Prior to that time only Indians were legal slaves but almost certainly there were some Africans among them.[1]

Very likely some of these Senegalese slaves were participants in the rebellion of 1637 occurring in the French quarter of St Kitts, the first uprising in the non-Spanish Caribbean. Numbers of slaves escaped from their estates in French St Christopher and went into the mountains where they constructed a fort in an isolated area. 500 well trained and equipped troops were sent to dislodge them by Governor de Poincy. Outgunned, the slaves were defeated after bloody skirmishes. Terrible retribution was taken against them. The leaders were drawn and quartered, or hanged.

One large, powerfully built man managed to elude the French for nearly three years. His several escapes were so miraculous that the slaves believed he possessed supernatural powers. At last an angry Governor de Poincy sent six men into the mountains to find and kill him. They succeeded in locating and surrounding him, but possibly because of wet weather, all the troops' muskets misfired and the slave then charged them with drawn sword. They broke and ran from him and he escaped. De Poincy sent a second detachment of men after him a day later. Once more, they found him, fired their muskets at close range, but all the shots missed. They continued to pursue him and at last he was felled by a pistol shot through the head fired by the sergeant. This was considered a stroke of luck, as he was so strong that the troops probably would have been unable to physically subdue him.

The impact of the companies organized to promote settlement, both English and French, was substantial. They were the forerunners of modern limited liability companies. Often royalty was given or bought substantial share holdings, thus lending indirect Crown support for these ventures. If the companies were very successful, as Warner's enterprise became because of sugar and the slave trade, the value of the shares was considerable and annual dividends could be as high as 40 or 50 per cent of the initial investment cost. At that early time Crown interest in new colonies was marginal, but as empires expanded the Crown ultimately would take over administration of the colonies from the companies and run them themselves. In both French and English Caribbean colonies this took place in the 1660s.

While the changes in the companies were considerable in the long run, locally they sometimes made little difference with the same people taking the same position with the new company as they held with the old. This occurred in 1665 in St Kitts when the Compagnie de Saint-Christophe was dissolved and the French West Indies Company immediately took its place. The local agent retained the same position and in his journal wrote this droll account of the change:

> Having received the key, I opened and shut the doors. I entered and came out again. I went down to the offices, where I had a fire made, and

smoked. I drank and I ate. I went into the chapel and had mass performed after the clock struck. I went into the guard house; and I made the Garrison go out, and I made them re-enter, under the authority of the West India Company. I raked the ground, and took up the stones. I cut down the trees by the root, and pulled up the herbs and replanted others; and at last I went out on the terrace, where I had the guns fired, and cried out 'God save the King and the Company'.[2]

5
The Coming of 'King Sugar'

The earliest cash crop in St Kitts was tobacco and to a lesser extent, ginger and indigo. One or two acres of tobacco would yield sufficient annual income for one or two people to prosper and little land needed to be cleared for this purpose. The population of St Kitts was higher at that time than perhaps even today as many indentured servants from Europe migrated to the islands and established small farms. In 1640, Barbados was the most densely populated place on earth and the other Caribbean islands were not far behind. In 1665 it was estimated that the population of St Kitts was 30,000. It was written in that year that ' ... this island is almost worne out by the multituds that live upon it'.[1]

Indentured servants were, in effect, contract slaves who worked from two to seven years to pay off their masters' costs in transporting them across the Atlantic. Often they were recruited by ships' masters and their indentures sold upon arrival to landholding citizens. They were often badly treated and their lives were usually short. Only a minority survived their indenture time. Many succumbed to diseases which were uncommon in Europe, such as malaria, dysentery and yellow fever. Like African slaves, they could be and were whipped for their transgressions. In 1701 the Lieutenant Governor of St Kitts ordered a white indentured servant ' ... to be whipt in the pillory and the pickle of beef brine to be put on his back'.[2] In addition, they were often people recently released from prison for minor offences, or were convicts who were 'transported' to the new world rather than serving a prison sentence at home. These were often not the best and most willing workers and some gravitated to piracy or crime rather than working on the land, yet they were sought after eagerly by landholders. Following Oliver Cromwell's bloody conquest of Ireland, in 1652 it was related 25,000 Irish were sold into slavery in the various islands of the West Indies. It was related that if any escaped and were recaptured, the letters FT were branded upon their foreheads, meaning 'Fugitive Traitor'.

In the seventeenth century Christopher Jeaffreson sought to have 300 prisoners transported from London to St Kitts to work on his plantation, Wingfield Manor. He was able to get only about half that number, and complained he had to give 'gifts', which were really bribes, to court officials in

London. It seemed that whoever made the most generous 'gifts' got the prisoners. It was a lucrative practice indeed for corrupt court officials. An eighteenth-century priest from neighbouring Nevis declared in 1733 that:

> Our Mother Nation has indeed been liberally dispensing her Filth and Putrefaction in her Sugar and Tobacco colonies for the last sixty or seventy years; people (it seems) that were not bad enough for the Gallows, and yet too bad to live among their virtuous Countrymen at home … the Mother-Nation now and then replenishes them with whole Ship-Loads of Pick-Pockets, Whores, Rogues, Vagrants, Thieves, Sodomites and other Filth and Cut-Throats of Society.[3]

The French and English both used similar systems and a predictable result was that a disproportionate number of early settlers were men, and drinking, fighting, sodomy and fornication were commonplace. A seventeenth-century writer observed that when a new colony was established, the first thing the Spanish did was to build a church, the Dutch to build a fort and the English to build a tavern. He was not far wrong.

The cultivation of tobacco in Virginia had proven to be successful and it was of a better quality than that which was grown in the islands. Competition between the Caribbean and North American colonies in tobacco production was causing friction in England as well. The price of tobacco was falling because of high production, and in St Kitts in 1639 the English and French settlers signed an agreement to uproot growing tobacco and not to plant any more for 18 months in order to increase prices in the world market. James I believed smoking tobacco was a filthy habit and considered banning its use in England, but when the exchequer showed him the profit made for the Crown by the tobacco trade, he changed his mind.

In the sixteenth century Spain conquered neighbouring Portugal and imposed control over Brazil, a Portuguese colony. Along with Spanish control came the Inquisition. The church had been liberal in Brazil prior to that time and it had become a refuge for Sephardic Jews who had fled from the Iberian Peninsula to escape the Inquisition. Once more, the Jews had to flee, this time from Brazil and many went from there to the Protestant Caribbean islands. Holland had established trading connections early on with Brazil, and their ships carried the Jewish refugees to the Caribbean. These refugees along with their Dutch transporters brought the secret of crystallizing sugar to the British islands.

Windmills were soon built to crush the canes, and within a century almost 100 had been built in St Kitts. They were faster than animal-powered mills when the trade winds were constant but like animal mills they were not able to press more than 50 to 60 per cent of the juice out of the canes.

Sugar cane evidently grew in the islands and was used by Indians to make 'cane wine' and chewed by them for its sweetness. The Spanish and Portuguese had discovered the process of crystallizing sugar by means of boiling the juice from crushed sugar cane in a line (called a train) of large pots called 'coppers', adding lime and skimming the waste from the top as the juice thickened into syrup. The syrup was then poured into flat evaporating pans where it would crystallize into brown 'muscovado' sugar, which was made into conical loaves and then packed into large (65 imperial gallon) barrels called hogsheads.

When warehoused before shipping, molasses would drain from the loaves and barrels onto the smoothly mortared storehouse floor where it was channelled into a copper sunk into the floor. Along with insects and other creatures which had become stuck in the molasses and drowned, the residue was removed, mixed with skimmings from the boiling coppers, and distilled into rum. The fuel for the sugar boiling and distillation was the dried crushed sugar cane. The entire process was self-contained and quite efficient for its time.

No one knows exactly when and how sugar production began in the Leeward Islands, but it was almost certainly in the decade of the 1640s. According to French sources, the first sugar to be produced in St Kitts was in 1643. The first mention in English records of sugar being produced in the Caribbean came from Barbados in 1646 and the second from Nevis in 1648.

The Dutch were the major traders in the islands in the seventeenth century, and carried out produce to Europe and brought slaves in from Africa. It was also the Dutch who suggested the use of windmills in the islands to turn the triple cylindrical iron rollers which squeezed the juice from the cane, as they were widely used in Holland for milling grain. A boom in sugar production in these islands was good for the Dutch from a commercial point of view, and with the English for ending Caribbean competition with North America over tobacco production.

The strong Dutch early presence in St Kitts was indicated by the fact that an Admiral in the Dutch navy escorted merchant ships back to Europe in 1642 when all but one were sunk in a hurricane at St Kitts. The price of sugar in Europe was very high at the time, and sugar thrived in the islands. The price of a pound of sugar in England equalled a day's labour for the average worker in 1620 but by 1650 it had fallen to one-quarter of that. It made sugar-growing landowners in the islands rich almost immediately, but this was not achieved without cost and profound social and environmental change. There was a saying in seventeenth-century England that a wealthy person was 'As rich as a West India planter'.

A story is told that Charles I was riding through Hyde Park in his carriage and passed one far more luxurious than his own going in the opposite direction. The king turned to look at it and inquired of his companion as to who owned that magnificent conveyance. He was told it belonged to a West India planter. At a time when a person in England with an income of £100 a year was considered well off, some of the richest West India planters had incomes of thousands of pounds per annum.

In the seventeenth century Christopher Jeaffreson of St Kitts wrote to his sister in London, 'I praye you send me an embroidered and fashionable waist-belt and let everything be modish and creditable, for the better sort in these islands are great gallants'.[4] He needed all the help he could get. He was courting Frances Russell, daughter of Governor Sir James Russell of Nevis, the richest planter on the richest island in the Leewards. His first proposal of marriage to her resulted in a 'brusque denyall'.[5] However, because of love or money or a combination of the two, he persevered and married her when he was 31 and she 15.

The law of unintended consequences applied in St Kitts and all the other sugar islands. The smallholdings of independent farmers were amalgamated into sugar plantations as large tracts of land were needed for sugar cane planting. Because of this indentured servants were often without local work following their indentures.

Indentured servants were not good field workers for the most part, as they were not used to the constant heat of the islands and disliked the work. Planting and cutting sugar cane was one of the most difficult jobs imaginable. Cutters had to work all day in the hot sun bending over swinging a cutlass or using a hoe and were subjected to insect, scorpion and centipede bites. As a result, when their indentures were up (provided they survived), most departed St Kitts predominately for North America. However, whites were considered necessary for the defence of the islands and were pressed into the militias. Not only were the islands under a constant military threat from European powers and Indians, but from possible slave rebellions as well. Having enough white males to defend the islands was a matter of primary importance to local governments in the seventeenth and eighteenth centuries.

The need for large numbers of workers meant that slave importation substantially increased. The average productive life of a worker in the cane fields was only eight to twelve years. By the end of the seventeenth century the number of slaves in St Kitts was double that of Europeans and by the end of the eighteenth century, the proportion had increased to about ten to one.

In the seventeenth century slaves were sometimes considered by the more enlightened planters as individuals rather than property. Governor Sir Christopher Codrington admired the character and spirit of Corromante slaves in St Kitts and Nevis and wrote in 1701 that they were:

> ... the best and most faithful of our slaves, really all born Heroes. There is a difference between them and all other Negroes ... There never was a raskal or coward of that nation, intrepid to the last degree, not a man of

> them will stand to be cut to pieces without a sigh or a groan, grateful and
> obedient to a kind master, but implacably revengeful when ill-treated ...
> no man deserves a Corromante that would not treat him like a Friend
> rather than a slave.[6]

Unfortunately, the increasing numbers of slaves in the islands caused them to be treated more as property rather than persons. They were more and more often demeaned as individuals and a race as the fear of rebellion in the islands grew and increasing justification for slavery was sought by Europeans.

In the eighteenth century, it was noted that nearly two-fifths of newly imported slaves died within a year of arrival, and that on plantations where the annual sugar production averaged one hogshead per slave, slaves died faster than the natural increase of population. On plantations where the average was two slaves per hogshead of sugar produced, the slave population increased faster than it died.[7]

Tragically, some owners found it more economical to work slaves to death and replace them with fresh ones than to ease their work burden and allow them to live longer. Nor did they wish to support old or disabled slaves who were not productive. This practice was not followed in the northern colonies (which would become the United States) as it was more expensive to bring slaves inland long distances from the coast.

As the number of slaves increased proportionately to Europeans, the laws to control them grew more and more harsh. A slave could not testify in a trial of a white person, and could be put to death for striking a white and drawing blood. If a white killed a slave he could not be prosecuted for murder but only had to compensate the slave's owner for his loss. Slavery permanently changed the racial composition of not only St Kitts but all the sugar islands.

The first Caribbean island to shift fully to growing sugar was Nevis where it was noted in 1652 as being the richest British possession in the western hemisphere because of that fact. In spite of rocky and steep land, the soil at that time was the richest of any of the lesser Antilles and it produced more than double the amount of sugar grown by all the other English Leewards combined. Barbados surpassed it in the seventeenth century because it had much more land available for cultivation but Nevis still outproduced Jamaica in 1700.

However, by the early eighteenth century, St Kitts moved to the forefront of the Leewards sugar production and remains there today. It was the wealthiest of all the Leewards in the eighteenth century and it was said that at the outbreak of the American Revolution in 1776, St Kitts was, per capita, the richest colony in the entire British Empire.

A Frenchman visiting St Kitts in 1649 described the island as ' ... the most noble and most famous of all the Carribies'. He declared:

> It is conceived that there is a Silver-mine in St Christophers; but in regard the Salt-pits, Woods Havens, and Mines are common to both nations [France and England], no body looks after it: Besides, such an enterprise would require a great stock, and an infinite number of Slaves. The true Silver-mine of this Island is Sugar ... The delightful bright-green of the Tobacco, planted exactly by the line, the pale-yellow of the Sugar-Canes, when come to maturity, and the dark-green of Ginger and Potatoes, make so delightful a Landskip, as must cause an extraordinary recreation to the unwearied eye.[8]

The writer declared that there were in 1648 more English than French inhabitants, but the French sectors were better fortified, with four forts. The English had only two. The French forts were armed with larger cannon which could fire far out to sea. The English had five well built churches of fine wood, and the French only two, but the largest French church in Basseterre was impressive. 'The structure is of wood, rais'd on a foundation of Free-stone: instead of Glass-windows there are only turned Pillars, after the fashion of a Balcony. It is covered with red Slate'.[9] That church was the Roman Catholic forerunner of today's St George's church.

There was also a French hospital considered to be very good, an orphanage and a hall of justice. Planters' homes in both the French and English quarters were distinctive, with red or glazed slate roofs, and all the roads had fruit or flowering trees planted on both sides for shade. Orchards and small gardens dotted the landscape. Goods such as wine, liquor, beer, silks and woollen cloth were readily available at low prices from French and Dutch merchants. However, planter Christopher Jeaffreson, in a 1687 letter to a friend in England, declared that 'Life here without Madera wine is an impossibility'.[10]

Early St Kitts seemed a Garden of Eden from this writing. However, it is not beyond the realm of reason that the writer may have been subsidized by the French West India Company and painted a glowing picture to encourage investors or would-be immigrants to become involved in the settlement and development of St Kitts. Others declared that the island was not as prosperous as they were led to believe in Europe, and a mason or carpenter could name his price for any job done as they were in such short supply.

In 1655, following the beheading of Charles I, Oliver Cromwell and his Puritans decided to declare war on Spain and move against them in the Caribbean. Although Cromwell was unpopular in the English Caribbean colonies, he set out to gather volunteers in St Kitts and the neighbouring islands. He was able to obtain between 800 and 900 volunteers from St Kitts but only 300 from more populous and prosperous Nevis, and a minuscule 80 from mostly Roman Catholic Montserrat. The relatively large numbers from

St Kitts indicated conditions were not as good there as they were made out to be.

The Puritan Commissioner Gregory Butler of Nevis sailed to St Kitts to help raise troops there for the expedition and became so boisterously intoxicated that he fell from his horse and vomited in front of his own and French officers, much to the embarrassment of all concerned.

These volunteers were not the best of soldiers. Many were drunkards, transported felons and indentured servants who were of little use for fighting and could not care less about Cromwell's plan for taking Santo Domingo from the Spanish. Under the leadership of General Venables and Admiral Penn, they embarked and sailed to Hispaniola. The Spanish were waiting for them and the military adventure turned into a rout when the English broke and ran at the first sign of Spanish resistance.

It has been said that the Spanish gave credit for their victory to land crabs. The English landed at night during the mating season of these creatures, which were making their way to the sea noisily in the dark by the thousand. The invading soldiers had as an objective the secret encirclement of the enemy's major coastal fortification. Believing the crabs were advancing Spanish soldiers, the English turned tail and ran for the beaches. Their failure to capture this fort enabled the Spanish to drive off the troops easily which remained on land as well as the English ships attempting to bombard it by sea.[11]

As if this ignominious defeat was not enough, some troops back on board the English fleet broke into the purser's quarters of HMS *Discovery* and attempted to draw off brandy from a barrel by candlelight. The brandy ignited and could not be extinguished. The alarm was given and the ship was quickly abandoned when the fire went out of control. When it reached the powder magazine, *Discovery* disintegrated in a huge explosion.

Venables and Penn gave up on the capture of Santo Domingo and sailed to Spanish Jamaica. There they managed to overwhelm a garrison of 57 Spanish militiamen and took the island. The Spanish surrendered but many of their loyal slaves did not and retreated to the mountains where they formed the nucleus of the famous Jamaica Maroons. They successfully fought the English until, keeping their freedom, they came to terms over a century later.

The Santo Domingo fiasco was so embarrassing to Cromwell that he had both Venables and Penn thrown in prison for a time after their return to England. Their defenders blamed the defeat in Santo Domingo on the troops, calling them ' … the very scum of scums, and meer dregs of corruption'. Venables himself noted that ' … the men of St Christophers lead all the disorder and confusion'.[12] However, after a half century as a pirate haven and a drain on the English treasury, Jamaica would later became its richest sugar colony.

In St Kitts in the seventeenth and eighteenth centuries there was hardly any circulating small coinage, an annoyance to all settlers, as it required barter for use in trade, usually pounds of sugar. When sugar's value rose or fell a windfall profit could arise for either debtors or creditors, to the detriment of the other group. Spanish pieces-of-eight circulated but their value was too great for small purchases. In today's money a piece-of-eight at that time would have been worth about US$24. They were sometimes cut into eight 'bits' and circulated in small pie-shaped wedges, but were easily lost and not popular for that reason. They are still found today, sometimes with 'SK' punched on them. Those bits and other such countermarked coins are valued by collectors and are quite rare.[13]

The silver mine mentioned by the French writer apparently did exist. A map of St Christopher made in 1687 and reproduced in the illustrations section in this book shows it located roughly between Brimstone Hill and Old Road in the mountains. It was mentioned in the 1627 treaty between the French and English, and in passing in some other old documents, but it would appear the production of the mine must have been relatively low and not very profitable.

6

The Birth of the French Caribbean Empire

St Kitts was the first French settlement in the Caribbean in 1625, established by the privateer Sieur Belain d'Esnambuc, who acted as Governor until his death in December 1635. In spite of the fact that there were some disagreements between the French and English, they joined forces to first eliminate the Indian threat in 1626 and then to fight the Spanish in 1629.

Thomas Warner and Belain d'Esnambuc prepared a formal agreement dated 13 May 1627 establishing boundaries in St Kitts. The salt pans on the southeast peninsula, and the silver mine between Brimstone Hill and Old Road in the English section were jointly administered. Roads, anchorages, wood cutting (for both construction and dyeing), hunting, and fishing were available to both nationalities anywhere in the island without restriction. In the event hostilities broke out between France and England, the side first receiving notice was obliged to give the other 72 hours' warning before commencing military action in St Kitts. This treaty was modified five times between 1627 and 1662 to address changing circumstances, but remained basically the same and was honoured (more or less) by both sides until 1713. That year the French gave up their portion of St Kitts to the British following the War of the Spanish Succession.

The English had settled Nevis, Barbados, Montserrat and Antigua by 1632, and the French cast an eye about for other islands to settle. D'Esnambuc sent an expedition to Antigua in 1632 for a potential settlement but upon arrival they discovered the English had arrived shortly beforehand. They returned to St Kitts.

In July 1635 d'Esnambuc dispatched troops to Guadeloupe under command of the wealthy landowner and aristocrat Lienard d'Olive of St Kitts. D'Olive was a hard but capable commander. Upon arrival he constructed a crude fort and very shortly afterwards the indigenous Indians attacked in large numbers. The French had the foresight to carry several cannons with them and when the Indians charged the fort a cannon was fired with a load of grapeshot cutting many down. The Indians fled the field in utter panic. They had never seen or heard a cannon before. They quickly came to terms with d'Olive and signed a peace treaty. The gratified d'Olive sent one of his officers back to St Kitts in a small vessel to inform d'Esnambuc and request additional supplies but on the way the ship was captured by the Spanish and the unfortunate officer was carried to Puerto Rico where he was imprisoned for a year and a half.

D'Olive had requested food, reinforcements and military ordnance be sent to Guadeloupe as soon as possible as the small garrison was in danger of starvation and possible Indian attack. D'Esnambuc did not get word of d'Olive's success for 18 months and as a result the supplies were not immediately forthcoming. By the time a relief ship did arrive, the French had not only boiled their boot leather and eaten it, but the survivors had cannibalized the dead to stay alive.

Also in 1635 d'Esnambuc led a group of settlers to Martinique where a successful colony was planted and the town of St Pierre established. In a few years it became the most prosperous of the French colonies except for St Kitts and would later become the seat of the French Caribbean Empire.

The French Caribbean Empire expanded more rapidly than did the English. By 1648, St Martin, St Barthélemy, the Saintes, La Desirade and Mariegalante had become parts of it. By 1650, St Lucia, St Croix and Grenada had been added. In 1664 Cayenne (French Guiana), the home of the infamous prison on Devil's Island, was also incorporated into it.

It should be mentioned that the city of St Pierre in Martinique, founded by d'Esnambuc in 1635, met a tragic end in 1902. It had been built below a volcano which blew out through the side in an unexpected eruption and a cloud of superheated gas blasted down over the city and harbour. Over 35,000 people were incinerated in seconds when the city and even ships at anchor exploded instantly into flame. One person survived – a badly burnt prisoner in a windowless dungeon who was found three days later by a search party. So hot was the gas cloud that it melted the exposed side of a large bronze church bell while leaving the other side perfectly intact.

It was in the best interests of both France and England to keep the peace on St Kitts. There were disagreements and occasional skirmishes over the salt ponds and other minor matters between the two nations from the outset, but they lived together in relative harmony for some years. A writer in 1708 declared that they ' ... were lovingly together ... '[1] until 1665, but that was a slight exaggeration.

In 1629, a few days prior to the Spanish attack on St Kitts, a French squadron carrying 300 settlers captured four English merchant ships, grounding and pillaging them. There were threats of war over this incident but the matter was settled expeditiously when Spanish galleons were sighted attacking nearby Nevis.

In 1635, the English had accidentally or on purpose sent some settlers across the borderline into French territory near Fig Tree at Sandy Point and d'Esnambuc sent in troops to drive out the interlopers. With the soldiers were about 250 armed slaves who were promised freedom if the attack succeeded. The slaves fought with excessive zeal: burning, pillaging and raping to an extent which shocked even the French. It seemed the slaves intended to gain their freedom by any means open to them, but ultimately the French did not honour their promise. Once again, the dispute was settled without a full-scale war with the English. The so-called Battle of Fig Tree would remain a sore point between the two nations in St Kitts for many years. In 1639 a disagreement arose over use of the salt ponds on the southeast peninsula, but once again the differences were settled without war.

Following the death in 1635 of d'Esnambuc, the privateer who had become governor and built a small empire in nine years, the French remained without an official governor until the arrival of Philippe de Longvilliers de Poincy on 20 February 1639. De Poincy was rich, a nobleman and a member of the powerful and secretive order of the Knights of Malta. The King of France gave the 56-year-old knight the title of Lieutenant General of the Isles of America and Captain-General of St Christopher.

De Poincy was a complete autocrat but ruled the French quarter of the island very capably and refused to recognize the authority of the king when he chose not to. The king had sold the French portion of the island to the Knights of Malta and de Poincy, their representative, governed as he saw fit in spite of the fact that in name the Crown still retained considerable power over French St Christopher.[2]

The King of France became dissatisfied with de Poincy and dispatched Noel de Patrocles de Thoisy to St Kitts to take his place in 1645. De Poincy refused to let him land in St Kitts, even though he had already stopped in Martinique and Guadeloupe and been accepted there as governor.

De Thoisy went instead to Nevis. From there he organized a force which sailed at night to Sandy Point in St Kitts and abducted de Poincy's two nephews, carrying them back to Nevis. De Poincy retaliated by sending a force of 2000 men across to Nevis where he recovered his nephews. De Thoisy escaped to Martinique and de Poincy pursued with a force of 800 and captured him there. De Thoisy was sent back to France and his followers banished from St Kitts to St Croix in the Virgin Islands. Never again did the King of France challenge de Poincy's authority in the West Indies.

The Capuchin monks in St Kitts joined the side of de Thoisy and when de Poincy emerged victorious, they were summarily ejected from the island

and replaced by the Jesuit order. The Jesuits established a college above Basseterre for which College Street is named.

This peculiar situation arose from what was a joint governance by the Crown, the Knights of Malta and private companies established to settle and handle the affairs of St Kitts. The first of these companies was the Company of St Christopher (Compagnie de Saint-Christophe), later succeeded by the West Indies Company, which had been hastily founded by Cardinal Richelieu in 1626. It collapsed after nine years and was succeeded by the Company of the Isles of America. This company assisted in the settlement of several additional French colonies but like its predecessor, was not profitable. It ultimately sold its holdings in the islands to individuals who conducted business as they saw fit, and succeeded in making profits.

In 1642 Governor de Poincy began construction of his chateau above Basseterre, which was one of the grandest dwellings in the entire Caribbean at the time. De Poincy lived there until he died in 1650 at the age of 77 years, still in charge and beloved (for the most part) by his subjects in St Christopher. He was buried in the churchyard of St George's in Basseterre but the exact location of his grave has been lost. It is possible that earth deposited during the flood of 1792 or that of 1880 buried it. An account written in the 1920s declared the oldest gravestones in the churchyard had been covered by mud during a flood many years before and their location had been forgotten by all but a few persons.

A citizen named Buisson who opposed de Poincy's successor, Governor de Sales, in 1651 shot and wounded the new governor's representative in the leg when the man came to call on him for official business. Eager to show his authority, de Sales had Buisson arrested, shot, beheaded, and then drawn and quartered. His head was placed on a stake in the Basseterre market and the four quarters of his body hung from surrounding trees.

The key to prosperity of the new French settlements was trade and the Dutch completely dominated it and skimmed off the profits for themselves. The French aristocracy as well as the English believed that participation in commerce was unseemly and best left to the lower orders. The Dutch did not feel this way at all and looked upon business as not only a suitable but a desirable occupation. The Dutch supplied needed items to St Christopher at prices lower than the French, and for that matter the English, and were able to do because of an absence of Dutch duties and tariffs.

The Dutch carried out produce in their ships and brokered it worldwide. Jean-Baptiste Colbert, Minister of Finance for the Crown, became interested in the colonies and firmly believed that the means of assuring prosperity and resulting income for the Crown was to correct this problem by lowering duties and increasing income by charging less on expanded trade. He was the person who brought Antoine Le Febvre de la Barré into the picture in the French Caribbean Empire as Colbert's personal representative. We will hear more of de la Barré later.

By 1664, from its base in St Kitts, the French Caribbean Empire had expanded to include Martinique, Grenada, St Lucia, Guadeloupe, Mariegalante, St Martin, St Eustatius, St Barthélemy, St Croix and Tortuga (north of Santo Domingo, and later the base for settlement of Haiti).

The omnipresent fear of Spanish or Indian retribution was a strong and successful impetus for cooperation between the French and English in St Kitts. Guards were posted on the roads going from one nation's district of the island to the other, but the conflicts which arose between them were minor until 1665.

The Dutch were content to profit from carrying cargo to and from both French and English islands, and in the early seventeenth century, the Dutch owned an estimated three-quarters of the world's merchant shipping. The Dutch navy in that era was the best officered and had the most modern ships. Their shipbuilding was the most advanced and the Dutch built and designed 'flutes' and 'flyboats' which were the backbone of world shipping commerce in the seventeenth century.

Establishing plantation colonies in the Caribbean interested the Dutch less than did trade. The only colonies they possessed were small islands such as St Eustatius (at one time French and only seven miles from St Kitts), Saba, and Curaçao near the South American coast, all of which were primarily trading settlements. Settled in the 1630s, Statia (as the English called St Eustatius) almost immediately became a slave trading post and furnished St Kitts and Nevis with commercial goods and numbers of African slaves in the early days of settlement.

These islands were also widely used by buccaneers of all nations for purchasing of vessel provisions and sale of captured merchandise at low prices. Statia and Danish St Thomas were the 'discount stores' of the seventeenth and eighteenth centuries. Ordinary items such as cloth, shoes, ropes and sails, salt beef and fish, liquors and hand tools were cheaper there than in French, English or Spanish islands, and their harbours were always filled with ships of every nation as well as many pirate vessels.

This was especially true in the case of the French colonies. The French West India Company and its successors charged very high prices for their cargoes and for carrying freight. The French simply had so few merchantmen that they were unable to supply their own settlements adequately or at reasonable prices. The same was true with England and Spain, but to a lesser degree. The French government charged excessive duties on goods produced in the islands. The duty on sugar was 50 per cent and ginger a huge 275 per cent.

Comparatively, the English duty on agricultural produce was 4.5 per cent. The resulting excessive costs in France constrained healthy markets for island produce from developing at home for many years.

These were the primary reasons for the financial failure of the early French colonizing companies. In June 1666 Colbert obtained a Royal Order immediately barring Dutch traders from the French Caribbean possessions. This caused sudden economic dislocation as there were insufficient French ships available to replace them, but the problem was quickly patched up when France and Holland joined to fight England in the Second Anglo-Dutch war that same year. Some of the men sent to the Caribbean to enforce Colbert's order proved to be very capable and helpful to the French in that war. Ultimately Colbert's anti-Dutch policies would triumph when the French defeated the Dutch in a huge battle off Tobago years later in 1678 and effectively ended their trade dominance in the French Caribbean Empire.

An amusing story was related by a French priest who stayed in St Kitts for a time near the end of the seventeenth century. By then monkeys, which had been brought into the island from Africa by the French shortly after settlement, had escaped and multiplied to such an extent that they were hunted and in some cases eaten. A hunting party had gone out and shot several, including a mother whose baby continued to cling to her body. The baby was given to a priest named Father Cabasson who raised it and became very attached to his pet as it grew up.

One Sunday morning the priest left for church in Basseterre and locked the monkey in his home. The service was under way when the priest noticed some of his parishioners were smiling and soon isolated laughter broke out. The priest became angry as he was preaching a serious sermon and there was nothing whatsoever funny about what he was saying. Before long the entire congregation was laughing loudly.

It seemed Father Cabasson's pet monkey had escaped from the house and followed him to the church. It made its way inside and climbed onto a ledge above and slightly behind the priest, and unbeknown to him was there imitating Father Cabasson's every movement and gesture, much to the amusement of the congregation. Upon discovering his pet's presence, the priest joined in their laughter and gave up on the completion of his sermon.[3]

7

The Birth of the British Caribbean Empire

Following St Kitts, nearby Nevis was settled officially in 1628, and in 1632 settlement of Montserrat and Antigua followed. All of these islands were proprietary colonies of the Earl of Carlisle called 'The Province of Cariola' granted under King James's Patent. Later that name was changed to the Leeward Islands. Carlisle sold his patent to the Willoughby family in 1660 and they assumed command in the name of the English West India Company with agreement from the Crown. The Leeward Islands were initially under the control of Sir Thomas Warner in St Kitts and after his death on 10 March 1648, his successors in the Company of Adventurers, although each island had its own governor.

In 1642 one Captain Jackson, an English privateer, recruited 250 men from St Kitts and 650 from Barbados and successfully raided the city of Maracaibo in Spanish Venezuela, and then went on to Spanish Jamaica, captured Spanish Town, and plundered it. A good many of the participants liked Jamaica so much they remained there under Spanish rule and did not return home.

The English settlements prospered more in the seventeenth century than did the French, primarily because of lower tariffs and taxes on their products. One situation which restrained prosperity in both the English and French islands and the homelands was their small merchant shipping fleets in comparison to the Dutch. Although the English merchant fleet was larger than that of the French, it soon became evident that the Dutch were skimming off the lion's share of profits from commerce and trade in the western hemisphere from both nations. Following the First Anglo-Dutch war in 1650 which began over fishing rights in the North Sea and was called the 'Herring War', the English government saw that it was necessary to increase the size of its merchant fleet. The result was the passage of the first of the English Navigation Acts in 1656.

The Navigation Act of 1656 limited trading in English colonies to English-made products carried in English ships except in times of emergencies or when there was special dispensation granted. The Act was unpopular in the islands and often ignored. Smuggling became rampant. Dutch traders still could undersell the English as the Dutch wisely did not levy high duties and taxes upon produce imported into Holland, but the law ultimately did have its intended result and the English merchant fleet grew considerably, especially when in the islands sugar replaced tobacco as the major export crop and the slave trade burgeoned.

'King Sugar' totally changed St Kitts and the other English islands. It was an extremely valuable commodity and in great demand in all of Europe and the prices which could be charged for it, especially in the mid-seventeenth century, were extremely high. Hand-in-hand with sugar cultivation came a vast increase in the African slave trade and the English cashed in on it, as did the Dutch. By the eighteenth century, the English would become the foremost of the European nations involved in the slave trade and make huge profits from it.

As the number of English merchant ships increased, so did the necessity for protecting them from the enemy in time of war and from pirates all of the time. The Royal Navy grew for that reason and its expansion was largely financed through the profits from sugar and slaves. By the mid-eighteenth century, following the Seven Years' War with France, Britain truly ruled the waves and would do so for another two centuries.

The French followed England's lead in increasing their merchant fleet, but not as effectively. The competition between England and France increased, with the Dutch keeping a low profile and protecting their trade with both nations as much as possible. However, the pressure was mounting year by year.

In the seventeenth century the English Caribbean empire was more successful than the French. The primary reasons were that the English recognized earlier than did the French that profit lay in establishing a national merchant shipping fleet and that excessive duties and tariffs hampered colonial development. However, the Dutch still managed to corner a substantial part of the shipping trade. In 1687 an English Customs officer investigating the situation wrote:

> There are generally several great ships lying at Statia [St Eustatius], any two of which of them large enough to carry a year's produce of that island ... on their way from Holland they generally touch at all our islands on pretext of watering, they generally stay a week, when all the planters go aboard and not only agree for what is on board, but watch the opportunity to get it ashore, to the loss of revenue of the merchants, who having paid the duty, can not sell so cheaply ... ships go to Statia where they wait for planters to send their sugar, which they punctually do, though the English merchants, their creditors owed for thousands, cannot get a pound of sugar from them ... the Dutch ships ... send their

long boats to St Christopher, once or twice a week, to get the sugar ... sail direct to Holland, without paying the King a penny of duty. Brandy and wine are also smuggled into the islands from French St Christopher.[1]

There were problems with trade between English North America and the West Indies as far as the collection of customs duties was concerned. Robert Quary who was the English Surveyor-General of Customs, visited several places in North America in 1707 and found corruption to be widespread. Customs duties on tobacco and molasses were subject to manipulation. In New London, Connecticut, he noted '... the Collector was one Mr. Withred a Pillar of their Church but a great Rogue which I'm sure your Lordships will believe when I tell you that there is no villainy that a man in his post could doe but was constantly practiced by him ...'[2]

In the eighteenth century, the flow of sugar would begin to go the other way into rather than out of the British Empire. When the British islands' production of sugar began to decline because of soil exhaustion, French molasses and sugar started flowing illegally into the British islands and North America, unbranded and carried by the Dutch and smugglers of every nationality, to be resold as British-produced sugar to take advantage of the British monopoly on sugar produced within their empire and the resulting high prices. Prices of sugar and especially molasses in Britain and North America had increased by then to almost double those of France because of lower British Empire production and increased demand. Additionally, the French discouraged rum production which used molasses because rum produced in their islands interfered with the sales of French brandy and wine.

Tea had become a popular drink in Great Britain and the demand for sugar with tea had grown so rapidly that prices had gone sky high and the Caribbean islands could no longer meet the demand at home.

The economic dislocations caused by this sugar monopoly created stresses within the British Empire which would have a significant effect on the movement for American independence coming later that century. The mercantilist practice of confining trade to individual empires which began in the Caribbean caused not only economic dislocation but contempt for the laws creating it among imperial subjects of every empire.

8

Imperial Conflicts

The Second Anglo-Dutch War

After the First Anglo-Dutch war in 1650, even though the Dutch navy was superior in the quality of its ships and officers to the English, Holland was too small to defeat England alone. The shrewd Dutch recognized this and when it appeared another war was possible, they courted France. The French had a powerful wartime navy. In 1663 Basseterre was swept by a fire which destroyed 60 Dutch-owned warehouses, an indication of their strong presence in French St Kitts. In the Caribbean, the French were allied with the Carib Indians, which was to prove a matter of critical importance. When war between the French and Dutch and the English broke out in 1665, the Caribbean exploded.

Both the French and English governors of St Kitts were aware tensions were mounting in their homelands and each side prepared for war as best they could without provoking or revealing their intentions to the other. Military supplies were shipped in quietly and militias on both sides were increased and intensively trained.

Word that war had been declared reached English Governor William Watts first and according to the agreement between the two nations in St Kitts, he gave notice to French Governor Charles de Sales. The agreement declared in the event of war between the two nations, after notification of both governors, there would be a 72- hour truce before hostilities commenced in St Kitts.

De Sales had learnt from a spy that the English were making preparations in Nevis to raise 1000 troops and land them in English St Kitts to reinforce their St Kitts garrison. On that basis, he took 800 troops to Palmetto Point on the Pentecost River (the name has since changed), which was the southern boundary between their territories, to launch a surprise attack against the English there on 21 April 1666. Following victory, he intended to move along the coast north to Sandy Point. He divided his army, giving the Chevalier de Saint-Laurent command of the other half. Should de Sales fall in battle, Saint-Laurent was to take full command in the field and as governor. With the troops he had a band of between 150 and 200 slaves who were commanded to burn buildings in the English quarter and if the attack was a success, they were promised freedom.

At first the French prevailed but the English rallied for a time before their smaller forces broke and retreated in disorder with the French in pursuit. The French slaves commenced an orgy of looting and destruction as the English army retreated. They burnt cane fields, houses, and allegedly dragged white women back into the French sector where they raped them. The slaves supposedly had been told they could have a white wife as well as freedom if they fought the English, but this was most likely a false story generated to discredit the French.

In the area of Hamilton River (again, the name has changed), 400 fresh English troops hiding in the bush ambushed the advancing French. While attempting to rally his troops Governor de Sales was hit by two musket balls and fell dead. Saint-Laurent immediately took command and shouted to the soldiers that it was their duty to avenge de Sales's death. They counter-attacked and fell upon the English. The onslaught succeeded and the English broke and ran, leaving the field to the French.

Meanwhile English Governor William Watts waited at Sandy Point, the northern territorial boundary, with his own army. On the morning of 22 April he saw smoke in the sky from the burning plantations and retreating English troops began straggling into his lines and reported what had happened. Watts was furious at the French for violating the 72-hour truce and called one Colonel Morgan to his quarters, and proposed that an attack on Basseterre be made by Morgan and the buccaneers he commanded. Watts's plan was not sound and Morgan took issue with him, calling him a coward and pointing a pistol at Watts's chest. Morgan demanded that Watts advance to the northern end of the island and meet a strong French army which was gathered there.

The Battle of Sandy Point

In the afternoon of 22 April, Governor Watts and Colonel Morgan with an army of 1400 topped a hill near Sandy Point and observed a small French army of 350 men on the field below. A French priest named Father Boulogne had dressed himself in a uniform and was galloping up and down the French line, shouting to the men to fight and defend their families and homes, adding that they also defended the Catholic faith against the English Protestant heretics.

Watts and Morgan believed they would make short work of this small force which they outnumbered four to one. They sent slaves over the border into the French lands to fire the cane fields, hoping the French troops would move to protect their lands, but they did not fall for this ruse and remained in battle formation. Watts's army then established a battle line near an English plantation house in a cane field. At that point the wind shifted and the canny French commander immediately ordered the field to be set afire and dispatched some troops to advance through the smoke and attack the enemy. This move succeeded and the plantation house was itself set afire and the English were thoroughly surprised.

Angry at the French success, Colonel Morgan ordered his men to charge and when they reached the French compound they were met with a blast of grapeshot fired from a cannon mounted in a farm waggon and were stopped cold. The French then counter-attacked and drove Morgan's buccaneers back. Of the 260 men under Morgan's command, all but 17 were killed or wounded in this fierce engagement.

Watts decided to take command himself, and advanced with a group of volunteers and officers on the French compound to overrun it and put the cannon out of action. However, a squad of expert French musketeers opened fire on them at close range, killing Watts instantly with a ball to the brain, as well as four other officers. For two more hours the battle raged until the French ran out of powder and then charged with sabres and bayonets, driving the English from the field.

The English fell back to a fort about a quarter of a mile away but rather than reorganizing for a fresh attack, they spiked the guns and fled to Old Road. There the troops, cursing Watts for a coward, pillaged his home. The French had won the Battle of Sandy Point, which was the decisive local battle of the war, and they completely controlled the island. English St Kitts was then surrendered to the French by Watt's successor.

Under the terms of the agreement the English were to remain in St Kitts under French guard and surrender their arms. In spite of this, a considerable number of men, women and slaves stole away to Nevis in small boats in the night. St Kitts was now under French control and well fortified. The English were in a state of confusion. Attempting to take advantage of this, the French launched a somewhat haphazard amphibious attack against Nevis. Hardly any details of the attack survive, but the Nevis militia, combined with refugees from St Kitts, turned back the French invasion when they landed at Pinneys Beach on the west side of Nevis.

Governor James (later Sir James) Russell of Nevis commanded the English forces, and was made a baronet later for his efforts, as is noted on his tombstone in Bristol Cathedral. He immediately wrote to the Governor of the English islands, Francis, Lord Willoughby, located in Barbados, urging him to either reinforce Nevis or evacuate it. He declared they were too weak to turn back another attack from French-held St Kitts.

The French, Russell wrote, would have prevailed had they not made a poor attack and failed to follow up the initial landings with additional troops.

He noted that Nevis had 1500 militia available but only 900 muskets and insufficient gunpowder and food. Willoughby in Barbados acted as quickly as he could. He put together a fleet of 17 men of war and boarded 1500 Barbados militiamen, 2000 muskets, and quantities of food and gunpowder and set out to reinforce Nevis for a future attempt to invade St Kitts.

The reinforcements never arrived. The whole fleet and Willoughby himself along with 2000 men, were lost in a mighty hurricane off Guadeloupe on 15 August 1666. The French took full advantage of this catastrophe. Seeing a deliverance by the hand of God, from St Kitts the French military commander, General Le Fevre de la Barré, put together a fleet of ships to raid nearby Antigua. His allies, the Carib Indians, landed from their canoes in remote bays along Antigua's extensive coastline and proceeded to wreak havoc on coastal plantations. The fleet fired their initial broadsides into the small fort guarding St John's harbour and after returning a single volley, the English troops abandoned the fort and fled inland.

De la Barré had not planned to invade but he saw the opportunity and landed what troops he had and under a flag of truce the English governor appeared and offered to surrender the island. De la Barré had insufficient troops to occupy Antigua, and the surrender agreement stated that he would leave and return in three days with an occupying force. By then the English were to have the slaves and money they agreed to pay as tribute ready and the occupation would commence.

Upon their return, the French found the English had not done what they had agreed to do and had to fight a second battle, which they won easily. The British defeat was attributed to a lack of naval superiority caused by the loss of Willoughby's fleet as well as fear of the Caribs, and the fact that the considerable number of Irish militiamen were 'strangely passive' and would not fight. At the cost of one man killed, the French had taken a wealthy English colony.

The French commanders returned victorious to St Kitts and voted to attack Montserrat, about 20 miles distant. The fleet was assembled and the attack launched after de la Barré received intelligence that of the 900 Irish militia in Montserrat, half would go over to the French. Over 400 did. Again the Caribs participated and their depredations were so extreme that some French officers wanted to end the alliance with them then and there, but it was impossible to argue with success and it remained in effect.

Montserrat was not as easy to capture as Antigua had been. Even with the defection of half the Irish militiamen, the remaining English and Irish troops under the command of Governor Osborne put up stubborn and effective resistance. Falling back to the mountainous interior of the island, they fought for five days until their ammunition and food was exhausted and then surrendered after the French took 80 prisoners, including Osborne's wife. Following the surrender Montserrat was pillaged with only the homes and slave quarters belonging to the Irish turncoats spared.

Upon his victorious return to St Kitts, de la Barré was '... accorded a Roman triumph'.[1] The French could taste complete victory in the Leewards but Nevis still remained in English hands, a dagger pointed at St Kitts. Nevis was only two miles distant and French observers on the mountains in St Kitts noted arriving English ships unloading troops and supplies, and considerable military activity taking place. De la Barré believed that an attempt would soon be made by the enemy to invade St Kitts from Nevis.

Wooden Ships and Iron men – A Moonlight Duel to the Death

In early April 1667, an English squadron of ten sail was sighted anchoring off the west coast of Nevis. Earlier in March a Dutch sea captain had informed his French allies that he had information that an English war fleet was putting to sea from Barbados bound for Nevis. These had to be the ships. De la Barré believed the expected attack on St Kitts was imminent and that it was necessary to alert the strong French command in Martinique and have reinforcements dispatched from there to St Kitts at once to repel the English.[2]

At noon the following day de la Barré set out of Basseterre harbour in the 24-gun warship *Armes d'Angleterre* accompanied by a brigantine. His Captain was named Bourdet, an experienced man and a skilful mariner, but stubborn. The year before Bourdet had lost his ship at Guadeloupe when he refused to take shelter from the 1666 hurricane which had destroyed Lord Willoughby's fleet. His stubbornness would, however, serve the French well on this occasion. As they departed from Basseterre they spotted a large English frigate on patrol off the coast of Nevis. She was HMS *Winchester*. Upon sighting the French frigate, *Winchester* immediately moved to intercept her.

The French frigate had begun life as HMS *Coventry*, and had been one of only two ships in Lord Willoughby's ill-fated 1666 fleet to survive more or less intact. Driven aground in the Isles of the Saintes with her masts and bowsprit cut away, the French had refitted and renamed her and added two guns. She was a 'flute', a Dutch-designed vessel which was not a fast sailer but a sturdy and seaworthy vessel. Flutes were the backbone of the world's commerce fleet in the seventeenth century; broad beamed and between 150 and 200 feet in length, they had a large cargo capacity and could be converted easily into warships.

De la Barré called a meeting of his officers and ordered them to return to St Kitts in the brigantine. He refused to turn back his ship as he believed such an act would demoralize his troops and that it was absolutely necessary to get word to Martinique of the English build-up in Nevis. He ran for Martinique at top speed with the enemy frigate in hot pursuit.

The faster English frigate immediately began to draw closer to *Armes d'Angleterre*. As the day wore on the winds increased to gale force and the ships were buffeted by rising seas. Both vessels were running with all possible sails set and *Winchester* continued to gain on the French frigate. De la Barré resolved not to strike at the enemy under any circumstances and hoped to be able to keep ahead until nightfall when they might be able to elude the swifter and more powerful enemy under cover of darkness.

It was not to be. Near sunset the range between the two ships closed to half a mile and *Armes d' Angleterre* ran out her stern chase guns to fire at her pursuer. Chase guns were mounted in pairs in the vessel's bow and stern and were long-barrelled six- or nine-pounders, usually bronze, and more accurate than a standard cannon. Sometimes a lucky shot could damage a target's rigging or even bring down a mast. Under the prevailing gale force conditions any hit would have been a lucky one with both ships rolling and pitching in the heavy seas.

Realizing that close action was inevitable, the French frigate quickly came about into the wind, rolling over almost onto her beam ends. When she righted herself, Bourdet fired a full broadside at the pursuing *Winchester*. The normal response would have been for *Winchester* to also come about and return the broadside, as enemy cannonballs flying the length of a vessel could kill or maim sailors, upend cannon, or wreck the rigging. The master of *Winchester* accepted the risk of being raked by enemy fire and did not change course, perhaps believing that the heavy seas would throw off his enemy's aim. *Winchester* headed straight for *Armes d' Angleterre* with all sails set and attempted to ram the smaller vessel amidships. *Armes d' Angleterre* turned as quickly as possible to avoid the collision but *Winchester* struck her a glancing blow amidships, her bowsprit ripping out *Armes d'Angleterre's* mainsail. At the same time English marines in *Winchester's* rigging peppered the enemy's deck with musket fire.

De la Barré ordered the ship's cannon to be loaded with double shot and fired into the enemy's hull. This was a risky procedure. The additional pressure inside the barrel of the cannon could cause it to crack or burst, but the velocity of the balls fired dropped from 1200 feet per second to 600 feet and the slower balls did not penetrate the hull cleanly but threw great quantities of wood splinters inside the ship, killing or maiming sailors. Standard French practice was to aim for the enemy's rigging and disable her. De la Barré and Captain Bourdet planned a fight to the finish and did not worry about exploding guns or conserving ammunition and aimed for the enemy's hull.

The sun dipped below the horizon but a brilliant quarter moon illuminated the tossing sea enough for the battle to continue into the night. The two frigates hammered each other unmercifully for over three hours. Neither ship would strike to the other. *Winchester* then slowly drew away from *Armes d' Angleterre* and sank, her colours still flying. The double-shotted cannon had holed *Winchester* so badly that the pounding seas filled her with water and she could no longer stay afloat.

De la Barré had defeated a superior enemy, but his ship was so badly damaged that he was unable to continue to Martinique and had to struggle just to keep her afloat. He turned back to St Kitts, and upon reaching the island discovered the English had instituted a naval blockade and he was unable to land. He pressed on to St Eustatius and from there made his way back to St Kitts days later.

A French writer observed of both the French and English that '… their subjects in St Christopher's fought with a degree of obstinacy that was not found elsewhere'.[3] This naval engagement and the loss of both the French and English governors on the battlefield was proof his observation was correct.

The Battle of Nevis

In the meantime the English had taken the Dutch colony of New Amsterdam in North America and renamed it New York. Dutch Admiral Abraham de Crynsens struck back by capturing the English colony of Surinam in South America and then sailed for Martinique where he joined the French. De la Barré and his commanders in St Kitts had decided that the English had to be beaten in Nevis or they would certainly attack and possibly recapture St Kitts. He had amassed a fleet of 16 French men of war ranging in size from 16 to 38 guns, to which de Crynsens's three Dutch men of war, two of 28 and one of 38 guns, were added. The fleet of 19 ships carried a total of 452 cannons. De la Barré also carried 1100 troops from Martinique and Guadeloupe in his vessels to effect a landing in Nevis.

De la Barré's plan was to sail past St Kitts to Nevis and engage the English ships present there. He was confident he outgunned and outnumbered the English and could make short work of them. In addition, his Carib Indian allies were to approach Nevis from the windward side in canoes and drive inland, forcing the English forces to split and defend both sides of the island at the same time. De la Barré intended to land his troops and reinforce them with additional French forces from St Kitts after the initial landing was completed. He ringingly declared that he would take Nevis and give no quarter, and all the Leewards would then be in French hands for good. A war council was called wherein de Crynsens and de la Barré agreed to a joint command and to attack the enemy fleet in two columns. It was a carefully designed plan with an excellent chance of success.

On 14 May 1667, the French fleet reached St Kitts and sailed onward towards Nevis, where Captain (later Admiral Sir John) Berry waited with ten large men of war headed by the powerful *Coronation* of 50 guns, two frigates, and two fireships. Berry formed a battle line off the southwest coast of Nevis in a favourable position with the wind at his back and awaited the enemy. He had sent out the two frigates as watch ships, both of which were ordered away from the action as the French drew closer.

Upon sighting the English at 6 a.m., de la Barré noted that although he outnumbered the enemy, the English squadron contained at least one very large ship and was more powerful than he had expected. Another meeting of his captains was called. De la Barré was a land rather than a sea commander and in short, he got cold feet and became indecisive. De Crynsens strongly urged an aggressive attack as they had the more numerous fleet which mounted more guns than the English carried. De la Barré spent considerable time attempting to form a battle line while sailing close to the wind and then changed the battle plan after the action commenced without informing all his captains and his Dutch allies. The result was confusion and a bad attack. Captain Berry was in a good position and waited patiently while his enemy dithered.

At 8 a.m. the vanguard of de la Barré's fleet commenced action against the English in a disorderly fashion and the return fire punished his ships badly. De la Barré brought his flagship, *Lys Couronne*, of 38 guns, into action with *Coronation*. The remainder of the fleet did not follow and de la Barré soon found himself surrounded by English ships and, badly damaged by their fire, barely managed to escape.

Admiral de Crynsens was beside himself with impatience and anger at the lubbery attack and finally removed his three ships from the line and led them against Berry's *Coronation*, giving her a severe pounding until one of the English fireships was sent against his vessels and forced them to break off action. The fireships were filled with flammable material and barrels of pitch. Manned by a skeleton crew they would sail downwind towards an enemy. The crew would come alongside the target ship and using grappling hooks entangle it with their own. They would then ignite their ship and put out from their burning vessel in longboats. The fire would then engulf both ships.

In the thick of the battle an English man of war took a hit in her powder magazine and blew up and sank with most of her crew, and a 30-gun French man of war and a smaller French flyboat were destroyed by fireships. By 2 p.m., de la Barré ordered his fleet to withdraw from Nevis to Basseterre harbour in St Kitts. Captain Berry's squadron had beaten a stronger enemy fleet and the French conquest of the Leewards had been stopped in its tracks.

Berry informed England by letter that he was unable to launch an attack against the French fleet in Basseterre because his squadron had exhausted its powder and shot in the engagement, and complained that he had not been able to capture any enemy ships because of their 'cowardice'.[4] He concluded, inaccurately as it would turn out, that the battle had been inconclusive.

A furious Admiral de Crynsens confronted de la Barré in Basseterre and told him they should have won the battle and that if de la Barré had been in the Dutch navy, he would have been court martialled for incompetence. Disgusted, he withdrew his ships from the French fleet and sailed north to Virginia, where he did considerable damage to English shipping until the end of the war. De la Barré would be sent to Canada after the war, where he was appointed governor of New France.

The French fleet withdrew to Martinique, and the English went on the offensive. Montserrat and Antigua as well as Surinam were retaken but St Kitts was considered impregnable and remained in French hands. Soon afterwards Berry's ships combined with Admiral Sir John Harman's fleet out of Barbados and attacked the French fleet at Martinique. After four days of vicious sporadic fighting, 33 French ships were sunk or captured and the English were left in full naval command of the Caribbean.

The English decided the time was ripe for an invasion of St Kitts following the French reverses. On 16 June 1667, a force of 2000 men were transported at night from Nevis under the command of Henry Willoughby, brother of William, Lord Willoughby, the current Governor and the late Francis, Lord Willoughby, who had gone down with his fleet the year before.

The troops landed in the dark on a beach near Palmetto Point where there were few French troops located. Luck was not with them, however. The spot they went ashore was not the correct location and they found themselves stuck below high bluffs. The few French soldiers in the area were under the leadership of Governor Saint-Laurent who quickly demonstrated his military ability. By first light when the English troops attempted to make their way down the beach or climb over the bluff, the French picked them off one by one and the English were helpless.

Seeing their position was untenable, the English organized the troops to attempt to fight their way out through a nearby ghaut. In the meantime, the French commander had sent for artillery and the only cannon close by had been removed from its carriage and securely roped onto a heavy farm waggon. It was moved as quickly as possible, placed at the head of the ghaut, and loaded to the muzzle with grapeshot. On a drum signal the English charged out of the ghaut and the cannon, still in the back of the waggon, was fired directly into the concentrated troops at close range and the effect was devastating. Many fell dead and wounded and after the second cannon charge was fired, their lines broke and they fell back in full retreat to the beach.

Colonel William (later Leeward Islands Governor, Sir William) Stapleton of Montserrat distinguished himself by saving the colours and simultaneously having his arm broken by a musket ball. The English were pinned below the bluffs and although protected from musket fire from above, were trapped. The French were throwing grenades and rolling huge rocks down on them and casualties were mounting quickly.

Evacuation was the only possible solution. More and more French soldiers were arriving on the scene and the English sent longboats out from their ships to pick up the troops. Many were successfully lifted off but 550, including the wounded Colonel Stapleton, sought quarter and surrendered to the enemy. French artillery soon began hitting the longboats and caused heavy losses. When this fiasco ended nearly 700 English were killed or wounded in addition to the 550 captured.

Bitter recriminations over the failed assault followed. It was alleged that Henry Willoughby lay the whole morning in a drunken stupor on board ship, incapable of command. No action was taken against him, however, possibly because of his brother's powerful position as Governor of the West Indies. Following this failed attack the English concluded St Kitts could not be taken in spite of their superior sea power and no further attempts to do so were made.

Shortly thereafter the war ended. The Treaty of Breda was signed between the warring powers and the situation in the Leewards was returned to what it had been before the war started. There were two interesting features of this treaty which were historically significant. In order to regain their half of St Kitts, the English gave the French all of Nova Scotia in Canada. The Dutch had the choice of keeping either Surinam or New York. They selected Surinam.

The cost of this war in lives, lost trade and destruction of property was vast. It was the first of a series of wars which would devastate the Caribbean and especially St Kitts in the late seventeenth and early eighteenth centuries. Being the only island jointly and uncomfortably held by France and England, it would suffer devastation three times until a period of peace lasting from 1713 until 1780 allowed it to prosper to a degree which its early settlers could not have imagined.

The destruction of St Kitts during the war convinced the French to move their Caribbean capital to Martinique in 1669. They believed that an island shared with the English, with English Nevis close at hand, rendered St Kitts too vulnerable to serve as administrative centre for their empire.

There was considerable difficulty for the English in the return of their part of the island after the war. Estates had been destroyed and new buildings constructed, and it was difficult to place a value on the improvements. As a result the actual return of the French held lands to the English did not take place until 1669. The more-or-less happy joint occupation of the island had ended with this explosive conflict and would never return to the prewar situation.

The Nine Years' War

The peace which followed the Second Anglo-Dutch War was brief. By 1689 England and France were again poised for conflict. In the interim, the Treaty of Madrid had been signed in 1670 and Spain grudgingly recognized colonies of other European countries in the Caribbean in return for the other nations curtailing activities of pirates in the area. The Leeward Islands had been separated from Barbados and were formed into a new colony in 1671 with Nevis as its seat. In 1673, in the Third Anglo-Dutch war the Dutch raided the Leewards but no serious battles had occurred. Admiral Cornelius Evertson led a squadron which attacked Montserrat, Nevis and St Kitts and had captured a French ship in Basseterre harbour and killed a soldier and five civilians with cannon fire.

On 7 March 1689 France declared war on England and Holland. In 1686 in St Kitts the French and English had signed a treaty declaring, among other things, that in spite of a war in Europe between the parent countries, conflict in the island would not occur. This was a far-fetched hope. A French fleet of 17 sail and 1200 troops under Count de Blenac arrived at St Eustatius and took it from the Dutch on 3 April and was poised for an attack on English St Kitts.

Governor Thomas Hill had done his best, but militarily speaking, English St Kitts was in sad shape. The 600 militia were disorganized and had not been paid for six years. Cannon, muskets and powder were in short supply. A hundred and thirty Irish settlers had deserted to the French for religious reasons, and were welcomed by them. Hill had rebuilt Fort Charles below Brimstone Hill and moved into it with his troops awaiting French action.

Under French Governor de Salnave troops were sent to plunder the English section of the island, and the Irish not only plundered but took over English plantations for themselves as settlers. Count de Blenac sailed his ships from Saba into Basseterre harbour, disembarked his troops, surrounded Fort Charles and ordered his fleet to bombard it. It was reported the French fired 1138 cannonballs and 22 bombs into it, killing 'only a dog or two, one Christian man, three children and a negro'.[5]

Governor Hill and his men accounted well for themselves. With indifferent ordnance and little powder, they held out against the enemy for two weeks until Jean du Casse, the French naval commander, carried up six cannons to Brimstone Hill and fired down upon the fort. The defenders' guns could not reach the crest of the hill and on 15 August Hill surrendered the fort and the island. The English were sent to Nevis and the Irish stayed on St Kitts under the French, as they wished to do.

At that inauspicious moment Sir Christopher Codrington arrived in Nevis from England to assume governorship of the Leeward Islands colony. With only two ships and no troops, he acted decisively by disarming all the Irish in Antigua and Barbuda and confining them to their plantations.

On 24 August Sir Timothy Thornhill arrived in Nevis with 800 troops eager for action. He was expecting to reinforce the English forces in St Kitts but arrived too late, as the island had surrendered nine days earlier. He and Codrington were of like mind and knowing they were too weak to recapture St Kitts, they decided to use their forces to strike at poorly defended French islands. Many, if not most, of their troops were pirates which was the rule rather than the exception for all sides except Spain in the Caribbean.

The first target island was Mariegalante, near Guadeloupe, where after five days of fighting the French surrendered and the pirates looted and then burnt every building on the island. One of the leaders of this attack was the infamous pirate Captain William Kidd, then fighting for the Crown as a privateer.

Codrington's other targets were St Martin and St Barthélemy. The English attack on these islands under Sir Timothy Thornhill had not gone well. A swift French schooner had sighted the five small English ships approaching St Martin and warned the inhabitants who drove off two landing attempts. The English ships went on to St Barthélemy where the landing succeeded and the island was quickly surrendered and then plundered. The French Governor signed the surrender in his house, a 12-by-12-foot stone building so small and unimpressive that the English termed it a 'pigeon house'.

Encouraged, the English returned to St Martin and this time secured a landing. They drove inland with little trouble when on the horizon they sighted an approaching French squadron of three men of war and three brigantines. Under the command of Jean du Casse they had left St Kitts the day before when word of the English invasion had reached them. Du Casse, himself a privateer, attacked the five small English vessels and drove them off, capturing one in the process, and landed 600 French troops carried there from St Kitts.

The remaining vessels raced to Nevis bearing news of the attack. The raiding party from Mariegalante had just returned. Codrington realized Thornhill and his 600 men were in grave danger of capture by the enemy, and he immediately dispatched Captain Thomas Hewetson in the frigate HMS *Lion*, Captain Kidd in the privateer *Blessed William*, and one other privateer to go to their rescue.

Hewetson sighted the French squadron, formed a battle line, and launched an attack against the larger force without hesitation. Twice his column passed the French line with broadsides blazing from both squadrons.

After the second run Hewetson attempted to lift off Thornhill's troops which had gathered on the beach, but du Casse counter-attacked and drove him off. Two additional French men of war appeared and joined du Casse, forcing Hewetson to turn away and withdraw for the night. In the morning he returned with the wind in his favour and once again attacked the French squadron, which was anchored between Hewetson and Thornhill's men on the beach. After a short but fierce engagement, du Casse withdrew and bore away to Anguilla. Thornhill's men were quickly evacuated and returned to Nevis. Among the English troops rescued was Captain Bartholomew Sharpe, a well known pirate who had spent three years pillaging Spanish settlements and ships on the Pacific coast of Central and South America. More will be heard of Sharpe later.

Codrington was receiving reinforcements from other islands in Nevis, including Montserrat. Montserrat had been a worry for him, as the majority of settlers there were Irish and it was believed they would go over to the French at the first opportunity as they had done in St Kitts. Many Irish had been forcibly resettled in the Leewards following Cromwell's conquest of Ireland and had no love for the English. Codrington must have been a persuasive man, as he had journeyed to Montserrat and convinced the Irish they would be better off under the English than the French.

With 3000 men at his disposal, on 24 June 1690 the troops in Nevis were loaded onto ships which had recently arrived from England and set out for St Kitts. They intended to land at Frigate Bay but Codrington determined that it was too strongly fortified. The ships opened fire on the French position to soften it up, however. Commanded by Sir Timothy Thornhill, troops were landed at night on an adjoining bay near a small salt pond on the southeast peninsula, today called Timothy's Beach. A steep hill separated it from Frigate Bay. In the morning Codrington ordered his ships to sail to Basseterre, which caused the French to move 300 troops away from their position to the city to protect it.

At daybreak Thornhill and his men appeared at the top of the hill between the two beaches, and stormed down upon the French position. Codrington then landed 600 men at Frigate Bay in the thick of the fight. His men attacked the French flank and their troops fled the field. Thornhill ordered his men to pursue the French, but in the meantime they had been reinforced and were blocking the advancing English at a strong point on the narrow neck of the island. The French fought hard and the English fell back, but under the command of Governor Williams of Antigua they re-formed and drove the French from the field.

After delaying overnight at the Jesuit College on what is now College Street, the English marched into Basseterre. Thornhill held them back that night as warehouses in the town held large supplies of French brandy and wine and he knew if the soldiers reached there in a disorganized state they would consume the liquor in short order and be vulnerable to a French counter-attack. Basseterre was taken in the morning without difficulty.

The French retreated past Old Road and Brimstone Hill into Fort Charles located on the shore just north of Brimstone Hill where they prepared for a siege. Codrington took Brimstone Hill and moved up two six-pounders and two chase guns, which took two days, and fired 'hot shot' down on the fort's defenders. The first shot fired hit its mark and the red-hot cannon balls soon set the wooden barracks afire, forcing the defenders into the open. At the same time ships of the English fleet began firing into the fort with little effect. HMS *Assistance*, 44 guns, was hit at the base of the main mast by a 24-pound ball fired from the fort which killed the gunner, wounded a sailor, and sprung the mast. *Assistance* withdrew from the action.

The French held out stubbornly until 16 July. They had tried to evacuate the fort the previous night in small boats but had been discovered and stopped. The Governor then surrendered the fort and the island to the English the following morning.

Codrington gave hard terms. He sent all the French settlers to distant Santo Domingo rather than to closer Guadeloupe or Martinique to keep them out of future action in the Leewards and break French power in St Kitts. However, some Frenchmen fled to the mountains with loyal slaves and formed military units. Operating from there they harassed the English until the end of the war. An English officer wrote that slave troops under a French commander had ambushed an English Regiment of Foot and killed 15 men.

Except for minor episodes the war was over in the Leewards. The English invaded Guadeloupe in the Windwards but failed to hold it. The Spaniards entered the picture in Santo Domingo and tried to drive out French settlers, most of whom had been sent from St Kitts, and massacred those they could find along with their slaves. The French retaliated against the Spanish by taking Cartagena (Colombia) after a bloody siege, and under the command of Jean du Casse of St Kitts, French buccaneers tortured, raped and robbed the inhabitants of this rich Spanish city. Enough plunder was taken to cover much of the French expenditure for this war.

In May 1697 the war was settled by the Treaty of Ryswick. The French and English retained their portions of St Kitts, and in the Caribbean. Spain ceded Santo Domingo to the French. The Treaty of Ryswick served only as a truce until the war of the Spanish Succession broke out in 1702.

Both sides expected further conflict in St Kitts. On 25 March 1699, a proposal was made to the French government that a new and substantial fortification be built at what was called 'Old Fort Point' where Fort Thomas is located. The 'Old Fort' they referred to was the one attacked by the Spanish in 1629, which protected Basseterre harbour. A map of the island was prepared

1 'The recapture of St Christopher' by Felix Castelo. Painting shows Spanish Admiral Don Fadrique de Toledo directing his troops in the 1629 attack upon the British fort located where Fort Thomas Hotel and Ocean Terrace are presently. Courtesy of Museo del Prado, Madrid.

*The Chateau of Phillipe de Poincy St. Christopher
from de Rochefort's Histoire des Iles Antilles
Published 1665*

2 Governor de Poincy's Chateau La Fontaine. Completed in 1649, it collapsed in the 1690 earthquake and was never rebuilt.

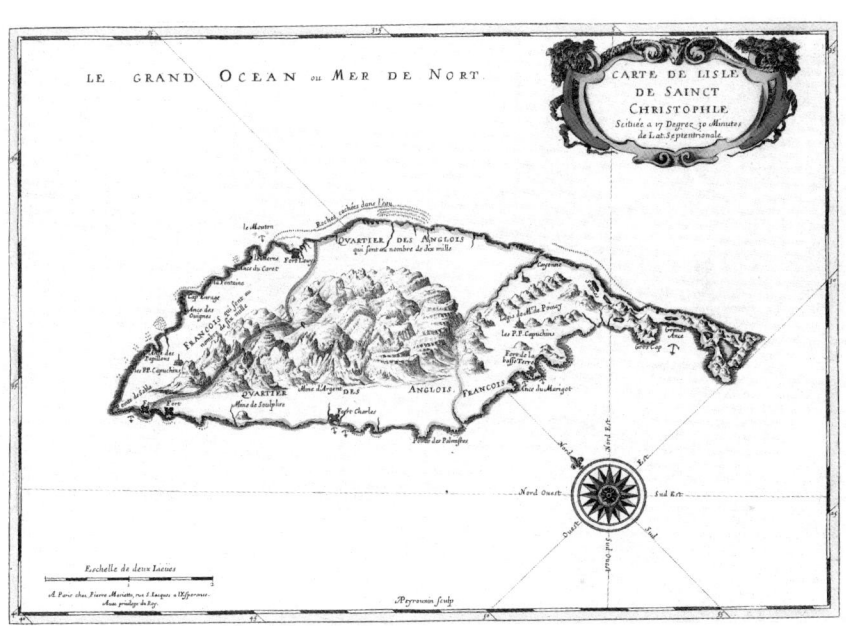

3 French map of St Kitts *c.* 1650 showing the French and English quarters and the silver mine.

4 The battle of Frigate Bay, 26 January 1782, with Nevis in the background. In the foreground a man pursues a horse terrified by the thunder of the cannon.

5 The Moravian church in Basseterre, *c.* 1795 from a German print of the time.

SHIPPED, by the Grace of God, in good Order and well-conditioned, by *Robt W. Pickwoad Esqr* in and upon the good Ship called the *Britannia* whereof is Master, under God, for this present Voyage, *Thomas Sharpe* and now riding at Anchor in the *Roads of Basseterre* and, by God's Grace, bound for *London* to say,

Twenty hogsheads Muscovado Sugar

being marked and numbered as in the Margin, and are to be delivered in the like good Order and well-conditioned, at the aforesaid Port of *London* (the Danger of the Seas only excepted) unto *Major Genl Christopher Jeaffreson* or to *his* Assigns, he or they paying Freight for the said Goods *six shillings per cwt Nett at the King's Beam* with Primage and Average accustomed. In Witness whereof the Master or Purser of the said Ship hath affirmed to *three* Bills of Lading, all of this Tenor and Date; the one of which *three* Bills being accomplished, the other *two* to stand void. And so God send the good Ship to her desired Port in safety. Amen. Dated in *St Christopher June 3rd 1809*

Thomas Sharpe

6 A receipt for 20 hogsheads of sugar shipped from St Kitts to London on the vessel *Britannia* 3 June 1809. The freight charge was 6 shillings per hundredweight.

7 Brimstone Hill 1812.

8 Basseterre c.1830.

showing the proposed location, and also suggesting the construction of a bastion where the road crossed the French and English border between Basseterre and Old Road. Whether this project was undertaken or completed before the War of the Spanish Succession commenced is not known, but from available records it appears likely it was not.

Another map of the island showing the largest estates was made about the same time which noted that persons with English or Irish names lived in the French areas and vice versa. That the populations had mixed to a certain degree is also indicated by the number of French surnames which still can be found in St Kitts, so obviously some French stayed on after they lost their portion of the island. In addition, this map calls the area of Nags Head on the southeast peninsula the Maroon Quarter, and Majors Bay as Maroon Bay, indicating this was an area where escaped slaves hid themselves.

The War of the Spanish Succession

In the seventeenth century, war succeeded war with fleeting periods of peace. While no territorial changes occurred in the Leewards, these were European wars and were fought between England and France for European military superiority. Wealthy but weak Spain remained in a defensive mode and was content to retain its great worldwide empire and let the other European countries expend their energies fighting one another. This was to cease when the King of Spain died without an heir in 1702 and named a French Prince to take the Spanish throne. Protestant England and Holland squared off with Catholic Spain and France. If France gained control of the Spanish throne and brought its wealth in behind French military adventures, the French would have been nearly unstoppable.

This war was the last in the series of conflicts which had inflicted great financial and material damage on the Leeward Islands, especially St Kitts, with few changes or improvements to follow. Only five years separated the Nine Year's War and this one. Once again, in St Kitts the problem of returning the captured French quarters to the English was causing difficulty and confusion. Many English had invested in French properties and Governor Codrington himself stood to lose £20,000 for that reason. Some English residents pulled down buildings they had constructed in the French lands and carried the lumber and fittings back to the English quarter of the island. Basseterre itself had been destroyed by the English except for the church and a few houses.

Upon returning to St Kitts the French were furious at the vandalism done to their sections of the island. Arrangements were made between the two sides to return purchased properties for the prices paid for them and they were to be given back in the same condition as they were in 1690. Damage done by the

English was to be repaired and French slaves were to be returned to their former owners only if the slaves themselves wished it.

This return was not accomplished without difficulty and conflict. Count Jean-Baptiste de Gennes had been appointed Governor of French St Christopher and upon the death of his father, Sir Christopher Codrington the younger had taken over governorship of the English Leewards.

Père Labat, a French priest, lived in St Kitts at the time, and was invited in early 1702 to a dinner given by Governor de Gennes for Codrington. Codrington, born in St Kitts, had been educated in Paris and spoke perfect French. Père Labat noted Codrington '… was more sober than his countrymen usually were'. Labat, although a man of the cloth, appreciated good living. He declared in his journal that '… good wine is the soul of a meal'.[6]

At the dinner, de Gennes showed his guests a wonderful mechanical peacock,[7] which when wound up would bend its neck and pick up bits of corn from a plate in its beak. He also complained that St Kitts had been stripped of soldiers and defending it would be difficult in case of war. Codrington advised him to have the person who made the peacock manufacture a regiment of mechanical Irish troops which could load and fire muskets and use them to defend the French forts. They would not have to be fed or paid, an advantage according to Codrington.

Codrington's comment probably referred to Roman Catholic Irish in St Kitts who had gone over to the French side in the last war, just as Protestant French Huguenots had gone over to the English side at the same time.

De Gennes's apprehensions proved to be well founded, as war between France and England broke out shortly thereafter. Père Labat noted that a few days after the dinner when he departed St Kitts for Guadeloupe, without de Gennes's knowledge the ship secretly carried the valuables of several prominent French residents of St Kitts who expected an English victory in the island.

Before departing St Kitts, Labat dined also with Sir William Stapleton the younger, son of the former governor of the Leewards and owner of estates in St Kitts and Nevis. Labat noted Stapleton spoke French well, as he had been imprisoned in the Bastille in France for five years. While jailed, Stapleton studied mathematics and French. How he got there is not known, but he was most likely a prisoner of war. Labat commented that soon afterwards Stapleton was '… killed by a band of drunken men'.[8]

De Gennes had only 400 troops at his command in St Kitts and had already ordered women and children to Martinique. He himself had recently weathered a personal crisis. He had married a Protestant Huguenot woman and brought her to St Kitts with her teenage daughter. De Gennes was a devout Catholic who knew his Protestant wife was beyond conversion to his faith but he believed there was still hope for the daughter. He asked a Jesuit priest to meet with the girl and give her instruction in the faith. The instruction continued for an excessive length of time and with the help of English friends the priest and the girl sailed to Nevis by night. There the priest announced his conversion to Anglicanism, renounced his vows of celibacy and married de Gennes's step daughter.

Under instructions of Governor Codrington, Colonel Walter Hamilton of Nevis, a capable soldier who had been twice wounded in the ill-fated attack on St Martin in the last war, was sent to St Kitts to parley with de Gennes. Hamilton informed de Gennes that Governor Codrington had been ordered by Queen Anne to demand the surrender of French St Kitts, and he gave de Gennes two hours to comply before hostilities commenced.

De Gennes had only the 400 men, divided with 160 at Basseterre and 240 at Sandy Point, to face an English army of six times that size which had been landed the day before. In the meantime four English men of war and 20 smaller ships had anchored off the fort at Basseterre where de Gennes and his men were gathered. De Gennes first refused to give up but discussed the proposal with his council, and they voted twelve to five to surrender. Some field officers did not agree with de Gennes and the council and later ransacked the Governor's home in retaliation.

The surrender agreement was signed and the French inhabitants of St Kitts were removed to other islands. De Gennes was sent to Cayenne in South America at his request rather than to Martinique, where he knew French authorities would take a dim view of his quick surrender of St Kitts. Fate was not on de Gennes's side. His ship was captured by a Dutch privateer on the way to Cayenne, and he was taken to St Thomas in the Virgin Islands, and by some means carried on from there to Martinique where he was at once imprisoned in the city of St Pierre.

It can be said that de Gennes's surrender spared both sides, especially his own, considerable bloodshed. The outcome of any battle almost certainly would have been an English victory. The King of France did not see it that way. Count de Ponchartrain in France wrote to the Governor General of Martinique, de Machault de Bellemont as follows:

> The conduct of M. de Gennes on this occasion has so displeased His Majesty and has seemed to him so dishonorable for the nation that he has ordered me to write you that he wishes that as soon as you arrive in Martinique you will bring him to trial and have him judged by a council of war, so that if he is guilty of any understanding with the enemy, or of the outright cowardice that appears in his action he shall receive the punishment he deserves according to the articles of war.[9]

De Gennes had no chance because of the king's condemnation of his actions. In 1704 he was pronounced guilty of treason and flagrant cowardice and stripped of his nobility and all honorary positions he held. On the way back to

France his ship was taken by the English and he died in Plymouth a broken man. However, his widow in France appealed and in due time the king reinstated his nobility and privileges and gave his family a suitable pension.

The surrender of St Kitts was not the final event of this war in St Kitts and the Leewards. In 1705 and 1706, the French struck back, first against St Kitts and then Nevis with raids which would cause great damage to English St Kitts and devastate Nevis so completely that its economy would collapse and never recover.

The dates are in question. Some documents put the raids in February and March of one year, and others in the next. The attack on Nevis was definitely in 1706, but most give 1705 as the year of the St Kitts attack. Establishing precise dates in the seventeenth and early eighteenth centuries can sometimes be very difficult. Years were often written in correspondence as, for example, 1705/6 and the day changed at noon rather than midnight. In addition, there was a problem with calendars. The Julian calendar, established by Julius Caesar, was running ten or so days behind the new Gregorian calendar as it did not include leap years. Pope Gregory XIII devised the modern calendar in the sixteenth century and Spain immediately adopted it, as did her colonies. Mainland France adopted it in the seventeenth century, but her Caribbean colonies continued to use the old calendar for some time after. In Holland, for a time some of the seven provinces used one calendar and the rest used the other. England was the last European nation to change to the modern calendar in 1752. Dates of some events can vary depending on the nationality and location of the writer, and for some time the English and French quarters of St Kitts were ten days apart for official purposes.

The architect of the raids was Pierre LeMoyne d'Iberville. Born in Canada where he fought both the Indians and the English, he had been sent to the French colony of Louisiana in North America where he became military commander under Governor Bienville. He was a bold and skilful soldier who did not follow standard practices of warfare and took advantage of local terrain and conditions.

The first of two attacks was made by Admiral Count Louis-Henri de Chavagnac with 24 warships against well-fortified Nevis in 1705. For five days he bombarded its coastal forts with his fleet's cannon. Several times he attempted to land his 1200 troops but bad weather and determined defence led by Colonel Thomas Abbott with 450 Nevis militia and 125 British regulars held him off. In disgust at the failure, he turned his fleet towards St Kitts.

Governor Walter Hamilton, appointed after his successful engineering of de Gennes's surrender in 1702, had attempted to strengthen the fortifications of St Kitts. The Assembly, however, had refused to grant the funds Hamilton requested and the work had not been done. The military activity at nearby Nevis had been observed and whatever could have been done for defence at that late date was done, but St Kitts was woefully unprepared and offered only token resistance. De Chavanac landed troops at Frigate Bay consisting mainly of pirates and they rampaged through the English quarter of St Kitts, burning and pillaging, and carrying off between 600 and 700 slaves as booty. These slaves were sold afterwards to the Spanish in Vera Cruz to work the Mexican silver mines.

One of the many claims later made to the British government for damage in St Kitts read as follows: 'The Church of the Parish of St Thomas Middle Island, about 50 foot long × 20 foot broad: Boarded and Shingled, with good Ironwood Catches: With Pews & Work all burnt to the value of £250, s 0, d 0'.[10]

The present stone church was built to replace this destroyed wooden building sometime after 1713. The British parliament voted £103,000 in 1707 for relief of St Kitts and Nevis after the French depredations, but the funds were not paid until 1715 by lottery as the British treasury was bare because of the cost of the war. Of this sum, St Kitts received £23,000 and Nevis £80,000.

Two months later the French would attack Nevis a second time with 36 men of war and over 2000 troops under d'Iberville on Good Friday 1706. He did not storm the forts directly as was common practice but hid 900 men on supply ships off the southwest coast of the island while his fleet lined up along the beach fortifications further north. At daybreak the fleet opened fire and d'Iberville landed his men unopposed and swept north to Fort Charles and easily captured it from the rear. Charlestown was taken, looted and burnt.

Nevis had armed some slaves for defence and d'Iberville knew he could not control the island without coming to terms with them. Under a flag of truce, he met with the leaders of the slave troops and promised them a life of freedom on French islands if they would go over to the French side. Some did, but others were suspicious and took to the mountains. The French army then chased the Nevis militia to a defensive point high in the mountains where, on Easter morning, the English commander surrendered the island to the enemy without firing a shot.

The slaves did not give up so easily. When those who had gone over to the French were being loaded on some of the 22 English ships the French had taken, one slave learnt that the French had lied to them and intended to sell them to the Spanish as had been done with the St Kitts slaves the year before. He jumped over the side of the ship, swam ashore, and spread word of the deception. The slaves remaining in Nevis turned on the French in fury. 'They fell on the French and cut their throats …'.[11] wrote an English historian in 1708.

D'Iberville took 3400 slaves from Nevis and demanded 1200 more from the Nevis planters or £30 per slave. He had attempted to capture the slaves with his army, but they took to the mountains and at what is now called

Maroon Hill, near Zetland, organized an army and faced the French on the battlefield – the first time a slave army fought a European army in the Caribbean. For two weeks the French tried to dislodge the slaves from their defensive position, but failed because '... they drove back the invaders time and again by their murderous fire'.[12] An English militiaman would write that '... their brave behavior and defence there shamed what some of their masters did and they don't shrink to tell us so'.[13]

The resistance of the Nevis slaves spared St Kitts from what would have been a devastating attack. The French were delayed in Nevis before they could launch a campaign against St Kitts. While attempting to dislodge the slaves in the mountains of Nevis, the French were informed that a squadron of English ships was making for the area at top speed so they hastily departed. Ironically, the ships later proved to be their own, not English. The French left Nevis a shattered wreck with only about 20 houses still standing and all the sugar works destroyed. Even the slave quarters were plundered and burnt. In their zeal for loot the pirates dug up bodies from the churchyards to look for jewellery buried with them.

The Treaty of Utrecht ended the war in 1713. This time there was a change to the Leewards. The French gave up their part of St Christopher permanently to the British. After the French were driven out and before the treaty was signed, there were internal troubles within the island. Some slaves loyal to their French masters had run to the barren southeast peninsula around Nags Head where they refused to surrender to the British. Their presence there prompted passage of a strong 1711 Assembly Act to control 'insolent' slaves which, among other things, declared that a reward of 20 pieces-of-eight would be offered for any runaway slave captured in the area of Nags Head.

This law did not stop internal low-level slave resistance which had reached a peak during the war because of their divided loyalties. A visitor in the 1720s commented that when he went with a group to climb Mt Misery they had to take with them for protection against runaway slaves ten armed men, six white and four slaves.

In 1722 the St Kitts Assembly passed 'An Act for Better Government of Negroes', which is called in legal terms a Bill of Attainder. It was a non-judicial legislative trial, conviction and sentencing to death of persons designated as outlaws. Bills of Attainder were specifically forbidden by the United States Constitution after independence and fell into disuse in English law in the nineteenth century. This Act read as follows:

> Whereas ... Great numbers have deserted the service of their Masters, and fled to the Mountainous parts of the island, and there have armed and assembled themselves into Bands, to oppose their Masters, and any who may come in pursuit of them, and in the Night-Time, when they cannot easily be discovered or taken, do frequently commit divers Thefts

and Robberies in the Plantations of this island ... That Johnny Congo, belonging to the Honourable Lieutenant General Mathew, Christopher, belonging to William McDowall, Esquire, and Antego Quamina, belonging to Marmaduke Bachelor, Esquire, have, and for a long while past, and still do, head several armed Bands or Companies of Fugitive Negroes in this island ... every one of them, be, and hereby are, convicted and attainted of Felony, and shall suffer the pains of Death.[14]

This and other such acts subdued the slaves but did not end the conflicts between masters and slaves in St Kitts.

Another internal problem arose regarding the disposition of French lands in St Kitts following the ending of the war. Various English people claimed the lands because of their services in the conflict, or for wrongs (real or imagined) done to them by the French. There were proposals about how to divide the estates into large and medium-sized holdings to encourage more whites to emigrate to the island, as the proportion of whites to blacks was declining and the colonial government believed whites were needed for administrative and military purposes. This was a growing problem for the English throughout the Caribbean, but the fact was that large plantations were the most profitable.

It was claimed by the French that '... a rapacious English Governor ...'[15] took several of the estates for himself. This could have been none other than the infamous Governor Daniel Parke II, formerly of Virginia. He had little experience which would qualify him for the governorship of the Leeward Islands, but had political connections with Queen Anne and was thus appointed to the post. Most influential people in the islands had favoured Sir Christopher Codrington the younger for this position.

Parke was an inveterate womanizer, who shortly following his arrival in Antigua, was caught in the bedroom of the wife of one of the island's most prominent planters. After his death a personal diary was discovered which gave details of his lurid debaucheries on the island. In addition, he was somewhat unbalanced mentally. Upon entering people's homes, he would sometimes look behind curtains to see if there were any French spies hiding there. At a dinner party given in his honour, during the meal he crawled beneath the table, once more looking for spies. He would sometimes go out at night in disguise and listen to conversations outside tavern windows to determine who his enemies were. He confiscated considerable real and personal property for his own enrichment by claiming he was enforcing the Navigation Acts and trying to stop smuggling. Most often the persons affected by the seizures were or would become his political enemies.

Sir Christopher Codrington had been given a fine 763-acre formerly French estate in St Kitts by the council for his success in driving out the French. Parke considered Codrington an enemy and seized the plantation and took it for himself on the pretext that Codrington had disrespected the authority of the Crown and was an absentee owner residing in Antigua. It seems Parke regarded the part of St Kitts which had been French as fertile territory for enriching himself, and helped himself to other estates there in addition to Codrington's.

By 1710, the people had had enough of him. There had been riots and demonstrations in every one of the Leewards and on 7 December a crowd surrounded Government House in Antigua (located where the cathedral now stands) and demanded that Parke resign. He refused, and barricaded himself inside with armed troops. The standoff continued overnight. At mid-morning on 8 December, Parke ordered a cannon to be fired into the crowd, which amounted to about 800 by that time, to disperse them. Following that, the crowd reacted, overwhelmed the soldiers guarding him, and broke into the building.

In an exchange of gunfire inside the building, Parke shot and killed Captain Piggott, the leader of the opposition, and was himself shot in the thigh and fell to the floor. Accounts vary as to the events immediately following, but as best can be determined. Parke was then stripped naked and severely beaten with musket butts almost to the point of death and then dragged down the stairs to the street by an arm and a leg. Witnesses declared that his head could be heard thumping against each step on the way down. He was then laid in the street in the blazing sun while Government House was ransacked and pillaged.

Whether he died there or was killed by being dragged behind a horse into the centre of town '... which rak'd the Skin from his Bones ...'[16] is not clear, but the people so hated him that they prevented his burial and left his corpse in the street in the sun for several days. They destroyed Parke's pew in the church where he was to be buried before the service took place. Upon hearing the news of Parke's murder, the Queen did not send a military force to restore order but instead appointed a new governor who was much better regarded by the people of the Leewards.

Sir Christopher Codrington died in 1710 before Parke did and he never recovered his St Kitts estate. There was so much contention over titles to the formerly French lands that in 1717 the British parliament decided to sell all the estates at auction and cancelled all earlier grants. The proceeds of £48,000 were used to pay the dowry for the marriage of the daughter of King George I.

Most of the estates sold were large, and the medium-sized ones were gradually amalgamated into bigger ones. There was much discussion as to what should be the size of the estates sold. One group wanted them divided into small estates in order to bring more white settlers into St Kitts, but others favoured large and medium-sized estates as small ones were not consistently profitable. The latter group won out.

Placing the formerly French properties into full cultivation and the ending of the destruction of plantations which had occurred in previous wars between the English and French caused sugar production in St Kitts to rocket upwards in the eighteenth century and instituted a period of unprecedented prosperity for planters which would continue until the outbreak of the American Revolution in 1776.

9
Pirates and Privateers

The years 1680 to 1730 were the heyday of pirates in the Caribbean. They had existed before and continued to do so afterwards, but that half-century saw the growth of piracy to a point that pirate ships seemed almost as common in the Caribbean as merchantmen. In times of war some pirates were given letters of marque or commissions which made their activities legal. They then temporarily became privateers, preying on enemy shipping. During those years they were widely used by European powers during the almost continuous wars not only on the seas but on land as well. The rule was no prey, no pay. They were paid only by what they could plunder from an enemy and drew no wages from their respective governments.

Pirates were democratic, electing their captains and voting on division of spoils. They devised the first workman's compensation as well. For the loss of an eye or a limb, the payment was usually 500 to 600 Spanish pieces-of-eight, but the amounts varied according to the circumstances and the parts of the body damaged. The downside of the democratic regimen was that they were bound to answer to their captain only during battle and when not fighting they were practically uncontrollable. In age the average pirate crewman was in his late teens or early twenties and the captain in his late twenties to early forties. Life was short and brutal in those times and anyone, especially a pirate, living past 50 was a rarity in the Caribbean.

Many pirates began life in the islands as indentured servants rather than seamen. Their lives on land were so hard that fewer than half survived their indenture time. Others were convicts transported from English and French prisons to work as indentured servants slipped back easily into a life of crime. In those times a man could survive in England on £3 a year and it is difficult to blame a young man facing a difficult and short life to take the opportunity to make as much in a year in piracy as he would in a lifetime of honest labour.

A considerable number of pirates and privateers were black. Whether they served as free men or slaves on board ship is not known but most likely in both capacities. They often shared booty in the same proportion as did others serving in the same position and although they usually performed the hardest shipboard jobs, some skilled slaves served as sail makers and carpenters. As an example, the English frigate *Francis* captured and burnt the 32-gun French pirate ship *La Trompeuse* in Danish St Thomas in 1673 and noted that of the crew captured on board, 33 were white and 16 black.

Francis was dispatched from Nevis by Leeward Islands' Governor Sir William Stapleton specifically to destroy *La Trompeuse* and kill or capture Jean Hamlin, her French Captain, who had taken nine ships in the vicinity of St Kitts, seven of which were English. Governor Esmit of the Danish Virgin Islands was a rogue of the first order. His brother had preceded him in that post, but Esmit wanted the position for himself and had his brother declared insane and placed him in an asylum. There was then no asylum on the island so Esmit built one for that specific purpose. After this was done Esmit welcomed pirates and allowed them to sell their ill-gotten merchandise there and collected 10 per cent of the proceeds for himself.

When *Francis* burnt *La Trompeuse*, two other ships in the harbour caught fire. In the conflagration, Captain Hamlin and his officers escaped ashore and Governor Esmit refused to turn them over to the English. When Governor Stapleton learnt of this, he was furious. Never a man to mince words, the hot-tempered Irishman wrote Esmit:

> If you do not deliver him or make some atonement for the injuries you have inflicted on the English, I warn you, have a care. I shall come from the Leeward Islands with an armed force, blow you up as the Trompeuse, and pound any pirate you may have fitted out.[1]

An English writer in the seventeenth century complained that privateers in wartime were nurseries for pirates in peacetime. The first pirate and privateer captains in the Caribbean were sixteenth century Dutch freebooters, followed by French buccaneers and English pirates. Later they would be joined by Spaniards and Americans. The crewmen were of almost every nationality. St Kitts and all the Leewards were at the heart of piracy from the outset. The aim of the earliest 'Brethren of the Coast', as they sometimes called themselves, was to skim off as much Spanish treasure as possible.

By 1730, pirates were adversely affecting commerce to the extent that their benefits to warring nations were outweighed by losses caused by them. They preferred to plunder wealthy Spanish shipping but would attack and capture any vessel they could regardless of nationality or cargo. At that point the European nations turned against them with their navies and thereby curtailed their activities but never completely eliminated them.

Today modern pirates transport drugs through the Caribbean from South America to the United States and Europe where they are ultimately consumed. The outlawing of drugs makes the profits to all involved in the trade risky and therefore spectacularly high. Today's pirates corrupt island governments with United States dollars as surely as their forebears did with Spanish pieces-of-eight centuries ago.

For understandable reasons pirates did not record their activities. Most were illiterate and if they were not, they had no wish to have their log books and journals fall into the hands of law enforcement authorities and be used against them. In the safety of retirement some successful pirates or those allegedly pressed into service against their will wrote memoirs. Along with transcripts of trial evidence those are the best accounts of what transpired in those early times.

Captain William Kidd began his nefarious career in St Kitts. During the Nine Years' War in 1690, the 45-year-old Kidd was a crewman on a 20-gun French privateer anchored at Basseterre. Born in Greenock, Scotland, to a Presbyterian minister, he had done nothing to distinguish himself from his contemporaries until he organized the members of his crew who were from the British Isles and stole the ship at night from its French captain in Basseterre harbour and sailed it to neighbouring Nevis. There he presented the ship to Governor Sir Christopher Codrington of the Leeward Islands Colony. Codrington was impressed with Kidd's feat and very pleased to add that substantial vessel to his small forces, as the French were entrenched in St Kitts and threatened Nevis with invasion.

Codrington changed the name of the ship to *Blessed William* in honour of William of Orange, who had recently assumed the English throne, and gave Kidd command of it in recognition of his daring theft of the vessel under the very nose of the French enemy. Kidd was ordered to report to Captain Thomas Hewetson of the frigate *Lion* and accompany him on a raid to the French Island of Mariegalant, about 100 miles distant. Named by Christopher Columbus in honour of his ship *Santa Maria*, that small island was devastated by the raid. A satisfied Captain Kidd returned to Nevis carrying plunder worth £2000 on board *Blessed William*.

As soon as the expedition returned, the participants were dispatched to French St Martin to rescue an English raiding party which had been surprised by a French force and was in danger of being captured. After success in a blazing battle with a superior French fleet commanded by Jean de Casse, a French privateer who would become the first governor of Saint Domingue (now Haiti), the English troops were successfully evacuated to Nevis. Upon returning, Kidd was invited to a victory celebration. While he was on land his crew took a leaf from his book and stole *Blessed William* and the £2000 worth of booty and successfully made off with it.

The furious Kidd begged Governor Codrington for another vessel which was given to him. She was a captured French vessel renamed *Antigua*. Kidd searched for but never retook his ship. He went on to New York to refit the ship, married a wealthy woman, and later commenced a generally unsuccessful career as a pirate.

Kidd was at last captured by the English and tried as a pirate in London in 1701. At his trial Captain Hewetson was a witness. As to Kidd's conduct in the

Leewards, Hewetson testified Kidd 'was a mighty man' and 'fought as bravely as any man I ever saw'.[2] Hewetson's testimony was not enough, however, and Kidd was hanged, his body covered with tar and displayed in a iron cage at a curve in the Thames near London until it rotted away. It was a powerful example to anyone considering a career as a pirate.

Another pirate involved in the same action in St Martin, and possibly evacuated on Kidd's ship, was Bartholomew Sharpe. Sharpe led a regiment of buccaneers when the English invaded and recaptured St Kitts from the French in 1690. Not as well known today as Kidd, Sharpe was one of the few pirates who died of old age.

He had led a pirate fleet from Port Royal, Jamaica, to the isthmus of Panama in 1679, where he hoped to cross it and capture Panama City as Henry Morgan had done a few years earlier. He captured a Spaniard in a land battle who had abducted and raped the daughter of the Indian King of Darien (today Panama) and left her pregnant. The Spaniard begged Sharpe not to turn him over to the king and in return for protection from the king's wrath the Spaniard would guide Sharpe '... to the very bedchamber door of the Governor of Panama'.[3]

True to his word, the grateful Spaniard led Sharpe to Panama City but it was too strong to attack. In a spectacular and extremely bloody battle Sharpe and his men attacked three Spanish warships using small boats and captured two of them. He and his 'merry boys', as he called them, used the ships to terrorize the Pacific coast of the Americas from Panama to Chile for three years. Sharpe at one point took a galleon named *San Rosario* carrying a Spanish Admiral with a full set of charts for the Pacific coast These charts would save his life in an unexpected way two years later. Another passenger was a lovely Spanish lady whom Sharpe described as '... the beautifullest creature I ever laid eyes on in the South Seas'.[4]

Sailing the two captured Spanish ships around Cape Horn to Barbados, he and his men did not land because of the presence of an English frigate which it was feared would arrest the vessels and their crews. He continued onward to Antigua where, in spite of a substantial bribe of emeralds and pieces-of-eight tendered to and refused by the Governor, he and his crew were not allowed to land. He continued onward to Nevis where the Governor apparently had fewer scruples and allowed Sharpe and his men to land and dispose of his cargo there and in St Kitts. They had stolen so much indigo that when it came onto the world market the price dropped and a portion of it was warehoused in both islands until prices rose again.

The now rich Sharpe returned to London where he was promptly arrested along with Basil Ringrose, a colleague, at the demand of the Spanish Ambassador and locked up in the Tower of London where he would later face trial. This would be Sharpe's fifth trial for piracy and the fifth time he would be found innocent. In a seventeenth century plea-bargain, Sharpe offered to turn over the Spanish charts to the Royal Navy in return for his and Ringrose's freedom. The deal was accepted and Sharpe returned to the Leewards where he would command pirate troops in St Kitts and Nevis in 1690, and later proclaim himself Governor of Anguilla where he held court and was reputed to light his pipe from time to time with warrants for his arrest.

During the War of the Spanish Succession, French privateers wreaked havoc upon English shipping in the Leeward Islands. Governor Codrington complained that they not only took and plundered ships, but came ashore at night and stole slaves from coastal plantations in St Kitts and other islands.

As bad as privateering was during the war, when it ended in 1713 the privateers were no longer commissioned to prey upon enemy shipping and many slipped into outright piracy and continued their plundering. They no longer pillaged only enemy craft but went after their own nation's ships as well. By 1720 the situation had reached crisis proportions in St Kitts. That year pirates took ships several times in Basseterre, Old Road and Sandy Point harbours out from under the guns of the forts. The frustrated gunners in many cases dared not turn their cannon on the pirates for fear of hitting their innocent victims. Following one raid by Bartholomew Roberts in which several ships were taken, upon leaving he wrote a rude note to the Governor of St Kitts about the poor marksmanship and unpreparedness of his gunners.[5] Unfortunately the text of the note has not survived.

Two of the pirates who appeared in St Kitts that year were among the worst of the lot. One was Roberts, very successful and utterly ruthless. He first took two ships at Nevis and then crossed to St Kitts the next day and took two more out from under the guns of the fort at Basseterre. Roberts was a nominal Christian who would not take a ship on Sunday and was possibly the only teetotal pirate captain, preferring tea to rum. He tried to discourage excessive drinking by his crews but met with little success.

The other side of his personality was extremely unpleasant. He would use some of his prisoners for target practice by tying them to the masts and having his crew shoot at them from decreasing distances until the unfortunate victims died. At the end of his career he was active in West Africa. At one point he swept into a slave trading port and held all 18 ships anchored there to ransom. The captain of one British slaver named *Porcupine* refused to pay. The vessel was loaded with shackled slaves ready to be transported to the western hemisphere and Roberts's men decided to burn the vessel. The keys to the shackles were given to an African and he was ordered to release the slaves, but the process was too slow. Roberts reportedly tried to hold them back but his crew were impatient and fired the vessel while many of the slaves were still in chains. The man ordered to release them continued his job frantically with the ship burning around him. As the terrified slaves reached the deck of the burning

Porcupine, they had to decide whether to jump into shark-infested waters or burn to death. Only a few knew how to swim. Roberts's men took bets as to how long individuals on the burning deck could stand the heat before they jumped to certain death in the sea.

His career ended shortly thereafter when the frigate HMS *Swallow* attacked his ship off the coast of Guinea. During the first minutes of action Roberts was hit in chest and throat with a charge of grapeshot and killed. His crew threw his body into the sea and struck at the frigate. They were tried and almost all hanged. The court spared the African crewmen on his ship, however, in part because of the fiendish treatment of the slaves in *Porcupine*.

Another pirate who paid several calls to St Kitts at that time was the dreadful Edward Lowe, a depraved psychopathic killer. His ship was the grotesquely misnamed *Merry Christmas* and his flag was a blood-red skeleton against a black background. Governor John Hart of St Kitts wrote to England, 25 March 1723, that:

> I did not hear that there are any more pirates, except a ship commanded by one Lowe with about fifty pirates in his crew ... This Lowe is notorious also for his cruelty even to subjects of the British Nation; and as a greater monster never infested the seas, I submit it to your Lordships' superior judgement whether it ought not to [be] recommended to His Majesty that a Proclamation be issued, even with pardon to his accomplices, offering an ample reward to such as should bring him in dead or alive.[6]

Lowe, born in Westminster, was truly a monster and looked the part. His face had been cut open by one of his drunken crewmen who slashed at a prisoner with a cutlass and missed, hitting Lowe. The ship's surgeon, also drunk, was ordered to stitch up the wound. Lowe cursed him for his rough work and the surgeon took offence and punched Lowe in the face full force, ripping out the stitches and reopening the wound. The surgeon shouted to Lowe to 'Sew up your Chops yourself and be damned!'[7]

Lowe hated the Spanish, Portuguese and New Englanders in that order. He usually murdered the Spanish and Portuguese after cutting off their noses and ears. He burnt New England ships as he had worked in Boston and disliked the people there. He once raised two captured Portuguese friars into the ship's rigging bound in ropes and dropped them repeatedly to the decks until they died. He also cut off the lips of a Portuguese captain, fried and seasoned them and forced a prisoner to eat them, and then disembowelled the captain.

His most horrible act of barbarity was performed upon two masters of whaling sloops taken off Rhode Island. He disembowelled one, cut his heart out, cooked it, and forced the second master to eat it. Of all the pirates, Lowe is regarded by several experts as being the worst one ever.

Finally, even his crew of sadists had enough after Lowe shot and killed one of his sleeping crewmen. At that time killing a sleeping person was considered much worse than killing someone awake, and his crew put Lowe and two others in a longboat at sea near Guadeloupe. They were picked up by a French ship and the captain, upon determining who Lowe was, put him in irons and carried him into Martinique where he was immediately tried and hanged.

French pirates and privateers were as bad as the English. One of them bore the nickname of 'Half-Arse', as a portion of his buttocks had been carried away by a cannonball during battle. A possible rival to Edward Lowe as the worst ever pirate was Jean-David Nau, called L'Olonnais after his birthplace. He fortunately avoided St Kitts for the most part. At one time he ripped open the chest of a Spanish captain with a cutlass, pulled out his still beating heart, and tried to eat it. The muscle proved too tough and he could only gnaw on it. He met a fitting end when he was captured by cannibal Indians, roasted alive and eaten.

A French privateer who gained some notoriety in the Leewards was one Captain Daniel. A resident of French St Kitts wrote that in 1702 Daniel stopped in the French island of Mariegalante to get chickens and brandy for his crew and discovered a priest resided close by. Daniel decided it would be uplifting to have the priest conduct a mass on board the vessel for the benefit of his men. A makeshift altar was constructed on the ship and for dramatic effect when each prayer was completed a cannon was fired with a blank charge. During the elevation of the host a crewman shouted out a vile oath. Captain Daniel leapt to his feet and without hesitation shot the offender through the head. The man fell lifeless to the deck, and Daniel roared out that if anyone else interrupted the service he would meet the same fate. The startled priest continued the mass and when it was completed the body was thrown overboard and the shaken priest carried back to land.[8]

The French had an idea in the seventeenth century that supplying men inclined to piracy with wives would cause at least some of them to settle down and become productive citizens. The authorities in Paris swept the hospitals, streets and prisons and sent a shipload of whores to the French West Indies. One unrealistic French writer termed them 'timid orphans', but if there were any such on board, they were few.

According to accounts, the pirates were given a hour on board the vessel carrying the 'timid orphans' to choose one for themselves. Care was taken that fights did not break out over the women and when the choices were made, the pirates took the following oath and were married:

> I take thee without knowing, or caring to know, whom thou art. If any body from whence thou comest would have had thee, thou wouldst not have come in quest of me; but no matter. I do not desire thee to give me

an account of thy past conduct, because I have no right to be offended at it, at the time when thou wast at liberty to behave either well or ill, according to thine own pleasure; and because I shall have no reason to be ashamed of any thing thou wast guilty of when thou didst not belong to me. Give me only thy word for the future. I acquit thee of what is past [then striking his hand on the barrel of his pistol, he added] This will revenge me of thy breach of faith; if thou shouldst prove false, this will certainly be true to my aim.[9]

Evidently this well-intentioned effort did not succeed, as it was never repeated.

St Kitts was one of the last places in the Caribbean to have a mass hanging of pirates. In 1828 a pirate ship from Buenos Aires named *Las Damas Argentinas* was taken by the British frigate *Victor* at sea near neighbouring St Eustatius and along with her victim, the Liverpool brigantine *Carraboo*, sailed into Basseterre amidst the great excitement of the population of St Kitts. People climbed hills to watch the ships make their way from Statia across the channel.[10]

Las Damas Argentinas was a fast 90-ton schooner which had been built in Baltimore and outfitted as a privateer in 1826 when Buenos Aires (now Argentina) was at war with Spain for her independence. Her commander was Captain José Lazaro Buysan from Majorca in the Balearic Isles. He was of good family, educated in the local military academy, had been an officer in the Spanish Navy and had there seen action at sea against the South American rebels. The remainder of the officers were Spanish except for an American surgeon, but the crew was of mixed nationality consisting of British, Americans, Spaniards, French and a single German. One crew member was a black man from Tortola in the Virgin Islands.

For the first year of her career as a privateer she had followed her commission and acted under the articles of war but as so many of her predecessors had done, she crossed over the line into piracy when pickings became slim. The pirates boarded *Carraboo* off North Africa near the Canaries and determined she was bound for Buenos Aires with a cargo worth over £20,000. *Las Damas Argentinas* should have released *Carraboo* as soon as it was determined that her destination was to *Las Damas Argentinas*'s home port, but the value of the cargo made the temptation too great to resist. *Carraboo* was taken and her officers and men put into longboats at sea. Although the boats were overloaded, none of the sailors was badly mistreated by the pirates and all survived when they were picked up at sea by another vessel.

The crew of *Las Damas Argentinas* had been recruited in the Caribbean and it was decided by the pirates to take her to Dutch St Eustatius (commonly known as Statia) to dispose of the stolen cargo. Statia was known even at that late date as a nest of pirates where stolen cargo could be easily disposed of with no questions asked. It was related at the trial in St Kitts that unidentified vessels would frequently appear in Statia, be unloaded, and then sailed out to sea by a skeleton crew and sunk. However, some of Statia's leading citizens were disturbed about this trade and disliked the nature of the pirates and their local confederates and the general lawlessness which was a result of their activities.

Governor Stedman Rawlins of St Kitts had been informed of the taking of *Carraboo* and the fact she was reported to be in nearby Statia along with the pirate ship which had captured her. He sent an agent over to Statia and determined the truth of the situation. The Dutch authorities there were little inclined to cooperate with their neighbouring island and would not let the Kittians take the ships in Dutch waters unless they could keep a third of the cargo. Governor Rawlin's agent, Lieutenant Colonel Thomas Harper, declared the harbour at Statia was filled with pirate ships and he believed any attempt to take the two vessels there would cause the pirates to join ranks against the British. Harper suggested they wait until a British warship could assist.

HMS *Victor* and the British packet *Emulous* arrived in St Kitts on 3 September and upon being advised of the situation by Governor Rawlins both agreed to assist. On 6 September a schooner answering the description of *Las Damas Argentinas* was seen leaving Statia and *Victor* moved to intercept her. The schooner raised the Dutch flag and attempted to run for it. When she left Statia's waters *Victor* fired several warning shots across her bows and *Las Damas Argentinas* then raised the Buenos Aires flag and heaved to only when *Victor* overtook her and ran out her 18 guns in preparation for an attack.

After brief discussions, *Victor's* officers took control of the schooner and sailed her towards St Kitts. Excitement was running so high there that Governor Rawlins declared martial law and ordered the militia on the windward side to assemble by firing guns in the forts and raising the flags. When the two ships arrived in Basseterre, 28 militia men along with Marines from *Victor* took control of the prisoners and marched them under guard to the prison. Hundreds of people gathered in the streets to witness the event and jeered the captives.

An 'Especial Court of Grand Sessions for the Trial of offences committed on the High Seas' was convened, and a Grand Jury indicted the defendants. The Reverend Enoch Wood of the Methodist Church and Reverend Daniel Gateward Davis of the Anglican Church immediately went to the prison to minister unto the prisoners, most of whom were Roman Catholic. There had been no Roman Catholic church in St Kitts since the French had left the island in 1713, but the prisoners for the most part accepted the assistance of the Protestant ministers. Three of the crew turned king's evidence and agreed to testify against the others.

A clever local lawyer named James George Piguenit was appointed to defend Captain Buysan. His first motion was to declare that because the defendants were mostly foreigners, it was necessary to have a jury of their peers convened to try them. This motion was dismissed as there were insufficient foreigners present in St Kitts to form such a jury. He then applied for a separate trial for Buysan and this was granted.

Captain Buysan behaved in an arrogant manner on the witness stand and the jury quickly found him guilty. Before sentencing Buysan was allowed through an interpreter to argue that he at all times conducted himself as a naval officer rather than a pirate but the judge rejected this argument and sentenced him to die by hanging. Buysan then cried out in English, 'Then I die an innocent man!'[11]

The rest of the crew were tried and convicted to die by hanging except for two teenage cabin boys, one Spanish and one Scottish, and a Scottish seaman who had been sick for the entire voyage and had not participated in the attack. The three men who had turned king's evidence were also spared.

A gallows was erected in Ponds Pasture near Basseterre next to the sea and the prisoners were marched to it from prison under guard with a cannon firing from the schooner each minute during the march until they reached the gallows. They were accompanied by the two ministers and most repented of their crimes. One exception was Alfred Cooper, a very tall Englishman and a hardened criminal, who had to be restrained until he was hanged and refused to join in final prayers.

The 28 men hanged were executed in three different groups by nationality, and for all of them the last sight they saw was their pirate ship anchored at sea in front of the gallows. Before hanging, Captain Buysan gave his pocket watch to the lawyer who defended him, and was kept by his family until the last century when it was stolen. All the deceased were buried in a trench dug next to the gallows.

An interesting footnote is that Ponds Pasture was developed as an industrial park in the 1980s, and archaeologists were invited to investigate the area prior to building. They discovered a mass grave on the site and determined that it was that of the hanged pirates. A sure identification was provided by the skeleton of Alfred Cooper, the unrepentant seaman. He was six feet five inches tall and his bones were among the first to be discovered. All were left where they were buried.

10
The Eighteenth Century – the Best of Times and the Worst of Times

The eighteenth century began and ended with England and France at war, but the intervening years saw growth and prosperity in St Kitts which would never be equalled. However, the distribution of the wealth was vastly disproportionate, with the planters being the beneficiaries and the slaves and indentured servants receiving only the crumbs from the table, if that.

The termination of the War of the Spanish Succession in 1713 left St Kitts in considerable disarray. The desolate Nags Head area on the southeast peninsula had been taken over by roving bands of rebellious slaves who would continue to use it and the central mountains to hide in until emancipation. The French lands at either end of the island had passed into English hands permanently, but there were problems in distributing these estates until they were finally sold off by auction in 1717.

Many of the privateers from the conflict could find no honest work afterwards (most did not look for it) and turned to piracy. They plagued commerce in the Leewards to such an extent that merchant ships feared to trade in the area. Carrying sugar out and bringing goods in became very dangerous and the price of imported necessities doubled in St Kitts for that reason. The crackdown on pirates began in 1730 by the Royal Navy and in a few years had eased the situation to a considerable degree.

As an example of how rich the Leeward Islands colony was, from 1715 to 1719, the value of exports, almost all sugar, from these five tiny islands exceeded the value of all exports from British North America. The 4.5 per cent tax on goods exported from North America amounted to £383,576 and that of the Leewards was £403,349 for that period of time. That was before the formerly French estates in St Christopher came into full production and Nevis was still trying to recover from the 1706 French attack. These were the only years that comparative statistics are available and is an indication of how valuable the British sugar islands were to the empire at that time.

There was a problem with the disproportionate numbers of slaves to whites, and laws were passed in England and in the islands to encourage white immigration for military reasons. For a time they appeared to work in St Kitts but the quality of the arriving whites was not good. Called Servant's Acts, these laws were generally ignored. Governor Mathew wrote in 1734 that '... these Laws hitherto procure such Unwilling, Worthless, Idle Vagabonds, as from whom but little Service can be hoped for, on Military Emergencies'.[1]

In 1720, the population of St Kitts exceeded that of Nevis for the first time and was 2740 white and 7321 black. The Servants' Acts caused the white population to grow to 4000 by 1724, but by then the black population had increased to 11,500. In 1729, the population was 3677 white, 14,663 black. By 1774 the numbers were 1900 white and 23,462 black.

It is interesting to note that the number of slaves carried into the Leewards in the eighteenth century averaged 6000 per year, approximately the same number as came into North America. Their death rate in the Leewards was far greater than in North America. It was calculated that on the Middle Passage journey from Africa to the islands, 22 per cent of the slaves died, and upon arriving in the islands another two-fifths would die within a year. Migrating whites died at a rate of 7 per cent coming over from Europe, but fared no better than slaves after arriving and died at approximately the same rate.

On 14 March 1737 a ship arrived in Basseterre carrying a full load of slaves. The captain noted that they were restive during the day, and at about 5 p.m. over 100 ran across the deck to the ship's rail and threw themselves over the side. All possible means were used to rescue them, but 33 succeeded in drowning themselves. A subsequent investigation revealed that morning a St Kitts slave who could speak their language had come aboard and he was instructed to inform them they were to be brought ashore and sold as workers on local estates. As a joke, he told them that upon reaching shore, their eyes would be put out and then they would be eaten. Many of the slaves, weak and confused by the long voyage from Africa, believed him.

Epidemics of smallpox, malaria, yellow fever and dysentery killed black and white alike. In 1723, a smallpox epidemic caused so many deaths in St Kitts that the island was quarantined by Governor John Hart, formerly Governor of Maryland, for several months and no ships were allowed in or out.

In December 1725 Governor Hart was informed that a plan for a slave insurrection in Nevis had been discovered and the militia had been called up to put it down. Hart commandeered a sloop and journeyed to Nevis from St Kitts with 100 St Kitts militia to assist the Nevis troops if needed. Upon arriving in Nevis the troops captured the two alleged leaders. They were burnt alive, protesting their innocence as they died. The rebellion was quashed before armed violence occurred.

Other than epidemics the reasons for death differed between the two groups. Slaves often died of overwork combined with a poor diet very low in protein. Whites, on the other hand, often weakened themselves by excessive drinking and succumbed to diseases which they would have otherwise survived. A historian writing in 1740 declared, 'Rum Punch is not improperly called Kill Devil, for thousands lose their lives by its Means'.[2] It was noted in a 1702 yellow fever epidemic the proportion of male to female deaths in St Kitts was ten to one. Women drank far less, and some physicians believed men's heavy consumption of drink made the difference. A Governor of Barbados wrote in the eighteenth century that hard drinking West Indians '... have bodies like Egyptian Mummies ... and murther [murder] their guests with drink ...'[3]

In 1758, Christopher Jeaffreson, living in London, rented Wingfield Manor in St Kitts to Lord Romney for £400 per annum, and '... 40 gallons of good, pure and sound rum for the use of Christopher Jeaffreson ... ' to be shipped from St Kitts to London every two years.[4] Evidently Jeaffreson retained his West Indian drinking habits in England.

Lead poisoning was also a factor, although that was not known until years afterwards. Lead pipe was often used in the distillation of rum and the raw alcohol absorbed it during the process. Almost every building had stone cisterns for the collection of drinking water and the downspouting collecting the water was often made of lead or soldered with it. Some cisterns were lined with lead as well. Insidious poisoning slowly debilitated those rich enough to use lead in their drinking water systems. People in the islands were frequently stricken with what was called 'the dry belly-ache' and were cured only by moving to a temperate climate. No one knew why that was effective until an English physician who had worked near the lead mines in Derby recognized it as a symptom of lead poisoning.

Not a few prominent men died in duels. One of the most interesting ones was fought on the sands of Frigate Bay beach on 19 November 1752. Matthew Mills, a rich planter from St Kitts, was involved in settling a bankrupt Nevis estate. At the sale he and John Barbot, a young attorney residing in Nevis representing the opposing side, had words. Mills called him '... an impertinent puppy ...', among other things, and Barbot called him out.[5]

Arrangements were made for the two to duel without seconds. Barbot had the choice of weapons and borrowed a pair of silver-chased brass barrelled duelling pistols from Mrs Dasent who lived at Dasent's estate in Nevis. He put out from Nevis early in the morning in a boat rowed by a young slave and met Mills at Frigate Bay in St Kitts. Events which occurred afterwards resulted in Barbot being tried and hanged for the murder of Mills.

The laws of that time did not allow a slave to testify against a white man in court, and the only two witnesses were slaves. The first inkling something was amiss was when a slave belonging to Mills galloped up on horseback to a nearby estate and pounded on the great house door shortly after daybreak. When the sleepy owner responded, the slave cried out, 'Oh Lord Master, make haste and come down, for my master is fighting with sword and pistols with a gentleman that is come from Nevis!'[6] The two raced to the beach where they saw Mills lying on the sand, and a figure seated in the back of a boat clad in a white greatcoat being rapidly rowed away towards Nevis.

Mills lay on his back dead from a chest wound. Later in the trial in Basseterre, forensic evidence showed powder burns on Mill's waistcoat which was evidence that the shot was fired from close up. In addition, the ball had penetrated four inches straight into his heart from the front.

The Crown's case was that had the two fought a duel by the rules of the day, the shot would have been fired from several paces away, rather than close up. In addition, it would have entered Mill's body on the right side rather than the front. The Crown contended Barbot shot Mills in the heart in cold blood at short range rather than in a duel, and he was guilty of murder.

The two slaves who had witnessed the event were unable by law to testify in the court proceeding. Anything they had told others concerning the crime was hearsay evidence and therefore inadmissable. The case drew much interest in England as legal authorities there strongly disagreed with the island law which prevented slaves from giving testimony against whites. Justice was done, however. On the basis of the circumstantial evidence given in court, the jury found Barbot guilty of murder and he was hanged on 5 January 1753. No doubt the slaves' account of the incident made its way unofficially to the ears of the jurors.

Duelling was commonplace in the Caribbean and the passions sometimes ran very high. A writer in the early nineteenth century related that a duel occurred in Antigua and when one participant's pistol misfired, he rushed his antagonist and knocked him to the ground with the butt of the pistol.

Militarily, the island had difficulties unrelated to the population. In 1711 and 1731, lightning struck the powder magazine at Brimstone Hill, blowing it up both times. Thomas Beake of St Kitts petitioned the Royal Navy for military ordnance on 25 December 1731, as follows:

> The said Island hath for some time past been in a very weak and impaired condition in regard to its Forts, Fortification and all manner of stores, and tho' its condition was so bad is now rendered much worse by an accident of having the principal magazine in the island lately blown up by lightning in which was contained the greatest part of the arms and ammunition belonging to said island whereby they were all destroyed ...[7]

There were too few whites in St Kitts to provide for an adequate defence. Various suggestions were put forth to increase their numbers including one by the Governor in 1734 that 'negro tradesmen such as carpenters, coopers, millwrights, masons ... be forbidden employment to encourage white immigration as only 200 men are capable of bearing arms'.[8]

Difficulties with Spain were becoming acute during those years. The Governor of the Leeward Islands wrote to the Duke of Newcastle in 1735 that:

> The Spaniards from Puerto Rico have begun an open war with His Majesty's subjects in these islands, with the advantage of carrying off all they meet from close under the shore of St Christopher's ... We have not one of His Majesty's ships of war at present in the Government that I know of.[9]

The War of Jenkins's Ear between England and Spain began and ended in the year 1739. The Spanish vessels referred to above were coastguard ships which were intended to stop illegal trade between the Spanish and English islands and curtail piracy. According to the English the Spanish coastguards were pirates themselves. One stopped Captain Jenkins's ship and in the process of boarding her a Spanish officer cut off the captain's ear. Jenkins, himself probably a pirate or a smuggler, carried his ear to England where he presented it to the king and requested retribution against Spain for the injury. He got it. In the resulting war, no direct military activity occurred in St Kitts, which was fortunate as the island was poorly prepared for it. The war was really about the lucrative trade between the two empires. It was illegal in both but the British believed enforcement by Spanish authorities was unduly harsh towards their Caribbean subjects.

In 1736, the fortifications in St Kitts consisted of Brimstone Hill, 49 guns, Charles Fort (also called Cleverley Point Fort), 40 guns, Londonderry Fort east of Basseterre, and six batteries at many landing places armed with 43 guns altogether. Brimstone Hill was being enlarged slowly and by 1782 would be formidable indeed when attacked by the French.

The constant fear of attack caused the Assembly to pass a series of Acts in the eighteenth century requiring all able-bodied men to make themselves available as militiamen in the event of war. In 1769 the Act required all European males between 16 and 60 years to equip themselves with uniforms and weapons at their expense and to report for duty dressed out on Sundays at noon for drill. Should '... three topsail ships or four ships of any kind ...'[10] be sighted standing, the island alarm guns were to be fired at three-minute intervals and the militia were to gather at designated spots.

Not only the militia but all white males between 15 and 70 had to appear ready for duty at designated points in each parish. If the men could not afford arms and uniforms, public money was available for their purchase. Every white man in St Kitts was fully armed. In addition, all customs officers and registrars were to report to their offices and remove all public records and secrete them in secure hiding places. Carts, cattle, horses and mules were also to be removed to designated areas. As ships of that day were slow there was ample time to perform these duties before an enemy arrived.

In 1776, after hostilities had broken out in North America between the rebels and the British Crown, the penalties for non-appearance at drills or at alarms were increased and the militia pool was expanded to include free coloured males. The serving age limits became 16 to 65 years. Top officers were to wear scarlet coats with gold piping and lower ranking officers wore blue coats. All were to wear

> ... a Decent plain cocked hatt a wig or his own hair ... and carry ... a pair of Pistoles, a Carbine ... a Cartouche box to hold twenty four Cartridges filled with glazed Powder ... twelve to fit the Carbine and twelve fitted for the Pistoles and two spare flints for the gun and four for the Pistoles and also one pound of powder and four pound of Spare Ball ...

The 1769 Act noted that

> ... any Person or Persons white or black free or in Slavery shall during the Continuance of any Christmas Guard or upon any other Occasion behave in a disorderly and riotous Manner or cause any Tumult or Disturbance in any part of this Island ... the Commanding Officer of the Guard ... shall forthwith order a Detachment of Militia Men to take such person or persons so offending as aforesaid into Custody ... [11]

The Christmas Guard was established during the holidays as bands of slaves would roam the island performing musical shows at the estates and getting food, drink and money in return. If they did not receive what they believed was due them or harboured resentments against specific planters, disturbances could result. The militia was always on stand-by at those times and Christmas was not a happy time for the planters. Many slave uprisings in the Caribbean occurred at or around Christmas, such as the one in Nevis in 1725 when militia from St Kitts were sent across to help put it down.

> It is worthy of remark that most of the insurrectionary movements of the Negroes in these islands have taken place, or have been meditated to have taken place, about Christmas. The first incidence of revolt occurred on the estate of Don Diego Columbus, in Hispaniola, on the 27th of December 1522.[12]

These problems eased in St Kitts with the arrival of the Moravian and Methodist missionaries who converted the slaves and made Christmas a religious occasion. Many slaves would attend services rather than join roving bands and by the end of the eighteenth century Christmas Guards were no longer required.

On 18 April 1795 an Enabling Act established a slave corps in St Kitts. They were to be called 'The St Christopher Corps of Embodied Slaves'. Five hundred men joined and 40, armed with pikes and cutlasses, served at Brimstone Hill full time. Within two years the number grew to 1000. They proved to be very good troops. The West Indies commander, Sir John Moore, complained they were unfairly treated and should have been enlisted as British regulars and given their freedom at the end of their service rather than being returned to slavery.

It took nearly half a century for the Assembly of St Kitts to follow the advice of Governor Payne given in 1757 when he called for slaves to serve in the militia. He declared then that 'The Negroes stood by their masters in Nevis in Queen Anne's war while our flag was flying, they are most of them (we see) good marksmen, they don't love the French'.[13]

The Decline of King Sugar

By the eighteenth century the soil of the long-settled British sugar Islands had lost much richness through heavy cultivation. Barbados's production began declining by 1690, and Nevis's had fallen off so precipitously after 1700 that in 1723 it was suggested by the Governor of the Leewards that its local government be abolished and it be governed through St Kitts. Nevis rejected this proposal out of hand.

St Kitts at that time had the richest soil of any British island other than Jamaica. In 1760 William Burke wrote 'St Christopher is by far the best Sugar Island, both for the quality of the Sugar, and the Quantity it produces in Proportion to Extent; but it is very small indeed, and not one inch uncultivated, and must wear out …'[14]

By the time of the outbreak of the American Revolution in 1776, on a *per capita* basis, St Kitts was judged to be the richest colony in the British Empire. It was also considered the healthiest of all to live in. Even so, it had become necessary to fertilize the soil heavily and replant canes every year to keep yields high. Originally, canes required replanting only once every three years.

For this labour the import of slaves grew rapidly and they had to be fed. Crop land suitable for sugar was too valuable to be used for food production so almost all of it was imported from North America. Salt fish, flour, corn meal and livestock were brought in and sugar and molasses were sent out. For a time the trade was more or less balanced, but that was soon to end.

Demand for sugar had grown dramatically in Europe at the same time. In England, tea was becoming a popular drink and sugar was needed to sweeten it. The British Caribbean islands were at that time the world's leading sugar producing area and had a monopoly for providing sugar and molasses to Great Britain and her colonies. Demand grew, but West Indian production did not increase to meet it. Prohibitive tariffs were levied by Parliament on sugar and molasses produced in other empires, most notably the French. Much French molasses was exported from the Caribbean to British North America from their Caribbean Empire and taxed at a very low level upon entry.

In the British islands the main ties of the planters were to Britain and as soon as they amassed large and profitable plantations they would often return home and become absentee landlords, living in grand style in London or Bristol. Management of their estates was left to overseers, who were often dishonest with the landowners and cruel to the slaves. Nowhere was this more evident than in St Kitts, where almost all the plantations were managed for absentee owners. Absentee owners were taxed double what resident owners were on their St Kitts properties. The law did little to bring them home, was widely ignored, and repealed a few years later.

The situation differed in the French colonies where most plantation owners settled permanently in the islands rather than returning home and renting out their estates. The French adopted advances in agriculture and sugar production faster than the British did for this reason, and their production of sugar first equalled and then surpassed the British. The French Revolution contributed to this situation in the late eighteenth century, as many planters in the islands were royalists and after the nobility lost control of the French government and were killed, the planters' connection to the home they had known was broken.

Plantation owners resident in England did not spend all their time living lavishly but put their money to work to influence the British government to keep their sugar monopoly firmly in place. They bought seats in 'rotten boroughs' and their interests were thereby disproportionately represented in the House of Commons. Murmuring was beginning in England over the rising price of sugar caused by increasing demand not being met by higher production in the islands. This upsetting of natural market forces created a vacuum which was filled by smuggling French and Spanish produced sugar and molasses into the outlying bays of the sugar islands, rebranding it as British produce, and selling it into the British market at the artificially high prices prevailing there. For that reason, sugar production figures for the British islands at that time are suspect and there is good reason to believe they were lower than indicated.

The French producers, being largely resident, used new agricultural techniques to their advantage and production costs declined or stayed level while those in the British islands increased as more slave labour was required. The

French government discouraged production of rum in their empire as it interfered with the sale of French brandy and wine, so French producers had molasses available at about half the loaded cost of their British counterparts, and their sugar cost less as well.

A great deal of French molasses production was sold in North America, more specifically Boston, where it was distilled into rum. There was supposed to be an enumeration charge on non-British molasses and sugar levied in colonial ports, but dishonest customs agents in the islands and in North America were commonly bribed and issued false papers and bills of lading for French produce. As prices increased this practice became commonplace and contempt for the law was a predictable result.

The rich West Indian planters wanted to close the loopholes. The price of sugar in England was double that in France, and they wanted to keep it that way. The result was the Molasses Acts of 1730 and 1733. The acts did what they were supposed to do by closing the loopholes, but provoked howls of outrage from North America when importation of French molasses was effectively prohibited by high customs duties and because of that smuggling became more costly as well. At the time, most molasses used in North America came from French Martinique.

John Adams, the second president of the United States, seriously contended that the American Revolution was caused by molasses. It was a trivial matter, he declared, but wars had been caused by even less significant happenings in the history of humankind. The ultimate price of appeasing West Indian sugar planters would be the loss to Great Britain of the thirteen North American colonies.

A St Kitts Estate

When Major John Jeaffreson arrived in St Kitts on the ship *Hopewell* in 1624, as a boyhood friend of Sir Thomas Warner he was soon granted 1000 acres of land for a plantation. The original indenture, dated 1628, still survives. Jeaffreson named it Wingfield Manor. The plantation was given '... at the yearly Rent of One Ear of Indian Corn to the King his heirs & successors (if demanded) forever'.[15]

It remained in the hands of the Jeaffreson family for 200 years. John Jeaffreson and later his son Christopher made it successful, first by growing tobacco, indigo and ginger and then adding sugar in the mid-seventeenth century. The family became rich and returned to England in the late seventeenth or early eighteenth century and lived very comfortably as absentee owners.

Fortunately, much documentation regarding Wingfield Manor has survived the years. A book was written in 1878 by a descendent about the first

Christopher Jeaffreson entitled *A Young Squire of the 17th Century* using these papers and others as background material.

From what documents survive, it can be seen that the estate was let for only £100 annually in 1692 for bare ground and with no slaves or buildings because of damage caused by the Nine Years' War. It was noted that '... of the 10 or 11 ships which departed carrying sugar only 2 have returned, because of Privateers'. The lease contained a clause increasing the rent by '... six score pounds per annum following the signing of a Peace Treaty'.[16]

For many years the pound sterling kept approximately the same value until the Napoleonic Wars. The normal annual rental of the estate varied from £400 to £700 per year until the first decades of the nineteenth century, except in times of war, when it could be reduced. Because of inflation the annual rental increased during the Napoleonic Wars to £1200. In spite of requests by the lessee, hurricane damage was not allowed as the basis of a rent reduction.

From 1713 to 1819, Lord Romney's family leased Wingfield Manor from the Jeaffresons. Romney owned an estate adjacent to it and could therefore cultivate both properties easily. Because of the 1758 lease clause promising Jeaffreson 40 gallons of rum from the estate every two years, problems arose between him and Lord Romney. Jeaffreson complained that the rum shipments were badly in arrears and what rum had been sent was of inferior quality. When the lease came up for renewal in 1819 following '... the annihilation of Bonaparte',[17] Jeaffreson believed that the sugar business would prosper and he expected a better price for the lease.

Romney was not so optimistic. He pointed out that slaves were almost impossible to purchase because of the cessation of the African slave trade and when Lieutenant General Christopher Jeaffreson asked for a rental sum of £1000 per annum, Romney countered with an offer of £600. Jeaffreson would have accepted £700, but he refused to negotiate because of his irritation over the rum. A Mr John Tyson offered a rental of £1200 per annum for the estate, which seemed too good to be true. It was, but Jeaffreson accepted it, much to his later regret.

Conflicts immediately arose over the harvesting of the cane crop which was in the ground. Romney demanded the value of it less the cost of cutting and processing it. Tyson took possession of the estate before he was supposed to and harvested the cane, but claimed a share of one third for his efforts. In addition, rent payments were slow and the required rum allotment was again not forthcoming.

Jeaffreson had wisely insisted that a reputable firm in Great Britain guarantee Tyson's rent and this had been done. By 1822 Tyson wrote that because of a precipitous drop in sugar prices he could not meet the terms of the lease and asked that a year's rent be excused. Jeaffreson refused and demanded the guarantors pay him. This was done after a 'long and tedious' lawsuit was instituted and the guarantors, Dennistoun of Glasgow, took over the operation of Wingfield Manor.

In addition, Jeaffreson sued Lord Romney over some slaves he accused Romney of taking from Wingfield Manor to Romney's adjoining estate upon expiry of the lease. The lawsuit noted the slaves carried the surname of Jeaffreson, but Jeaffreson's lawyer wrote confidentially that it would be nearly impossible to determine the origin of the slaves as they had been born in St Kitts rather than purchased and no recent records existed of slave births at Wingfield Manor.

The final result of the lawsuit is unknown, as the correspondence ended before the matter was finally settled. Romney's attorney in St Kitts had agreed to negotiate the matter, however. By this time the decline in the sugar industry in St Kitts was pronounced and it would never improve. These matters indicate how difficult and inefficient absentee ownership of a sugar estate was in those years.

From the early sales of tobacco, depredations of the French during the seventeenth century wars, the eighteenth century years of great prosperity, and finally the decline of the industry in the nineteenth century, a picture of the island's economic activity from the viewpoint of a rich absentee planter's family is very revealing.

The Seven Years' War

In 1756, the Seven Years' War broke out between France and Great Britain, and its outcome would determine which one of the two nations would become the world's greatest military power. No direct action would take place in St Kitts but there was considerable naval activity in the area. It would become the gathering spot for merchant ships carrying sugar to convoy and sail to England escorted by Royal Navy men of war.

In 1756 it was reported that 320 ships in a single convoy left Basseterre under escort. This activity put considerable funds into the local economy. Taverns, gaming houses and whorehouses for entertainment of sailors sprang up at harbour side. British privateers were also attracted to St Kitts and made Basseterre their home port in the Caribbean for activities against the French.

That same year, one of the Royal Navy convoy escorts was short-handed and the captain decided that he would send a longboat into Basseterre and press some of the seamen from privateers into service on his ship. Impressment of seamen was often the way the Royal Navy obtained full crews. They would simply take men off the streets or out of merchant ships and taverns and press them into service whether they wanted to go or not. Needless to say, this practice was extremely unpopular.

When the longboat landed at Basseterre and the sailors in it attempted to press unwilling men into service, a riot ensued. The Royal Navy sailors were overpowered and beaten by the crowd. Their longboat was taken and with considerable effort, dragged from the seafront to the centre of town, filled to the top with rum punch, and the privateers proceeded to drink it dry. No one attempted impressment in St Kitts after that incident for the remainder of the war.

In 1759 the British frigate *Crescent*, under Captain Collingwood, encountered two French frigates in the area, *Amethyste* and *Berkly*, and engaged them both at the same time. In the lopsided fight *Crescent* was the unexpected victor. She captured *Berkly* and brought her into Basseterre harbour as a prize.

In North America this war was called the French and Indian War, as Indians, allied with the French, attacked British settlements in New England with much bloodshed. Most Indian attacks were resisted by colonial troops, but in Canada a British Army under General Wolfe fought and defeated a French army under General Montcalm on the Plains of Abraham before Quebec City, and control of French Canada passed into British hands. When the war ended, the British were the clear victors worldwide from Canada to India.

When the terms of the peace treaty ending the war were concluded the French were given the option of keeping Canada or the Caribbean islands of Guadeloupe, Martinique and St Lucia. Today it seems absurd that such an apparently lopsided choice was given but then it was considered nearly an even trade. The value of the sugar exports of these three islands greatly exceeded that of furs and timber from Canada, and most of Canada was considered to be nothing but frozen wilderness. Sugar prices in Britain were too high and for that reason many wanted the French islands to be absorbed into the British Empire in order to increase sugar production and increase the supply. The land area of Canada was vast but empty, yet it had potential for future development.

The last thing the West Indian sugar planters wanted was for sugar and molasses prices to fall because of increased production within the British Empire. Increasingly inefficient in the British islands as compared to the French, they recognized that the inclusion of the French islands into the British Empire would result in plummeting prices and economic inconvenience to themselves. They brought their considerable assets into play to convince all concerned parties that the French should give up Canada rather than the three Caribbean islands. There was opposition to this in Britain but the planters prevailed. The result of the French decision to give up Canada had profound consequences in world history which continue to this day, but they were not immediately evident at that time.

With the elimination of the French military threat to the North American British colonies, the colonists there realized that they no longer needed British power to defend themselves from a foreign invader pressing down on them from the north. Anger resulting from the Molasses Acts of the 1730s had been long brewing and resulted in a deep anger towards interests in the mother country which ran contrary to those of the North American colonies. Even though the economies of the sugar islands benefited from the results of the war, the results were to be short lived.

In St Kitts the economy boomed. Profits were huge to the planters in the most fertile and productive of the sugar islands. Slaves benefited hardly at all but funds were available for local projects. In 1768 the Assembly passed Acts to bring water down from the mountains for drinking and irrigation of the sugar crop in times of drought. Roads were improved and fortifications, especially Brimstone Hill, were strengthened. The planters resident in St Kitts lived lavish lives and planted almost every bit of available land with sugar cane. It was reported that the planters would often consume huge meals eating as much as a pound of meat a day while slaves subsided on as little protein as a single kipper a day would provide.

There were grumblings in St Kitts about the perceived indifference of the mother country to all but the wealthiest planters. The Navigation Acts and their trade restrictions continued to annoy islanders. In 1765 the British Stamp Act did more than simply create annoyance. In St Christopher and Nevis there were demonstrations against the Act which developed into riots and tax stamps valued at £2000 were seized by rioters and burnt in protest. A report written that year declared:

> The populace suffered themselves to be so far imposed on by the crews of some New England vessels in their harbours, as to go even greater lengths than the New Englanders themselves; particularly, the population of St Christopher's who not content with the burning of the Stamped paper of their own island and making those appointed to distribute it to renounce that office went over in a body to assist their neighbours in Nevis in taking the same precautions against it.[18]

Another problem which was created by widespread trade restrictions was a lack of coinage in the islands. This problem existed from the time of earliest settlement to the mid-nineteenth century and was increasingly critical in St Kitts in the eighteenth century as the island became more prosperous. Governor Codrington had complained about the situation early in the century and declared scarcely one in a hundred Spanish pieces-of-eight circulating in the islands was of full weight, as they had been shaved on their edges for silver. When striking coins became more sophisticated in later years their edges were milled to prevent this practice.

A barter system then existed in all the British islands based on pounds of sugar. Even slaves were sold to planters by the Royal African Company in exchange for sugar until a temporary drop in sugar prices in the early eighteenth century caused them losses. The practice then ceased and specie payment was demanded for slaves. This aggravated the need for coinage considerably. North American and Dutch traders wanted specie as well in payment for their goods and as a natural result illegal trade with the Spanish grew. When St Kitts planters were short of coin, sometimes the solution was to sell slaves to the Spanish possessions.

Money called 'currency' or 'island pounds' was used throughout the British Caribbean. The value varied from island to island, but on average an island pound was worth around 45 per cent of a pound sterling. No paper or metal money was issued to reflect this, however. Coins from all nations were used interchangeably in St Kitts but Spanish pieces-of-eight, first called 'dólares' and later 'dollars', were the most common. Commonly used foreign coins were given a value in sterling by law, and some of these Acts also laid down the death penalty for conviction for counterfeiting or shaving coins.

The abolition of slavery first exacerbated then solved the coinage problem. Prior to emancipation it was determined that if former West Indian slaves would have to be paid in coinage, there was not enough available to do it. In 1809 a joint British-Portuguese force had invaded Cayenne (now French Guiana) in South America and confiscated the local coinage. These coins were of silver and silver bullion and bore the portrait of the King of France. Held by the British for some years and not melted down, the coins were of low value and were put into circulation in the Leewards for the purpose of paying wages to emancipated slaves. However these coins were often counterfeited.

However, there were problems. The coins were called 'black dogs' but the origin of that name is not known. In 1837 a petition was presented to the St Kitts Assembly declaring that 'The coin called the black dog has been generally refused ... the labouring class generally possess these coins ... measures should be adopted to alleviate the situation ...'.[19] The measure taken was to overstrike some of these coins with a punch showing the letters 'SK'. All the other Leewards used the same coins and overstruck them with the letters 'N' for Nevis, and 'M' for Montserrat. They then were accepted by local merchants.

In 1838 the coinage problem grew. The Treasurer of St Kitts complained to the Assembly that the Colonial Bank would take gold Spanish doubloons only at face value and would not give change in silver, nor would merchants change them. There was not enough silver coinage locally available to do it. Land taxes were in large amounts and often paid to the Treasury in doubloons. A doubloon then was valued at $16.00 local currency or £7 4s(hillings) British currency. As a result, the Treasurer stated that gold doubloons could be accepted for tax payments only at full face value and no silver change would be given.

The permanent solution was that the British mint sent quantities of small silver British coins to St Kitts and the other islands. At last the coinage problem was solved. By the early nineteenth century the British economy was the world's strongest and by then it had sufficient coinage to meet the needs of the West Indian colonies for the first time. Even so, in 1854 American gold Eagles valued at ten United States dollars and their 'silver pieces' were made legal tender in St Kitts by Act of the Assembly, which was an indication of growing United States economic strength and influence in the Caribbean.

Rebellion in North America

By the late eighteenth century in North America a growing number of residents believed that some adjustments would have to be made with Britain in order to allow full development of those colonies, especially as the French threat from Canada had ceased to exist. These feelings existed in the islands as well, but the French presence in the Caribbean had not diminished so the complaints were muted.

An excellent comparison in conditions between the islands and North America can be found in the journal of Miss Janet Schaw of Scotland, who visited both areas in 1775. Her family had estates near Wilmington, North Carolina, but she stopped on the way there in St Kitts to visit friends. Because of prevailing winds and currents, sailing ships from Columbus's time onwards would leave Europe and sail into the Caribbean, where they would pick up the Gulf Stream current and favourable winds and proceed northwards.

She paused briefly in both Antigua and St Kitts, and was enchanted with St Kitts. She noted that all the roads were shaded by flowering or fruit trees and that the plantations were neatly laid out with impressive dwelling houses. Her observations were confirmed by a French priest who visited at about the same time. He commented 'The taste for rural life, which the English have retained more than any other civilized nation in Europe, prevails in the highest degree in St Christopher's'.[20]

Miss Schaw, however, was critical of the agricultural practices used in comparison with those in Scotland. Scotland was then in the forefront of farming advances and almost any place would suffer by comparison. A major factor contributing to agricultural backwardness in the islands was the sugar monopoly. Planters in St Kitts did very well and in the opinion of most they did not need to mend something that was not broken. For instance, the use of the plough was never exploited as much as it could have been in the sugar islands. Hoes were used for cultivation instead.

The lady noted that Sunday market was the big day for slaves who grew produce and raised animals to bring them into Basseterre, and their produce was of better quality than the small amount raised by planters on their plantations. She commented that great quantities of manure were used for fertilizer and it was hoarded and placed in compost heaps for use in planting new cane.

A shrewd observer, she commented, 'St Christopher's, they tell me, is almost abandoned to Overseers and managers, owing to the amazing fortunes that belong to Individuals, who almost all reside in England'.[21] She stayed at Olivees Plantation, which was almost certainly the one which had belonged to Monsieur d'Olive, the Frenchman who led the French settlers to Guadeloupe from St Kitts early in the previous century. It was owned in 1775 by William Leslie Hamilton who was a prominent planter and attorney, speaker of the House of Assembly, member of the Council, and Attorney-General. Hamilton's wife, Lady Isabelle, was the daughter of the tenth Earl of Buchan, and a childhood friend of Miss Schaw.

She described the great house: 'It is between fifty and sixty feet long, has eight windows and three doors, all glazed; it is finished in Mahogany very well wrought, and the panels finished with mirrors'.[22] It was considered one of the best plantations in St Kitts at the time.

She went on to describe the slaves who worked the fields.

> The Negroes who are all in troops are sorted so as to match each other in size and strength. Every ten Negroes have a driver, who walks behind them, holding in his hand a short whip and a long one. You will too easily guess the use of these weapons; a circumstance of all others the most horrid. They are naked, male and female, down to the girdle, and you constantly observe where the application has been made.[23]

She noted that slaves were forced to jog uphill carrying cut cane and run downhill all day carrying composted manure for fertilizer. They were not allowed to walk or they would be whipped. In 1770, only a few years before she visited St Kitts, a plot for an alleged slave rebellion had been uncovered, but it was a false alarm. It turned out not to have been a rebellion at all, but only a large Sunday religious service held in the country.

Miss Schaw wrote later in her journal that in North Carolina the estates were far apart, disorderly in appearance and the dwellings were primitive compared to St Kitts. There was so much sentiment for independence there that ultimately her family gave up their properties and returned to Britain. She commented that she had not met such feelings in St Kitts. However, there were some which manifested themselves after her departure and had she visited St Kitts two years later, she would have found a different situation.

There was a powerful radical group in St Kitts, which Leewards Governor Burt in 1778 characterized as '… factious, disappointed and Gallo-American principled'. He continued '... your Lordship may rest satisfied I will eradicate these monsters or fall in the contest'.[24] In 1780 Burt wrote to England:

> The disposition of that assembly [St Kitts], as well as of others in this part of the world, having caught the infection from America and deeply tinged with the principles of Republicanism, attempt to bring all to a level and assume privileges to which I cannot think them constitutionally ... entitled.[25]

Miss Schaw's host, William Hamilton, was nearly bankrupted by events in St Kitts in the years following her visit. As Attorney-General, he left his plantation and moved into Basseterre because of the constant agitation caused by the pro-American contingent. He gave up his valuable private practice of law and spent much of his own money fulfilling the duties of his office.

Because of French military activity in the region Lady Isabelle returned to England in 1779. Many of their possessions were sent back on another vessel which was captured by the French. Hamilton followed in 1780, and died four days after arriving in England at the age of 31 years. In 1778 it was reported that 300 whites fled St Kitts to avoid bankruptcy court proceedings and evidently the exodus continued for years afterwards.

Some years later a friend of Lady Isabelle had occasion to dine with the Marquis de Bouille, conqueror of St Kitts in 1782 and Governor of the French Antilles, and noticed some of Lady Isabelle's family china on his sideboard in Martinique. It had been taken from the captured ship. Lady Isabelle wanted it back. The American Ambassador, whom she asked to help her have it returned by the Marquis, calmed her as best he could by pointing out such were the fortunes of war and little could be done about it.

In all the Leewards at that time government consisted of a locally elected Assembly and an appointed Council and a local Governor, or President, under the ultimate authority of the Governor of the Leeward Islands colony. The general rule was that the Assembly could pass Acts which lasted under a year and the Council passed Acts lasting longer than a year. Council Acts had to be approved by the British parliament.

In order to vote or serve on juries in St Kitts the voters, white males only, had to own property or be possessed of goods valued at £50 or more. Qualifications changed slightly from time to time, but females, poor whites and all blacks could not vote. A more subtle discrimination occurred with Grand Juries, upon which only voters could serve. Very often alleged criminals were not even indicted if they were influential or accused of violating an unpopular law.

In spite of these limitations, the Assembly sometimes proved to be difficult for the local establishment to control. In 1770 seven members of the

St Kitts Assembly were arrested and jailed by the speaker. A minor riot occurred and after legal proceedings the men were released but deprived of their seats. They ran again in the next election and all were re-elected. It was said that they had assumed advantages in St Kitts which were given to the House of Commons in Britain. What exactly those privileges were has been forgotten but that difficulty had the same origins as did the North American troubles; resentment against the Crown's authority.

Despite internal problems St Kitts remained loyal to the king when war broke out in 1775 in North America. However, the overall Caribbean situation changed when the Continental Army under General Horatio Gates soundly defeated a British Army commanded by General John Burgoyne at the Battle of Saratoga in 1778 and France allied with the Americans.

When the French heard of that victory they believed it was possible for the rebels in North America to actually win the war. The French were itching to get back at the British for their recent defeat in the Seven Years' War. French entry radically changed the situation in the Caribbean. A planter in Nevis wrote to England because of the French action he would '… go bankrupt or starve to death, or both'.[26] He was not far wrong.

The British had instituted a naval embargo upon the rebellious American colonies, but with their extensive coastline vessels slipped through in spite of it. Americans had no navy but their privateers immediately set upon British shipping, much of which was bound for the West Indies. Commerce was disrupted and shortages were soon felt in St Kitts. They were most acute in bulk products, such as salt fish, flour, livestock and timber. British ships carrying molasses and sugar northwards experienced difficulties as well.

At the beginning of the conflict neutral Dutch, French and Spanish shipping partially filled the trading void. The islands were far from self-sustaining in food production. Planters in St Kitts had believed it was more efficient to plant sugar everywhere possible and use the profits to buy foodstuffs from North America rather than grow it themselves on a large scale. In 1754 Governor Thomas of the Leeward Islands had written that 'Almost every Inche of the Leeward Islands is cultivated, from thence the Price of Fresh Provisions is double what it is in Jamaica, where they have great tracts of Pasture Land'.[27] As costly as it had been before, the war caused the price of food used to feed slaves to increase fourfold. The fortunes of the planters began to melt away.

Soon after the French, Spain entered the war on the American side with hopes of regaining their colony of Florida, which they had lost to the British in the War of Jenkins's Ear in 1739. The Dutch continued to be neutral and made fortunes trading with the British islands from St Eustatius near to St Kitts.

However, that would cease in 1781 when an angry Britain, fed up with the Dutch cross-traders, declared war on Holland. The rebellion in North

America had become a world war by eighteenth-century standards. What prompted the British declaration of war on Holland was an incident taking place in Statia in 1780. An American ship flying the new flag of the American colonies appeared in the harbour and lowered her colours as protocol required. The normal procedure in every port was for the guns in the harbour fortifications to fire a salute with blank charges recognizing the flag if the nations were not at war. If the procedure was not followed, it indicated the countries were at war.

The Governor of Statia did not know what to do. Officially, the thirteen colonies were still British and that was the flag the vessel should legally have flown, but the rebellion in North America was still going on after five years of fighting. The Governor hastily convened his council and the decision was made to recognize the American flag by firing the salute, and it was done. That salute was the first international recognition of the United States as an independent country.[28] The British were enraged. In 1781 a powerful fleet under the command of Admiral George Brydges Rodney attacked Statia and laid waste to it. The Admiral described Statia as:

> That nest of Vipers, which preyed on the vitals of Britain ... an Island inhabited by rebellious Americans and their agents, disaffected British Factors, who from base and lucrative Motives were the great support of the American Rebellion, Traitors to their King, and Patricides to their country ... [29]

He burnt the ships and warehouses which were filled with cargoes destined for the British Islands. That was not all. He rounded up the 101 Jewish inhabitants of Statia for banishment with one day's notice, and when they were gathered in a group all were all stripped naked and searched. Items valued at £8000 were taken from them. Rodney's ill treatment of the Jews was vigorously objected to by the Reverend James Ramsay of St John's Capisterre church in St Kitts. His intercession on behalf of the Jews stopped the plundering of their property and Admiral Rodney changed his mind and allowed those already banished to return. This active priest also spoke out against slavery in St Kitts and was pilloried by the establishment for doing so.

The planters had already paid for much of the destroyed goods with letters of credit and were furious at Rodney's destruction of them. St Kitts was the most hard hit by this because of its proximity to Statia. There was an angry outcry from merchants and planters and a letter was sent by John Glanville of St Kitts to the British Admiralty demanding Rodney be cashiered from the Royal Navy for destroying property legally owned and paid for by British subjects. Glanville's letter declared:

... that their property, fairly bought under the sanctions of the acts of parliament, had been taken from them; that insurances for some of these goods had been ordered to be made in England; that they held their excellencies answerable for all risks ... and they would seek redress by all means in their power.[30]

Rodney was a very capable commander but had a disagreeable personality. His career was very nearly ended by this action, as through the years he had offended many people who saw it as an opportunity to get back at him. Fortunately for Great Britain, the Admiralty recognized that his ability outweighed his personal unpleasantness. He retained his position and in the West Indies would win a great victory for his country the following year.

Rodney's fleet visited St Kitts after the reduction of Statia and offloaded at Sandy Point eight new 24-pounder cannon with 6000 round shot and two 15-inch mortars with 1500 explosive shells which were intended to be mounted in Brimstone Hill Fort. The laws of St Kitts required planters to supply the government periodically with healthy male slaves for maintenance of roads and fortifications but because of anger at Rodney the planters refused the St Kitts government's repeated requests for slave labour to move the guns up to the fort. This fit of pique on the part of the planters would cost St Kitts dearly in 1782.

Brimstone Hill – the Gibraltar of the Caribbean

In 1689 and then in 1690 in a war, first French and then English troops had climbed Brimstone Hill and successfully used it as a high point to fire down upon the enemy. In 1690 the English moved up four cannon with which they bombarded enemy troops entrenched in Fort Charles below the hill and the use of Brimstone Hill as a fortress began.

It was recognized as an excellent defensive position. A fort was constructed and heavy 24-pounder cannon were mounted in it. A 24-pounder of that era could be fired with reasonable accuracy up to a distance of half a mile, and with increasing inaccuracy up to a mile and a half. From its height of 972 feet, projectiles could reach ships anchored below the fort for a good distance because they were shooting downwards. By 1780 Brimstone Hill had expanded into a great fortress believed to be impregnable by its builders. It was not, and the French would prove it in 1782.

Until the Napoleonic Wars few British troops were sent to the West Indies. The primary reason was that a posting there was considered a death sentence both for officers and enlisted men. This was not because of war, but disease. Of all British soldiers sent from Europe to the West Indies during the Napoleonic Wars, it has been calculated 51 per cent died there.

Only a small fraction perished in battle. The remainder succumbed to yellow fever, malaria, dysentery, dropsy, and poisoning from lead and fusel oil found in poorly distilled rum. The annual death rate from disease was often as much as 18 per cent, and several times that number were ill. The average number of troops reporting sick in the West Indies per day was about 20 per cent and through the course of several years, entire armies would melt away from disease. Specific figures for Brimstone Hill are not available but there is no reason to think it differed from other fortifications in the area such as those in Antigua and Barbados. Evidence found in archaeological digs at Brimstone Hill confirms the high death rate there.

These appalling figures indicate why recruitment of slaves for military service in the West Indies increased and also in Africa (mostly Sierra Leone) for the West Indies Regiments began. Soldiers raised in tropical climates fared much better in the West Indies than did Europeans. Death rates for black troops were less than half those of Europeans, and the blacks did not drink to excess to the same extent as did the Europeans. Their rates of desertion were far lower as well. By the end of the Napoleonic Wars over one-third of the British forces in the West Indies was black.[31]

As a result of constant illness the rate of desertion of British troops was considerable and the punishment handed out for that and other offences would be considered inhuman today. Drunkenness was constant among both troops and officers and was tolerated as it was believed by the upper echelons of the British military establishment that, without alcohol, morale would plummet and desertion increase. They were probably correct.

Discipline was enforced by the whip. Punishment by flogging was commonplace and anywhere from 300 to 500 lashes were given for desertion, theft and insubordination. As many as 1000 were given for sodomy (which usually went unpunished unless especially flagrant). Execution of deserters by firing squad or hanging was not uncommon, nor was branding an offender in addition to lashing him.

It is interesting to compare the punishment of soldiers to that of slaves. At the same time as the punishments handed out to soldiers were as noted above, unwritten law in the Leewards limited the number of lashes given to disobedient slaves to 39. When in 1810 Edward Huggins of Nevis gave two slaves close to 300 lashes each in the public market the British public was justifiably outraged. Why was the even more extreme punishment regularly handed out to British soldiers and sailors ignored? Even when the Napoleonic Wars had ended it continued until the 1830s and 1840s. Discipline in the French army and other European forces was nowhere near as extreme as in the British army.

In 1779 the French fleet made its first major appearance in the West Indies. Commanded by Admiral Count d'Estaing, the island of Grenada was taken from the British and in September the fleet blockaded Nevis while the French considered an invasion. Their plans were thwarted by nature when a hurricane dispersed the fleet on 9 September and Nevis was spared. The French had their eye on St Kitts and believed that holding Nevis was necessary for the protection of a land force invading St Kitts. Their plans were merely postponed. With British sea power drawn off to North America the Caribbean islands were vulnerable and the French intended to take full advantage of it.

In 1781 under command of Admiral Count de Grasse, the French fleet was being prepared for action in the West Indies from Martinique. The King of France then ordered the fleet to go to North America and resupply the French and Continental armies fighting under General George Washington. De Grasse operated on a strict timetable. The Americans had use of the French fleet for a limited time only and if whatever they wanted it to accomplish could not be done within that time frame, so be it.

Washington and his French ally General Rochambeau had pinned British General Lord Cornwallis in Yorktown, Virginia, with the sea at his back but the outcome was by no means certain. The British still held the four largest cities in the rebellious colonies. The Continental and French forces were short of food, clothing and ammunition, and the rebel government was bankrupt.

At that point Admiral de Grasse appeared with his fleet from the West Indies carrying critically needed supplies. Cornwallis was awaiting a British fleet from New York carrying food, military ordnance and troops which would allow him to fight his way out of the trap or barring that, evacuate his army to fight elsewhere. When the British fleet, commanded by Admiral Thomas Graves, appeared off Yorktown they were very surprised to find de Grasse already there. The two fleets formed up to fight and the Battle of the Virginia Capes began.

De Grasse used the standard French tactics of refusing to engage in close action unless necessary and leading the slower British fleet on a merry chase. There were minor skirmishes but after a few days Graves realized he was helpless and returned to New York for reinforcements. De Grasse had won a critical victory. As a result, Cornwallis received no supplies and after a long siege, surrendered his starving army to Washington. Some historians have said that without de Grasse's victory, the surrender would have been the other way around.

The French were not finished. Returning to the Caribbean right on schedule, de Grasse and the Marquis de Bouille, Governor of the French West Indies, planned first an attack on Barbados and as a back-up plan, an all-out assault on Brimstone Hill in St Kitts. They intended to take Britain's rich West Indian sugar colonies while the British remained embroiled in the American Revolution.

In 1775 William Pitt had declared before Parliament that four-fifths of Britain's overseas wealth was in the Caribbean. Brimstone Hill was the key to the Leewards and if it was taken the entire colony could fall into French hands. The French fleet made for Barbados as planned but because of adverse winds they were unable to reach it. The fleet returned to Martinique, re-supplied, and set out for St Kitts.

The St Kitts government had been advised by British Intelligence on 22 December 1781 that the enemy was close by. 'It having been represented to this House that the French Fleet are out in considerable numbers …' [32], the Assembly took immediate measures to strengthen the military situation of the island. Two small bombproof powder magazines were ordered to be constructed at Brimstone Hill without delay, and 150 cords of wood and 100 hogsheads of coal were ordered to be delivered immediately to the fort for cooking purposes. However, the cannon and mortars landed earlier at Sandy Point by Admiral Rodney were still not mounted at Brimstone Hill as they should have been.

The Marquis de Bouille was in command of the ground forces and de Grasse was the naval commander. With more than 7000 troops and 50 warships, de Grasse left Martinique. De Grasse's flagship was the mighty three-decker ship of the line *Ville de Paris*, 110 guns, at that time the most powerful vessel on earth. The British knew he was on his way but as the war in North America was continuing they could muster no fleet of equal strength to oppose him in the West Indies. The French reached St Kitts on 11 January 1782, landed their considerable forces and proceeded to lay siege to Brimstone Hill.

The Battle of Frigate Bay – 'A sulphurous hell …'

On 22 January Rear Admiral Samuel Hood departed Antigua for St Kitts with a fleet of 22 ships of the line. De Grasse had 36 ships of the line and Hood realized a direct ship-to-ship battle would be risky indeed, but he was determined to go into action nevertheless.

The French had already disembarked their troops and de Grasse was prepared for such a contingency. On 25 January he attacked Hood's rear but was forced to withdraw because of unfavourable winds. Residents of both St Kitts and Nevis climbed hills and mountains to observe the engagement of the two fleets as soon as cannon fire was heard.

De Grasse's fleet was anchored in a battle line off Frigate Bay close to land, and when Hood was sighted coming around Nevis Point (Nags Head) closing for action, de Grasse moved his ships further out from land in order to fight more effectively upon the open sea, a move which would prove later to be a mistake.

Hood saw his opportunity. Knowing the wind and sea currents, he developed a brilliant plan. He ordered his ships to appear to be withdrawing but instead to suddenly tack around the end of the French line on the leeward side and come between de Grasse's fleet and the land, which they accomplished successfully. A helpless de Grasse immediately saw Hood's plan but could do nothing to stop him. Hood stole the favourable position and turned the tables on de Grasse. Because of the wind direction, de Grasse's ships would now have to run the length of Hood's line rather than the other way around.

The Battle of Frigate Bay was described as '… a sulphurous hell, with cannon vomiting forth flame and death'.[33] The description was accurate and the entire battle lasted from 7 a.m. to 6:30 p.m. The major action began in the afternoon with de Grasse signalling his lead ship, *Pluton*, 74 guns, to proceed down Hood's line with the rest of the fleet to follow.

> … the *Pluton*, commanded by the gallant D'Albert de Rions, and supported by the whole French Fleet, sailed down the English line, at anchor at Basseterre, receiving the crashing broadside of ship after ship until the splintered planking flew from her off side and her rigging hung in a tangled mass as she bore away to St Eustatius.[34]

The French were getting the worst of it, but they drew blood when *Ville de Paris* sailed down the line. Her massive broadside sent masts and spars tumbling and timbers flying from the British ships, but she took 84 hits at the waterline in return and had to have them plugged following the battle.

When the battle ended, neither side had clearly won and both had been badly punished. The French fleet suffered more damage and higher casualties than the British, but Hood lacked the power to drive de Grasse off and in the coming days could do little more than observe the action on land and harass the enemy whenever possible.

This he did very effectively. His ships captured the cutter carrying the heavy siege guns the French had planned to use to bombard Brimstone Hill. De Grasse dared not remove any cannon for that purpose from his ships as Hood posed a constant threat. However, the Marquis de Bouille had discovered the heavy guns and ammunition left the year before by Admiral Rodney at Sandy Point, and promptly turned them upon the British in Brimstone Hill.

Another ship had been dispatched from Martinique carrying additional cannon to replace the ones lost to Hood. However, the vessel carrying these guns grounded and sank off Sandy Point trying to evade Hood's ships, and the guns had to be slowly and laboriously salvaged one-by-one from the wreck by the French.

The Marquis de Bouille was in a quandary. He had carefully planned an attack expecting to have enough heavy cannon to batter down the walls of Brimstone Hill but he was short of the required number of guns. He and de Grasse conferred and it was decided de Grasse would take both Nevis and Montserrat and remove all the large British cannon from those islands to use in

St Kitts. Ultimately, the Marquis de Bouille obtained a total of 23 heavy cannon and 24 mortars, most of them British, to use against the fort.

The French fleet had passed within cannon range of Nevis on the way to St Kitts. The Nevis militia mustered out and manned Fort Charles at Charlestown, hoping fervently Nevis would be spared by the French. De Grasse held his fire as he sailed by and the Nevis forces, having only 26 'old and indifferent' cannon in Fort Charles, did the same.[35] On 1 February de Grasse dispatched the 74-gun ship of the line *Le Glorieux* to Nevis to demand its surrender, and commandeered 40 slaves to remove all the 18- and 24-pounder cannon from Nevis's fortifications for use in St Kitts. A delegation from Nevis was transported on that ship to St Kitts and the surrender of Nevis was signed on board *Ville de Paris* 3 February 1782.

De Grasse was a generous victor. He was appalled to discover that Nevis was so short of food that immature sugar cane was being crushed for molasses to feed the slaves. St Kitts was little better off. The President of the Nevis Council gave de Grasse '10 fat sheep' for his table. De Grasse accepted them as a gesture, but wrote that more gifts of food would be refused, as the slaves there were near starvation. In an unprecedented move he allowed British ships to pass in and out of Nevis without being taken as prizes because of its destitution.

De Grasse sent a small occupying force to Nevis and guaranteed no slaves would be taken but that any caught bearing arms of any kind could be executed. He was aware that in 1706 the slaves of Nevis had held off a French army for two weeks. He did not want anything to happen there in 1782 which would require troops to be removed from St Kitts to put down a slave uprising in Nevis.

A squadron of French ships of the line sailed to Montserrat and repeated the performance there, receiving a bloodless surrender and removing the largest guns and carrying them back to St Kitts.

The Siege of Brimstone Hill

The British defenders at Brimstone Hill numbered only 850, but they were under capable commanders, Generals Shirley and Fraser, and their position was very strong. They returned fire shot for shot against the French cannon emplacements below. Each side would periodically go out and retrieve as many of the solid iron cannonballs as they could and fire them back at the enemy, but food and the powder supply at Brimstone Hill was limited and rapidly diminishing.

Most of the British cannon fired solid iron shot weighing 24 pounds and the French heavy guns fired shot weighing about 22 pounds. As a result, the British could, with extra wadding, use the slightly smaller French cannonballs in their ordnance but the French could use British balls only in the 24-pounder British guns they had taken. This fact stretched British resources as far as ammunition was concerned, but did nothing to help the powder supply.

In the countryside a band of troops from the St Christopher Corps of Embodied Slaves fought very effectively.

> On St Kitts ... slave irregulars fought with such tenacity and daring (they almost managed to ambush and capture the enemy commander-in-chief) that the French threatened to lay waste to the entire island if their less courageous masters did not bring them to heel.[36]

De Bouille had surrounded Brimstone Hill with gun emplacements and concentrated his fire on a 200-yard length of stone wall at the top of the hill rather than firing shot randomly at the fortifications. Now that he had adequate cannon he kept them shooting night and day at that one target. The slaves who had constructed Brimstone Hill had done an excellent job erecting the masonry, which absorbed the punishment of thousands of cannonballs and still held after three weeks of bombardment.

In the meantime Hood and his ships were not idle. They landed 700 troops on the southeast peninsula under General Prescott with a plan to fight their way through the French forces into Brimstone Hill, if possible, in order to reinforce the defenders. The hopes of the British were dashed when they were confronted by 3000 French troops near Basseterre who had quickly marched overland from their camp at Brimstone Hill. The British withdrew and returned to their vessels without engaging the enemy.

De Bouille and de Grasse were gentlemen and treated the population of St Kitts respectfully. Plantations were taken over and French officers put in charge of them, but there was little plundering and no widespread destruction of anything but military installations.

After three weeks of bombardment the French tactics paid off when large sections of the target wall of Brimstone Hill finally collapsed, breaching the Fort's defences. By then only 500 of the 830 initial defenders were still capable of bearing arms. The Fort could be taken by a foot charge up the hill through the breach, but it would be costly in terms of lives lost for both sides.

A parley was arranged and the British surrendered the fort and all of St Kitts and Nevis to the French. The defenders had performed so gallantly that they were allowed by the French to march out of the fort with their band playing and colours flying. St Kitts militiamen were allowed to return to their homes, as were the armed slaves who had fought alongside the British troops. Some pressure had been put upon the British by the French who declared that unless a surrender was quickly arranged the island, spared up to that point, would be systematically pillaged and burnt. Fortunately this was avoided. Even so, the loss to St Kitts was considerable and later estimated to have exceeded £100,000.

Following the surrender Hood's fleet slipped away during the night. He feared being pursued and engaged at sea by a superior French fleet which had repaired some of its damage locally. Hood was not able to do the same as the French held St Kitts, Nevis and Montserrat and could conduct repairs in those port facilities. At night Hood ordered his fleet to cut their cables to avoid the noise made by raising anchors, and mounted false lights in open boats. He allowed his fleet to drift away silently on the current and when at sea distant from St Kitts, they raised their sails and made off. De Grasse did not realize they were gone until sunrise. By then Hood had disappeared and it was too late for de Grasse to go after him.

The agreement of 12 February purported to surrender Nevis as well as St Kitts. This was possibly not done on purpose, but a payment of 500 'joes' had to be made monthly to the French as long as they occupied St Kitts. A 'joe' was a small Portuguese gold coin and got its nickname as King Johannes's (João V's) portrait was on the face of the coin.

Nevis was bound to pay 150 of the total by the terms of the agreement. The Nevis Council took issue with this after the fall of Brimstone Hill and attempted to refuse payment of their share on the basis that the 3 February surrender agreement of Nevis superseded the St Kitts agreement as far as Nevis was concerned.

The President of the Nevis Council, John Herbert (the uncle of Frances Woolward Nisbet, later to become the wife of Lord Nelson), wrote to Lord Shelburne in England, that '... this little worn out island of Nevis ...' should not be forced to bear a quarter of the cost of maintaining the French occupying government of St Kitts. Further, he noted of the surrender agreement '... the inhabitants and legislature of Saint Kitts were eagerly maneuvring to turn it to their advantage ...' and that the agreement had been made without the '... privity and consent ...' of Nevis.[37] With his letter he included a copy of the Nevis surrender document.

In St Kitts, Count Dillon, the occupying French commander, dismissed the Nevis supplication and declared that according to his orders, he was to ignore the terms of any surrender agreement other than the one of 12 February 1782 and therefore Nevis was bound to pay the 150 joes per month. He further declared that '... the gentlemen of Nevis are much given to chicanery ...'[38]

The British Colonial Office ultimately decided the disagreement in favour of Nevis and the payments it had made were refunded to it by St Kitts after the peace treaty ending the war was signed.

The fall of Brimstone Hill and the capture of the Leewards (except for Antigua and its important naval base) encouraged the French to continue their military action against British possessions in the Caribbean.

In Martinique they prepared an expedition against Jamaica. Once more, Admiral de Grasse was naval commander. The British fleet which at that time had gathered in Antigua under the command of the much-maligned Admiral Rodney was far stronger than Hood's had been at St Kitts and more numerous than the French fleet. Near the Isles of the Saintes, close to Guadeloupe, the two fleets met on 9 April 1782.

After having chased de Grasse's faster vessels for two days without being able to close with him, Rodney found himself in a favourable position because of a wind shift and immediately went for the enemy's battle line. Rather than coming alongside de Grasse's fleet, which was the normal method of such an engagement, Rodney forged straight ahead and broke through the French line, bringing the full weight of his firepower against the rear portion of the French fleet and devastating it.

This had not been done in a naval battle for 125 years. By the time de Grasse's leading ships could reverse course and join the contest nearly a third of his vessels had been badly damaged or disabled and he had little hope of victory. Ultimately six French ships of the line were captured and one sunk, as against no losses for the British, and the irascible Rodney had won a great victory.

The battle lasted nine hours and the rumble of cannon fire could be heard throughout the islands. The 62-year-old Count de Grasse, six feet tall and heavy set, fought like a man half his age. After fighting *Ville de Paris* until no powder or shot remained, his adversary from the Battle of Frigate Bay, now Rear Admiral Sir Samuel Hood, came alongside. Hood's ship, *Barfleur*, 94 guns, pumped a full broadside into *Ville de Paris* at pistol shot range. De Grasse was unable to return fire. In addition to being out of ammunition, 300 of his 900 man crew were dead and his ship was taking water fast. He had no alternative to striking the *Barfleur*. It was related that not finding an uninjured man on deck, de Grasse lowered the colours himself and gave up his ship to Hood.

It has been pointed out by naval historians that Hood's action at Frigate Bay in St Kitts, although inconclusive, damaged the French fleet so badly that their proposed attack on Jamaica was delayed long enough to allow Rodney to assemble his fleet at Antigua and later win the Battle of the Saintes.

Both the brave de Grasse and his ship both met a sad fate. After the battle *Ville de Paris* was placed under British command, temporarily repaired, and sailed to Canada for a full refit. In heavy seas off the coast of Newfoundland, the damaged vessel foundered and sank with her crew of 800 officers and men. All were lost. De Grasse was not on board but had been transferred to Admiral Rodney's flagship as a prisoner.

Perhaps it would have been more merciful had he gone down with his ship, as his country never forgave him for losing the Battle of the Saintes. His wife left him and he died in isolation, pilloried by his countrymen in spite of an otherwise fine record as a naval commander and his gentlemanly conduct towards his defeated enemies in every instance.

The French occupation of St Kitts lasted for not quite a year following its capture. Shocked by the loss of Brimstone Hill, Britain at last came to the negotiating table with the United States and her allies and a treaty was hammered out. The victory in the Battle of the Saintes saved Britain from humiliating terms in the Treaty of Paris. St Kitts, Nevis and Montserrat were returned to Britain by the French. The thirteen North American colonies were granted full independence and Florida was returned to Spain. Canada was retained by Britain.

When the French departed from St Kitts and the Leewards under the terms of the treaty, they systematically spiked all the cannon they did not take away, and blew up the powder magazine at Brimstone Hill. However, St Kitts estates were spared the destruction which had accompanied the earlier Anglo-French wars. In spite of considerable financial losses to planters caused by the war, commerce returned to near normal afterwards.

However, the British Navigation Acts curtailed trade with the new United States. Enforcement of them was becoming more and more difficult as the islands depended heavily on North American trade. The Dutch still cross-traded with North America and the islands, but American ships would often fly false English colours and come openly into British colonial ports.

Pro-American sentiment grew in St Kitts. Admiral Rodney noted in his journal that on 18 March 1785 some Irish residents celebrated St Patrick's Day and American independence by throwing a boisterous party in central Basseterre. He wrote:

> Yesterday being St Patrick's Day, the Irish Colours with thirteen stripes in them was hoisted all over the Town. I was engaged to dine with the President but sent an excuse, as he suffered those Colours to fly. I mention it only to show the principle of these Vagabonds.[39]

No less a personage than Captain Horatio Nelson of the frigate *Boreas* commented on this sentiment when he was patrolling the Leeward Islands to enforce the Navigation Acts. In 1785 he declared in a letter that 'The residents of these islands are Americans by connection and interests, and are inimical to Great Britain. They are as great rebels as ever were in America, had they the power to show it'.[40]

Nelson spent much time in both St Kitts and Nevis, but more so in Nevis where he met and married Frances Woolward Nisbet, a wealthy young widow, there in 1787. Nelson had arrested four ships in Charlestown harbour which were disguised American vessels and seized the cargoes. He was sued for £40,000 by the Nevis merchants who owned the cargoes. He won the suit, but had to spend much time in Nevis because of it and was entertained by

Mrs Nisbet's uncle John Herbert, President of the Nevis Council. At a dinner at Herbert's plantation he met Frances and fell in love. When they married at Montpelier Plantation on 11 March 1787, Prince William Henry, later King William IV, was his best man.

In a professional sense Nelson put his time in the Leewards to good use. He studied Admiral Hood's tactic at Frigate Bay of getting between the enemy and the coast and used it against the French in the Battle of the Nile. At Trafalgar he improved upon Rodney's daring stroke of breaking the French line in one place in the Battle of the Saintes by breaking the enemy line in two places at Trafalgar, with spectacular results.

It has been calculated that in 1775 a tonne of West Indian sugar brought the equivalent of US$5000 in today's money.[41] That price would begin a slow and inexorable decline in the nineteenth and twentieth centuries. According to *The Economist* of 27 November 1999, bulk sugar on the world market sold for 0.04 United States cents per pound (in weight) and was expected to drop beneath its all-time 1983 low of 0.03 cents per pound in the year 2000 because of a growing glut of sugar. It did so, but in 2001, the price had rebounded to 0.04 cents per pound. Although the planters could not know this, the heyday of St Kitts and all the British sugar islands had ended. The loss of Haiti by the French to rebellious slaves in 1804 caused sugar prices to rise, but this increase was to be short lived.

Religion and Slavery

During the years of joint French and British occupation of St Kitts, the Roman Catholic Church was the established religion in the French quarters and the Church of England in the British quarters. Both churches were supported by stipends from the respective governments, but the Roman Catholic Church was sent packing when the French departed and in 1702 Roman Catholics were forbidden from settling in any of the Leewards and this law was not repealed until 1753. It was feared that in the event of the war Catholics would go over to the French or Spanish. This act was specifically aimed at the Irish, as many had settled in the islands. There was a substantial community of Irish in Irish Town, now part of Basseterre.

In 1777 the Moravian Church, also called the United Brethren Church, sent missionaries to St Kitts. They had a German background and were serious evangelical Christians, who believed slavery was wrong and said so. They were not a charismatic group and met with little initial success and by 1784 had only 40 converts, all black.

They were regarded by the power structure as being rather harmless religious fanatics but were closely watched. They were not encouraged in their mission and received no financial support from government. Funding of their efforts came from donations and grants from the main body of the Church overseas. However, by 1785 their numbers had increased to 279 and by 1790, 2500. The Moravian church in Basseterre was built in 1795. They were allowed to preach to slaves on 50 estates as it was believed by some planters that converted slaves would be less likely to rebel than non-Christians. By 1819 they had a new settlement at Cayon and the church there was consecrated on 21 February 1821.[42]

In 1788 the Methodists appeared in St Kitts. Bishop Thomas Coke, one of the early founders of the Church, made three trips to the Caribbean from 1788 to 1792, stopping in St Kitts on each one. His untiring efforts in organizing the new denomination were to a great extent responsible for the considerable success of the Church both in the Caribbean and North America.

On his first visit to St Kitts on 19 January 1788 he was invited to preach at the courthouse in Basseterre and he noted '... the Crowd was prodigious'.[43] Coke and Mr Hammett, the missionary assigned to St Kitts, also visited Sandy Point and stayed there in the home of a Mr Summersal.

Bishop Coke went to Statia from St Kitts and was pleased to find there a freed converted black man named Harry, who was such a powerful preacher that during his sermons on a single day 26 persons were so overcome by the spirit that they fainted. The Dutch Governor, however, was not pleased and ordered Coke and the other Methodists to leave at once. By the time of his second visit 27 December 1789, the number of Methodists on St Kitts was 700. He noted that on 28 December an earthquake shook the house he was staying in for several seconds and was felt in the surrounding islands as well.

Coke also visited Nevis and Statia. The Church was doing well in Nevis as it was in St Kitts, but Statia was a different story. Harry, the forceful preacher, had been horsewhipped and banished by the Governor from the island. As if that were not enough, a law had been passed that anyone publicly praying, if white, would be fined 50 pieces-of-eight and if black, would receive 39 lashes. Upon learning of the presence of Coke and his team of missionaries, the inhospitable Governor ordered them off Statia at once.

They chartered a sloop to carry them back to St Kitts. Upon setting forth they discovered the entire crew was drunk and they collided with a larger vessel, damaging the rigging of their ship. In spite of the accident they continued on. Heading into the Statia Channel, the drunken crew turned the damaged sloop towards the Caribbean rather than St Kitts. The inexperienced missionaries themselves had to take control of the vessel, bring her about, and return to the harbour. In doing so they damaged the rudder but arrived safely. When they returned, the Governor forbade them from preaching and told them to leave the next day without fail.

On 2 January 1789 Coke journeyed from St Kitts to Nevis and arrived at ten in the evening. It was too late to travel to the home of his host so he took a room in an inn at Charlestown. His room was next to one containing a billiard table:

> ... where the blaspheming, dissolute, reprobate Billiard players kept me awake until about two in the morning. Their horrid blasphemies tempted me beyond the bounds of charity: they almost made me thankful, that the irregular lives of these pests of Society must necessarily, in this torrid clime, soon root them out of the land of the living.[44]

Coke's host in St Kitts was a Dr Bull, who lived '… high on the side of a burning mountain …' and had as fine a garden as Coke had seen in the West Indies. There is little doubt that this man was Dr Zachariah Bull of Cayon in St Mary's parish, a member of the St Kitts Assembly. At the top of the mountain, Coke commented that '… the ground was so hot one could barely walk over it … but the mountain had not thrown up any lava since the first European visitation'.[45]

He preached to a 'love-feast' on 27 January in Basseterre where he noted that many slaves gave 'lively accounts' of their conversions. He declared that in St Kitts '… religion flourishes like an olive tree in the house of God'.[46]

He noted there were two missionaries in St Kitts, William Warrener and George Skerrit, and the Church had grown in numbers to 280 mulattos and 1120 blacks. In Nevis there were 1800 members. On his final visit to the islands in 1792 there were four missionaries in St Kitts: W. Black, John Harper, Robert Pattison and Joseph Telford. The number of Church members had grown to 1522.

The Methodists opposed slavery as did the Moravians, but were not so forward about it. The seeds of emancipation were being sown in the islands. The winds of change were blowing in Britain as well. William Wilberforce and others attacked the institution of slavery in Britain and their speeches fell on sympathetic ears. At that time slavery was not considered the evil by most people that it is today. The Bible itself bade slaves to serve their masters, and with religion a much more important factor in day-to-day life in those times, that admonition was good enough for many. However, accounts of the inhumane treatment of slaves in the Caribbean were publicized and repugnance towards the institution soon manifested itself.

Planters fought back with arguments and published treatises declaring that without slave labour sugar could not be economically produced and the effect of the loss of income and duties produced by sugar would cause Great Britain's economy to suffer greatly. It is very likely that slaves were not brutalized on many plantations, but there were so many instances of inhumane treatment that even pro-slavery planters could not deny they were widespread.

The pro-slavery arguments did not go unheeded, but public opinion in Britain was turning against it. There were cases of mistreatment of slaves in St Kitts where the perpetrators could not even be tried as no jury would indict them. Those guilty of misconduct were most often overseers or plantation managers, and so were the majority of voters and jurors. Even in cases where the perpetrators were tried, the penalties were usually no more than a slap on the wrist.

One Jordan Burke of Basseterre was indicted for cutting off one ear and slitting the other of a female slave named Clarissa. On 8 March 1785 he was fined £50 for the offence. Later that same year Mr Wadham Strode was fined £100 for doing the same thing to his male slave Peter. In England such an act would have been a misdemeanour and a conviction would have resulted in a severe penalty and a prison term.

In 1786 a Basseterre merchant named William Herbert was fined 60 shillings for severely beating a six-year-old slave boy named Billy and his sister. He had even torn out some of their hair. The children were taken from him by the court, treated by a physician and healed. Herbert threatened to sue the Attorney General to get them back and for damages for deprivation of the children's services after they were removed from his custody. Rather than bringing such an inflammatory case to trial where publicity adverse to St Kitts was bound to result, the children were returned to Herbert and no more questions were asked.[47]

Such outrages could not be ignored. Parliament passed the Amelioration Act in 1792 which specifically prohibited the cruel punishment of slaves, but sadly the situation in the Leewards did not greatly improve because of it. In 1810 a Nevis planter named Edward Huggins marched 30 slaves into the public market in Charlestown where he had three different drivers flog them, two almost to the point of death. Between 250 and 300 lashes were administered to a man and a woman. One of them, the woman, died the following day. Huggins was charged with cruelty under the Amelioration Act and acquitted by a 12-man jury, all but two of whom were overseers or planters. Following his acquittal, a St Kitts newspaper which printed a Nevis Assembly Resolution condemning Huggins was fined £15 in a court proceeding brought by him for libel.

The legal proceedings in the Huggins case were publicized in Britain by abolitionists and resulted in an outpouring of anti-slavery sentiment and ultimately an amendment of the Amelioration Act limiting the number of lashes which could be administered to a slave to 39. Also in Nevis in 1830 an overseer named John Walley working on Lord Combermere's estate had been brought before a Grand Jury on three charges of murder, one of manslaughter and one of mistreatment, all of slaves. Lord Combermere had been the Duke of Wellington's Chief of Staff at Waterloo.

In only one case did the Grand Jury return an indictment and in that trial the testimony of the slave witnesses was disallowed because the alleged murder took place before the law had been changed allowing slaves to testify against whites in court in October 1828. Of the twelve jurors sitting on the case, all but three were plantation owners, managers or overseers. Walley was freed.

This sorry incident was such an obvious miscarriage of justice that the Governor of the Leeward Islands William Charles Maxwell sent transcripts of the proceedings to England for review by the Privy Council. The Nevis courts then were under the jurisdiction of St Kitts. Viscount Goderich of the Privy Council reviewed the matter and corresponded with Lord Combermere about it. Combermere, who owned estates in both Nevis and St Kitts, wrote to Goderich that he had been in India at the time and was unaware of Walley's misconduct and had promptly sacked him upon hearing about it. He noted he had personally given orders to his estate managers in both islands that slaves were to be treated humanely, and had introduced both the plough and wheelbarrow on his estates to ease their working conditions. As far as future cases of punishment for brutality against slaves, Combermere hoped for it yet sadly observed '... but I fear we cannot expect a jury at Nevis or St Kitts to do their duty'.[48]

Planters in the British Islands had been horrified by the carnage in neighbouring French islands which had occurred after the French Revolution when slavery had been abolished, and then reinstated later by Napoleon Bonaparte at the instigation of his Martinique-born wife, Josephine. Haiti exploded in rebellion. In Guadeloupe the blacks rose up and killed many whites and to prevent such an occurrence in Martinique the British, in spite of being the traditional enemy of the French, were invited in for a time to administer the island and keep the peace, which they did successfully and departed as agreed.

British planters used all their power and influence to stop the anti-slavery forces in Great Britain, declaring that similar disorders would take place in British islands and wreck them economically if emancipation were granted to the slaves. This argument seemed logical to many. Because of this violence and the ongoing Anglo-French Napoleonic wars, the move for emancipation was slowed but not ended. Looking back, it would appear inevitable slavery would soon end but at the time it was by no means clear.

A New Power Emerges in the Caribbean

War made strange bedfellows in the 1790s. The infant United States of America by 1799 had constructed three excellent frigates which constituted their entire navy. Because of the French Revolution relations between the United States and their French ally had become strained and powerful French commerce raiders were taking American ships on the high seas. There was no declared war, but President Adams dispatched the frigate *Constellation* to patrol the Caribbean and protect American merchant ships. The British allowed American ships to use Basseterre harbour and provided necessities to *Constellation* there. At least one American seaman found the pleasures of the town too great to resist and jumped ship. With the help of a St Kitts constable, the man was found in 'a place frequented by sailors'[49] and was forcibly returned to his vessel.

On 9 February 1799, *Constellation* departed Basseterre and was patrolling north of Nevis under the command of Captain Thomas Truxtun when an unidentified ship was spotted. She was the French frigate *L'Insurgent*, 40 guns, France's most successful commerce raider which had taken 11 American prizes. When *Constellation* showed her colours, *L'Insurgent* raised the tricolour flag and fired a cannon to windward in defiance and ran for it in the direction of Saba. *Constellation* gave chase. The 38-gun American frigate was fast, solidly built, and carried heavier guns than her opponent and immediately began to gain on her. When a rain squall struck, the French frigate lost her top main mast in a sudden gust of wind, which slowed her considerably.

Off Indian Castle on the east coast of Nevis, *Constellation* overtook *L'Insurgent*. Off the enemy's port quarter, with all double-shotted guns bearing, *Constellation* fired a broadside into the enemy. *L'Insurgent* returned fire immediately and the first high seas battle fought by the United States Navy commenced.

L'Insurgent carried nearly a hundred more men than did her opponent and Captain Berrault attempted to close with the American frigate and board her, but his damaged ship was at a disadvantage in speed. After exchanging several broadsides, *Constellation* crossed the enemy's bows and raked her from stem to stern with a broadside. The battle then turned in favour of the Americans. After an hour and a half, *L'Insurgent* struck her colours. She had lost 42 men, killed only two on the American vessel, and a prize crew from *Constellation* boarded her intending to take her into Basseterre to repair the damage. However, she was leaking so badly that emergency repairs were required and it took three days to get her to St Kitts.

Excitement ran high in St Kitts when the victorious *Constellation* returned followed by her battered and defeated enemy and crowds rushed to the bay front to witness the event. Salutes were fired by the cannon in St Kitts forts to welcome her. The United States Navy had won its first high seas battle and when word reached America the nation joyfully celebrated. With this victory, the United States was recognized by the European nations as an emerging world naval power. The eighteenth century would end with a new power, the United States, competing with the old in the Caribbean which foretold the beginning of a new era for the sugar islands.

11

The Nineteenth Century – the Decline Sets In

The early years of the new century saw the continuance of the Napoleonic wars between Britain and France, and St Kitts was not immune to the consequences. Little direct military action took place other than two raids by French forces, but ocean-going commerce was often disturbed by privateers and warships.

In 1805 a French squadron under Admiral Edouard Missiessy raided St Kitts, burnt six ships, landed troops and again blew up the powder magazine at Brimstone Hill. The French also extracted a ransom of £18,000 in return for not laying waste to the island. After extracting ransoms from St Kitts, Nevis and Montserrat, Admiral Missiessy's fleet divided and some of the ships under his command crossed the Atlantic and joined the French fleet at Trafalgar where Admiral Nelson dealt severely with them. The remainder of the French squadron was destroyed or captured at the Battle of Point Palenque in the Dominican Republic by Admiral Sir John Duckworth.

In 1806 a small French squadron under the command of Jerome Bonaparte raided St Kitts and British merchant ships took refuge under the guns of Brimstone Hill. They were well protected by the fort's 24-pounders and none were taken. Bonaparte attempted to land troops at Sandy Point, but Brimstone Hill's cannon, fired at extreme range, held them off. This inconclusive action was the last military attack by anyone against St Kitts. Brimstone Hill had been repaired and considerably expanded by then, but its guns would never again fire in anger. In 1854 it was abandoned and closed, and the St Kitts militia disbanded.

Napoleon Bonaparte personally did more damage to the sugar islands than any raids by his forces. After losing Haiti in a bloody slave rebellion he offered a prize to anyone who could develop a process for crystallizing beet sugar. A German invented it and the sugar beet, which grew in the temperate climates of Europe and North America, provided ever increasing amounts of sugar even though its yield per acre was considerably less than from sugar cane. In its final form of white sugar it could not be differentiated from that made from cane. This was the first of many blows which would ultimately bring the Caribbean sugar industry to its knees.

In 1805 the population of St Kitts was 1800 white, 998 free coloured and 26,000 slaves. It was noted that year that the St Kitts sugar yield averaged one hogshead per acre, and required the labour of two slaves per hogshead. The yield was much higher than that of its nearest Leewards rival Antigua, which averaged only one-third of a hogshead per acre because of poorer soil and a drier climate. An English Atlas published in 1822 noted that St Kitts was the best island for producing sugar, and that a single acre on one plantation yielded five hogsheads per acre and another plantation had an overall yield of four hogsheads per acre.[1]

In 1807 Parliament abolished the African slave trade in the British Empire beginning in 1808. It had an unexpected beneficial effect in the sugar islands. Slaves were mostly better cared for as they could no longer be replaced. Their lifespans increased as did the birth of children. This Act, '... by which Parliament declared the slave trade to be founded on principles contrary to those of justice, humanity, and sound policy, and engaged to institute measures for the total abolition of the same' clearly sounded the death knell of slavery.[2] As always, smuggling of slaves into St Kitts continued from Statia and elsewhere, but the numbers dropped off to near nothing. Full abolition was on the way to becoming a reality although it would not occur for another 27 years.

In 1810 the John Hart Cotton plantation in St Peter's Parish in St Kitts was leased, and the portions of the lease agreement dealing with the slaves was more specific than most which have survived to the present day. The slaves working the estate were considered part of the leasehold. The plantation had 65 male and 36 female slaves, all of whom were named in the document. Of the males, the most valuable were those skilled in a trade. In local currency the carpenter and cooper were valued at £250 each, while the sugar boiler was valued at £230. Field workers were valued at £160 each except for nine who were ruptured. They were valued at £130 each. One male, Madingo Tom, was a runaway.

Of the 36 females, 12 were rated as being totally useless. Why we do not know, except for one who had a ruptured womb and another who was a runaway. A third was noted as being 'with the rose', which was a venereal disease. The value of the women not considered useless was about £65 each. One would suspect that the 'useless' ones were probably barren or elderly, or both. After the African slave trade ceased the ability of females to reproduce was of paramount importance. Sixteen children on the estate were aged 14 years or younger and valued at £40 to £130 each. There were also 16 infants, with no ages given. They were valued from £10 to £35 pounds each, except for one who was noted as being an idiot.

In 1812 Great Britain and the United States went to war primarily over the impressment of American seamen into the British Navy against their will. It was not a popular war in North America. The United States's attempted invasion of Canada was repelled and in retaliation the British Army invaded Washington DC and burnt the Capitol, the White House, the Library of Congress and many other buildings. A very heavy rainstorm, accompanied by strong winds which were the remnants of a Caribbean hurricane, saved the city from total destruction by fire. In St Kitts that very same hurricane had destroyed a few days before ten captured American prizes in Basseterre harbour before it moved north. Once again, this war curtailed the sugar trade and damaged the economy of St Kitts.

In 1820 a third serious blow hit the West Indian sugar planters. They lost their monopoly for sugar production in the British Empire and prices plunged. Conditions which had been bad became worse very quickly. It was noted that two estates in St Kitts which had sold for £45,000 in 1817 were resold in 1822 for half that price. This monopoly had arisen under the mercantilist theory of trade when in the seventeenth century, the various European empires restricted trade to products originating within their own empires and carried in their own ships. Caribbean sugar planters actively and successfully worked to keep sugar from French and Spanish colonies out of the British Empire for nearly 200 years. The result was that demand always exceeded supply and prices in Great Britain were artificially very high. As the British Empire expanded eastwards to tropical lands where sugar could be produced, free trade pressure mounted and sugar import restrictions were removed. The British government decided, correctly, that decreasing the cost of sugar for their subjects was more important than pleasing a few rich Caribbean sugar planters.

Historians have called the loss of the 13 American colonies the end of the first British Empire and following that, the eyes of Britain subsequently turned from the western hemisphere to the east. The second British Empire was to be India and the Far East. Cane sugar could be grown in the new eastern empire where labour was cheap and the soil rich. After 1820 eastern sugar flowed into Great Britain and was often labelled 'Not produced by slave labour'. Even though the price was the same, many who opposed slavery bought it in preference to West Indian sugar, or boycotted sugar entirely. The British Caribbean possessions were on their way from being a central concern of the British government to becoming marginal possessions by the end of the nineteenth century.

By 1822 the sugar industry in the Caribbean, including St Kitts, was in a severe depression. Planters were financially strapped and could hardly break even and many estates went into bankruptcy. The consequences were the worst in the Leewards where individual estate production was inefficient and the soil exhausted from years of cultivation.

In 1825 the Anglican Church appointed a Bishop for the West Indies and the seat of the diocese was Antigua, the seat of the Leeward Islands colony and the most populous island. Up to that time the West Indies had been under the authority of the Bishop of London. The new Bishop was Henry Nelson Coleridge, cousin of the poet Samuel Taylor Coleridge. Bishop Coleridge kept a journal during his 1825 visit to the islands. He wrote:

> I believe I have reason to say there is no colony, perhaps with the exception of Grenada; where the free-colored people are treated with so much justice as in St Kitt's. There are instances here of respectable white and colored persons intermarrying, which is a conquest over the last and most natural of prejudices.[3]

Bishop Coleridge was upset, however, by the sight of a dozen or so nude young women washing clothes in a stream near St Mary's Church in Cayon.

By 1830 a noticeable decline was evident in St Kitts as a result of falling sugar prices. A visitor commented that even though the great houses on the plantations for the most part were still in reasonable order, the outbuildings were almost always in poor repair and in some cases dilapidated.

> Many estates exhibit lamentable signs of departed opulence in the ruins of buildings, once designed for the residence of their wealthy owners, too many of whom have fallen victims to their own improvidence, and brought beggary upon their offspring, whom they had taught to expect unrestricted wealth.[4]

One St Kitts planter, he related, had imported wheelbarrows so that his slaves would not have to carry heavy bundles of sugar canes on their heads. After a brief demonstration to the slaves of how they worked, he returned to the fields to find they had placed the bundles of cane into the wheelbarrows and then balanced the filled wheelbarrows on their heads, spinning the wheel which was carried in the front, for their amusement. The purpose of the wheelbarrow had been entirely misunderstood.

Central Basseterre looked poverty stricken, he declared. He complained that stores were poorly lit and the goods were piled haphazardly in an unattractive fashion. In Nevis, he wrote, central Charlestown and the great houses were better kept and far more attractive than their counterparts in St Kitts. The courthouse in Basseterre was in particularly poor repair.

> The court-house is unquestionably suitable in its construction for the several purposes contemplated, but the same want of cleanliness and comfort, which marks almost all their buildings externally, characterize

every part of the structure. The unpainted panels and scantling, the 'Jack Spaniards' nests and cobwebs, and the absence of proper accommodation for visitors, give it in every direction a mean and unfinished appearance. A unit in the extraordinary expenditure of the colony would surely provide a few pounds of paint and a dozen brooms ... [5]

This was certainly a far cry from the laudatory descriptions of the town and its buildings found in earlier writings going back to the mid-seventeenth century. In spite of the sad state of the economy St Kitts' first bank, the Colonial Bank, opened in 1837 and as a result of a merger it later became a part of Barclay's Bank. This event solved several problems which had been present on the island for centuries. Letters of credit could now be easily obtained for international trade and the chronic shortage of coinage for local transactions was greatly alleviated. Following full emancipation in 1838, local merchants grew substantially in number.

Before then planters had negotiated directly with overseas suppliers for merchandise rather than purchase it locally. When the former slaves were paid wages they had the choice of buying what they wanted where they wanted. Without the presence of Colonial Bank, this economic change would have occurred much more slowly.

Not only was the economy in poor shape, but government was even worse. In 1830 an Act of the Assembly allowed by name 14 free men, black or of colour, to stand for office in St Kitts. In 1832 one of them, a man of colour by the name of Thomas Drew, had been elected to the Assembly and was one of its most active members. He was instrumental in passing two acts, the first 'Setting and Regulating the Trial of Criminal Slaves', and the second 'An Act to provide for the Compulsory Manumission of Slaves'. Debate on the Acts seemed to have been acrimonious and the Attorney General, Charles Thomson, attempted to fine Drew for words uttered in the Assembly which Thomson considered actionable.

Members of the Assembly were outraged regardless of their race. Words spoken by a member before a duly convened Assembly were privileged, the members claimed, and this protection had been '... entitled to and enjoyed since time immemorial'.[6] Legal proceedings commenced and continued for two months until the King's Bench Court declared it had no jurisdiction over the proceedings and dismissed the case. It was evident Drew had been singled out because of his colour. Other white members of the Assembly supported him and the court case was argued on behalf of the entire Assembly by J. G. Piguenit, a very able barrister. After the success in court, Piguenit presented a petition to the Assembly signed by more than 50 white men of influence in St Kitts '... praying that all the Privileges enjoyed by His Majesty's White

Freeholders and other white Subjects, be extended to the free coloured and free black Subjects ... which they have hitherto been excluded by the Laws of this Island'.[7]

In the 1838 election 25 Assembly seats were being filled and the results of the election approached the absurd. The voters numbered only 104. Requirements at the time were that voters had to own 10 or more acres freehold or have an income of £10 per year. To sit in the Assembly, 40 acres of land had to be owned or an income earned of £40 or more. All had to be male, but free coloured men meeting the requirements were allowed to vote from 1824 on and Roman Catholics from 1827 on. In 1829 both free coloured and Roman Catholics were allowed to sit in the Assembly.

Emancipation

Public opinion in Great Britain had turned against slavery to the point that emancipation finally became a reality. It was slow in coming, as the Parliament at all costs wanted to avoid the violence and bloodshed which had accompanied the first attempt at emancipation in the French islands. Planters had made their case for retaining slavery based on the fact that abolition without compensation to them would be illegal deprivation of their property, and they had no idea of what would follow freedom of the slaves.

One man in St Kitts who was very influential in the struggle for emancipation was the Reverend James Ramsay. He had been a physician in the Royal Navy and while in service had been called to treat slaves bound for the West Indies on board the British slaver *Arundel* in 1759. An epidemic had killed most of the slaves and many of the crew, including the surgeon. Ramsay was so sickened by the terrible conditions on the slaver that he fainted when he first went below. He revived himself and treated the sick, but was so shaken by the experience that when he returned to his warship he was unsteady on his feet and lost his footing on the deck, falling and breaking his thigh. For the rest of his life he had a pronounced limp from this accident. Ramsay could not forget his experience and resolved to take holy orders and go into the Anglican priesthood. He disliked being at sea. He learnt:

> ... that there was a deficiency of Clergymen in St Christopher, a thought suggested itself, that here was an opportunity of shaking off an employment, in which his heart had never been engaged, of quitting a sea life, which had never been pleasant to him, and assuming what he had ever considered as his intended calling.[8]

Ramsay was ordained priest at St John's Capisterre in 1762. His friends had urged him to go to St Kitts and practise as a physician rather than a priest, but he believed he could put his medical skills to work while a priest, and he did so. He could frequently be found in the slave quarters treating the sick and converting them. Ramsay dared to preach that the soul of a slave was as important to God as that of a planter.

He had become an abolitionist after his experience on *Arundel* and took an interest in the welfare of the slaves, urging their masters to allow them to attend church and to be more lenient in their treatment of them. Predictably, the planters turned against him and attempted to force him to leave the island. Ramsay was a stubborn man and stayed until 1781 when the vilification finally became too much for him to bear and he returned to England.

Some white parishioners refused to attend his church and one George Gillard, a prominent planter and a member of the vestry, went so far as to confront Ramsay at the altar of St John's church and curse him using foul and abusive language for being an abolitionist. At some vestry meetings the members insisted on drinking rum punch inside the church and resting themselves on the altar as they drank.

Shortly after his arrival a campaign began in the St Kitts press in which vicious and inaccurate personal attacks were made on him in the form of letters, mostly unsigned. Readers of the current local press in St Kitts would immediately recognize this sort of journalism, as it unfortunately continues to the present day. Personal smear tactics replaced the necessity of facing the critical issue of slavery and as a result nothing concrete was accomplished in that regard until years later.

The attacks continued even after Ramsay returned to England and up to his death in 1798. Ramsay was vulnerable to attack by pro-slavery forces as he had owned house slaves in St Kitts and sold them upon his departure. However, the real irritant to St Kitts slave holders was that Ramsay was 'one of them' who lived in the West Indies and should have supported the establishment, but turned against them.

It was hoped by planters that the situation in the islands would remain much as it had been before emancipation, except that freed workers would be paid wages. Planters believed it was necessary to retain strict control over the freed slaves or they would not work on the sugar estates. Even some of the slaves feared freedom as they had been housed, clothed and fed by their masters. They too did not know what would happen afterwards, but the vast majority wanted freedom desperately.

After much careful study Parliament had arrived at a solution which seemed viable. Masters would be financially compensated for loss of their slaves, but beginning in 1817 had to make lists every three years of all slaves they owned by name, age, sex and place of birth. These triennial lists would ensure as much as possible that there would be no cheating by moving slaves from estate to estate and counting them more than once. The Act would take effect on 1 August 1834, but slaves were required to continue working for their same masters for wages until 1838, when full emancipation would occur and they would be free to leave if they chose. However, this period of adjustment could be waived locally in each island if deemed desirable.

Bonds were to be floated in England to pay the cost of compensation. The British financier Baron Rothschild agreed to underwrite the bond issue and a committee was established to set the value for each slave, a formidable task. The compensation for the 19,780 slaves freed in St Kitts was £329,393. The slaves themselves received nothing for their years of labour.

All things considered, this plan proved overall to be a success. Bloodshed such as had transpired in the French islands was avoided. In America a devastating civil war had to be endured to accomplish the same end. Planters' complaints of not receiving full value for their slaves were muted by the compensation as many were in dire need of cash to pay outstanding debts. They hoped they could continue to keep labourers on the plantations and control them through payment of wages. In addition, they would no longer bear the expense of housing, clothing and feeding the slaves and would not have to support those who were no longer productive or were aged.

Abolitionists believed that adopting a wage economy in the sugar islands would result in lower production costs for sugar. Some planters believed this was possible as well. The major immediate problem would arise over this four-year apprenticeship period set to run from 1834 to 1838.

In Antigua the apprenticeship period was waived and full freedom was granted to all slaves on 1 August 1834. All the other islands retained the period. Antigua's action caused turmoil in St Kitts. Lord Romney, owner of Romney Manor, could see no valid reason for the waiting period and fully emancipated all his slaves on 1 August 1834. The other slaves in St Kitts believed that as full emancipation had occurred in Antigua and at Romney Manor, Deputy Governor Nixon in St Kitts was conniving with the planters to deprive them of their freedom.

A demonstration took place in the countryside which turned into a widespread riot and British marines were called in from a warship anchored in Basseterre harbour. They brought the situation under control after two days but St Kitts remained under martial law from 6 August to 18 August. The marines and St Kitts militia swept the hills in order to bring workers back to the estates from which they had fled. They had left their tools at the doors of their overseers' or former owners' homes as an indication they would no longer work in the fields.

Some of them joined the fugitive slave Marcus, who was known to his followers as the 'King of the Woods'. For some time prior to emancipation Marcus, an accused murderer, had led a band of fugitive slaves who were armed and would sometimes descend upon estates in the night, raiding them for food and arms. Marcus had declared freedom for all former slaves in spite of the four-year apprenticeship required by the Emancipation Act and capturing him and his band was therefore considered a matter of primary importance. By 18 August he had been taken. The situation calmed down and Martial Law was lifted. There were no casualties and no further disturbances afterwards. Five primary instigators were banished to Bermuda and several were whipped but there were no deaths or executions resulting from the matter.

The hopes of abolitionists that sugar production costs would fall after full emancipation in 1838 occurred only in Barbados where almost all land was under cultivation and freed slaves had no place to go. In large islands such as Jamaica many slaves left their old plantations for unused lands and began farming and refused to work in the sugar industry any longer. Severe economic disruption took place there.

In smaller islands such as St Kitts and Nevis there was little unused land available and as a result many people stayed on in their villages and continued to work the estates. The economic effect of emancipation was not as severe as a result, although after 1838 many migrated to Trinidad where more work was available and caused a local labour shortage. Throughout the Caribbean sugar production fell by a half following emancipation, but by 1860 it had returned to 1838 levels. Profits of the planters fell by a half from the late eighteenth century to the mid-nineteenth, and would never recover in spite of production gains because of declining prices.

The hopes of planters to keep the newly emancipated slaves on the plantations often failed. Demand for workers was high when the cane was being processed, but much less the rest of the time. Planters could not afford to pay wages all year when the demand for work was seasonal, and most labourers were unwilling to do nothing and earn no money for months at a time. Skilled former slaves such as coopers, blacksmiths, carpenters, and masons were often able to find employment full time. The unskilled had difficulties and suffered the greatest hardship. Migration began to grow and in time even some of the skilled left for higher pay elsewhere.

St Kitts planters who had been used to living under the protection of a monopoly were being exposed to the real world at last and competition had to be faced. In addition to everything else, sugar from Cuba and Brazil was coming onto the world market at one-third less than it could be produced in St Kitts. Planters had to modernize or face ruin.

Nature intervened in 1843 to deal the crippled economy of St Kitts another blow. A huge earthquake shook the island and wrecked many buildings. St George's church collapsed and was not rebuilt until 1856. The jail was destroyed and a new one constructed in 1844. Evidently it was more important to the Assembly to deal with felons than with souls. Especially hurt were estate sugar production facilities, almost all of which were made of stone. The cost of rebuilding them was considerable and beyond the means of some small owners who sold out at a loss or leased land to the workers.

Many planters were not financially able to obtain the latest agricultural developments as credit had dried up following emancipation and many were already deep in debt. Steam engines were able to extract 70 to 80 per cent of cane juice (when properly adjusted) compared to 50 to 60 per cent for wind and animal mills. They were purchased by planters who could afford them beginning in the 1830s and by 1846, there were 33 operating in St Kitts. By 1878 the number had grown to 74. They were more efficient but did not contribute to an increase in the quality of sugar produced.

Vacuum evaporating pans for crystallization did improve sugar quality and were invented in 1813. They were, however, expensive and few estates could afford them. The ones which did install them saw a distinct improvement in quality and income. Poorer planters tried mechanical substitutes which were cheaper but they did not work very well, if at all.

The use of the plough reduced the need for field labourers but it had a detrimental effect in that it caused more erosion than the usual practice of 'holing' cane did. Holing consisted of digging squares in which manure was worked into the soil and the cane planted in the prepared earth. The squares were surrounded by ridges which held in water.

New varieties of cane were also introduced at that time which improved yield per acre but they had an indirect detrimental effect as well. Higher and steeper land was cleared for cane planting which was not as rich as soil lower down the slopes and erosion was worse. The new fields played out quickly and were soon abandoned as fertility and yield declined.

The most effective means the planters had of keeping costs down was paying low wages, which they did whenever possible. Understandably, former slaves who had been forced to work in the cane fields in the past continued to do so only if no other options existed and few did, other than migration to other places. Cane field work was hot, hard and dirty. A shortage of workers kept the wages higher than the planters wished to pay, and they decided to try and relieve the situation.

Emigration of foreign workers into St Kitts seemed to be the answer. Planters believed immigrants would be more efficient than local labour. The first experiment was with imported British labour. Between 1835 and 1845, 200 were brought into St Kitts. They were '... ill-selected, ill-conducted, ignorant, infirm, and most unsuccessful'.[9] In 1849, 97 Africans came in as indentured servants and proved to be better workers than the British. More would follow.

These were called 'liberated' Africans, as they had been removed by the Royal Navy from illegal slave trading ships, and they were eagerly sought after as indentured servants by the government of St Kitts. In 1857 it was noted by the St Kitts Council that under the terms of an 1855 Act, 192 African indentured servants who would not or could not return to their homes had permanently migrated into St Kitts under its terms. They were welcomed. The

9 The American fleet at anchor in Basseterre 1901. During the construction of the Panama Canal (1903–1914) the United States considered purchasing St Kitts and Nevis for use as a coaling station for its war fleet protecting the canal. Courtesy of Pam Berry, Golden Rock Hotel, Nevis.

10 An American Vought Kingfisher aircraft of the same squadron from St Thomas as the one which crashed in St Kitts in 1944.

11 Robert Llewellyn Bradshaw, first popularly elected leader of St Kitts and Nevis. He set in motion many improvements in living standards, education and local services which have made the life of the average person far better than it had ever been before. Courtesy of the St Kitts Archives.

12 Dr Kennedy A. Simmonds first elected Prime Minister after independence and leader of the People's Action Movement. Following the loss of his seat in the last election he has resigned as head of PAM. Courtesy of the St Kitts Archives.

13 C. A. Paul Southwell, successor of R. A. Bradshaw. In poor health when he took over the leadership of the nation, he died a year later while still in office. Courtesy of the St Kitts Archives.

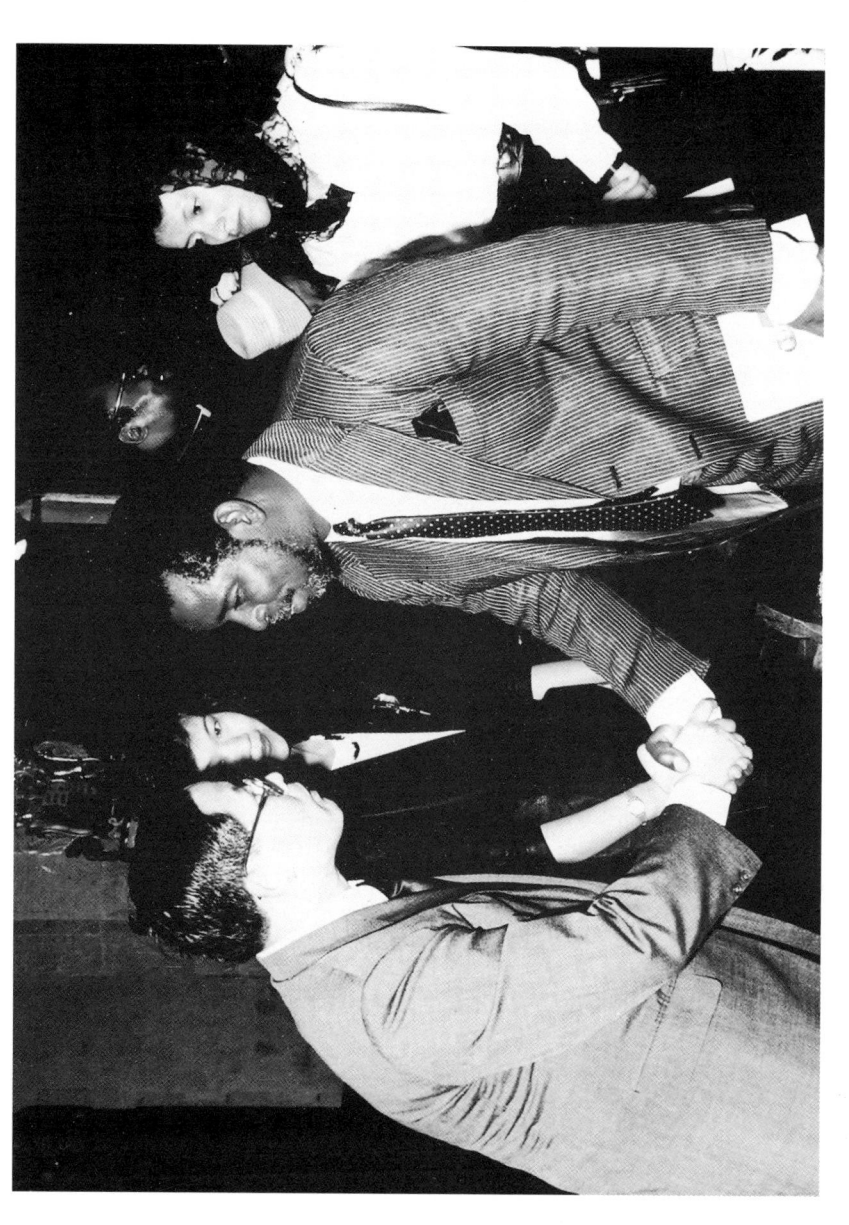

14 The Hon. Lee Moore, QC, followed by C. P. A. Southwell as Prime Minister and head of the Labour Party. He lost to Dr Simmonds in the following election. He has since died. Here he is shown greeting the Ambassador of the People's Republic of China. Courtesy of the St Kitts Archives.

15 Dr Denzil Douglas current Prime Minister and Leader of the Labour Party. Courtesy of the St Kitts Archives.

16 Women washing clothes at Old Road *c.* 1890.

Duke of Newcastle wrote to Governor Hamilton of the Leewards that the liberated Africans were good workers and much cheaper to obtain than 'coolies or chinese' for labour.[10]

The St Kitts Council took note in 1858 that 452 immigrants from the Portuguese island of Madeira had arrived in St Kitts in the past four years. By 1887, there were 295 Africans, 838 Portuguese, 61 East Indians, and 218 from Ireland and Britain residing in St Kitts as immigrants. The total population was then about 25,000. Between 1838 and 1917, 300 East Indians had emigrated to St Kitts. A number of Lebanese arrived during the same time period, coming as pedlars and later establishing shops and stores. A considerable number of people moved across to St Kitts from poorer Nevis during this time but no record was kept of their numbers.

In 1845 it was noted that '... the gaol contained 44 men, 6 women, and 6 debtors'. The Poor House contained 60 inmates. 'The state of the colony is altogether unsatisfactory; the depression is general; it applies to Planters Merchants Artificers and Day Labourers'.[11]

In 1849, it was related that in St Kitts:

> ... in the northwest quarter there were eighteen estates. In nine the cultivation of cane had been given up and the land had either been let to labourers, for growing provisions, at the rate of from nine to fourteen dollars a year the acre, or had been neglected, or used for pasture; a neglect indicated by many of the sugar works in ruins, and some of the estate-houses.[12]

In addition to lower sugar prices and lack of credit there was a depression in Britain in 1848 which caused demand for sugar to decline. In 1846 the British parliament had passed the Sugar Duties Act which, by 1854, would eliminate duties on non-British sugar. Sugar prices dropped yet again. Parliament believed that reducing prices for British consumers was better policy than protecting their increasingly less important West Indian sugar colonies. The sugar islands were no longer of primary economic concern to Great Britain. It no longer depended upon their produce and as the slave trade had been abolished, the profits from it had vanished. The replacement of mercantilism by free trade resulted in the loss of the protected status of the sugar islands.

Following the final defeat of Napoleon Bonaparte, Britain had emerged as the world's leading military and economic power. The Industrial Revolution had propelled British imperial power worldwide. In the Caribbean it had no rivals. Spain had lost its Central and South American empire and was left with only Cuba, Puerto Rico and the Philippines. Those she would lose to the United States in 1898 in the Spanish-American War.

Holland remained prosperous but was too small to be a significant power. France was a world power and had its own substantial empire but was no longer a military rival in the Caribbean. The United States was a growing power but was concentrating upon expansion westward to the Pacific and not hungry for overseas territories.

In 1853 and 1854 a cholera epidemic swept the Caribbean islands, killing thousands. St Kitts suffered more deaths, 3920, in proportion to its population than did any other, a full one-sixth of the population. The St Kitts Council declared the deaths were '... the deplorable results of the neglect of sanitary facilities..'.[13] Steps were taken by the government to improve sanitation by introducing 'earth closets' as toilets and stopping the use of drainage ditches for this purpose. These measures were moderately effective and no more epidemics of cholera or dysentery would ravage St Kitts.

On 23 October 1853 a dispatch was sent to the St Kitts Council by the Secretary of State for Colonial Affairs, the Duke of Newcastle, that the British garrison at Brimstone Hill would be withdrawn. In 1814 a British Commission had studied Brimstone Hill and determined that it was suitable only as a defensive position. Its guns did not cover Basseterre or the harbour.

Following withdrawal of the troops the structure was to be abandoned. Arms and buildings were to be turned over to the local government and what they did not want would be sold to the public or carried back to England. A year later instructions were given to the Council that whatever was left and not wanted by government would be abandoned. Most British military installations were officially closed in the Caribbean in the 1850s as they were no longer required for defence. In a few years this great citadel would become an overgrown but not forgotten ruin.

In 1854 the militia in St Kitts and on all the islands were disbanded as they too were no longer needed. The West Indies' time as a focus of worldwide imperial struggles was over and it would slowly settle into genteel obscurity and poverty. In St Kitts, however, the militia was reconstituted in 1858 following labour disorders in Antigua. They consisted of a detachment of horse troops called the St Christopher Yeomanry Cavalry and a regiment of infantrymen organized into the Basseterre Volunteers. Different groups of each were formed on the windward and leeward sides of the island and they were to drill weekly on Saturdays at designated spots until they were sufficiently trained, and then drills were to be monthly.

Membership in these militia groups was voluntary rather than being required by law and no racial restrictions were included in the Acts. By 1859 there were 847 officers and enlisted men in the two groups.

What made the declining economic situation even worse was the fact that the governments of St Kitts and the other islands were inefficient and what funds they had available were often misspent. With very low numbers of voters participating in elections, the oligarchies in the islands perpetuated their own interests to the detriment of the working people. Government was far from being representative and the poor suffered because of it. The bloody Morant Bay rebellion in Jamaica in 1865 brought home to Britain that local governments in the sugar islands were not up to the job.

The solution proposed by Britain was to make all the sugar islands into crown colonies. Alternatively, the franchise could have been expanded and government made more representative, but the local establishments in the islands were not ready or willing to do this. In 1866 the St Kitts Assembly voted for a single chamber, eliminating the Council, and with a majority of members appointed rather than elected. That same year it was noted that of a population of 25,000, only 300 were qualified to vote under the requirements then in effect.

Other islands in the Leewards followed suit. The British Governor wrote to the Colonial Office in London that the government of Antigua was the best, but bankrupt. In St Kitts the government was rich but the Assembly and the President were deadlocked and little could be accomplished. In Nevis the government was 'bad' and '... Montserrat was, if possible, even worse'.[14]

Governor Hamilton of the Leewards wrote the Duke of Newcastle a letter on 23 October 1862 in which he succinctly set forth an accurate analysis of the Leeward Islands' political situation – true then and still true today.

> Antigua, St Kitts, Montserrat and Nevis are all within view of each other; I frequently see them all at one view. They are minute Monarchies with separate Legislatures, different tariffs, distinct provincialisms, and with antipathies strong in the ratio of approximation. A gentleman of Nevis says it is a duty he has inherited to abhor everything belonging to St Kitts, which, he adds, is the faith of all true Nevisians. The isolation and the consequent difference might be surmounted by the consolidation of the Civil Establishments of the Islands.[15]

It can be seen from this letter that the animosity between St Kitts and Nevis was nothing new. The Federation of the Leeward Islands followed and was imposed on the islands in 1871 by Great Britain at the pinnacle of her imperial strength; otherwise it would certainly have failed.

The 1871 conversion from very restricted self-government to crown colony status was described as follows: 'The greatest tragedy of all lay in the officially acknowledged abandonment and promise for the ex-slaves and their descendants'.[16]

In the 1860s the American Civil War caused great disruption in the sugar islands. In 1861 the St Kitts Council noted that the fort on the eastern bluff overlooking Basseterre harbour (Fort Thomas) mounted eight 24-pounders and a cannonade covering the harbour, and two 32s and an 18- pointing out to sea. The fort was in good condition and could protect shipping against privateers. The Council also considered mounting some 24s in old Londonderry Fort as well, but whether that was done or not, we do not know.

By then the majority of sales of sugar and molasses from the islands were to the United States and Canada rather than Great Britain. Sales of sugar declined and the cost of clothing increased 100 per cent because of the war, as cotton supplied by the southern states to Britain was cut off and there were shortages worldwide. Poor sales of St Kitts sugar in England were caused '... by the unhappy war that wages between the two different sections of the Great American Republic'.[17] By 1864 sales rebounded but because of a drought the crop failed in St Kitts and the poor were suffering.

In 1865 the St Kitts Council repealed a law which had allowed distillers on the island to make rum out of ships' bilge water into which molasses from sugar barrels had drained. Brave tasters had pronounced the rum good, but members of Council believed that the remains of rubbish, human and animal waste, and other such vile accumulations in bilge water rendered the rum unfit for human consumption. One must certainly agree with the council.

In 1867 a great fire swept Basseterre. A fire brigade had been organized in May 1865, but could not control the blaze. Of all cities in the Caribbean, there are none which have burnt as often. Accidental fires destroyed great parts of the city in 1660, 1776 and 1867. It was burnt during wars in 1667 and 1690. Many structures in 1867 were wooden and a great majority of all buildings had wooden shake roofs. Once a fire began and the wind caught it, little could be done to stop it. The fire began around 11:30 at night in a bakery at the corner of West Square and Central Street and destroyed over 500 houses, five-sixths of the dwellings in the city. 5000 persons were made homeless and took refuge in Irish Town and New Town, both of which had not been damaged. Food was in short supply as stores and warehouses holding produce had been destroyed.

The newly rebuilt St George's church was burnt down but the new jail constructed after the 1843 earthquake was spared and is still in use. The excellent library, said to be the finest in the West Indies, was lost but the courthouse, in which the archives were located, survived the fire only to burn in 1982. The Basseterre one sees today is essentially what was reconstructed by plans from the Department of Public Works made after the 1867 fire. Few structures exist in the city which were built before that time.

Some new streets were constructed and others were straightened or widened, and the Circus was built, modelled on Piccadilly Circus in London. The fountain in the centre, dedicated to The Honourable Thomas Berkeley Hardtman Berkeley, was not built until 1883. It was dedicated by Lord Combermere, a descendent of the first Lord Combermere who assisted the Duke of Wellington at Waterloo.

In 1871 the Leeward Islands became a federated colony. The elected members of the St Kitts Assembly were replaced by members appointed by the Crown. The Assembly had 20 members, three were ex-officio, seven nominated and 10 elected. The Crown exercised a tie vote. The same was true of the other Leewards, and in all of them the final political authority became the Royal Governor of the Leeward Islands located in Antigua. There was an appointed local Governor who held power in each island. St Kitts remained the richest of the Leewards, but in comparison it was far from the economic powerhouse it had been a century earlier.

On 1 January 1883 St Kitts, Nevis and Anguilla became a 'Presidency' and all authority over the three islands was centred in St Kitts. This move was very unpopular in Nevis and there were demonstrations against it in Charlestown. Neither was St Kitts happy about the new arrangement. It was believed that St Kitts' relatively prosperous treasury would be drained by supporting the two poorer islands. To a certain extent that supposition proved to be true. In 1956 the islands were freed from the federation and once again became a colony. This was done in preparation for membership of the short-lived West Indies Federation which would appear in 1958.

The Nevis court system had come under St Kitts overall authority in the late eighteenth century. Around 1900 a judge in St Kitts asked a lawyer in his court where he practised. The lawyer answered, 'Between St Kitts and Nevis'. The judge replied, 'Ah, on Booby Island, I presume'.[18]

The Portuguese Riots

By the 1860s about one quarter of the world's sugar production was made from beet rather than cane. Beet sugar yield was considerably less per acre than cane sugar but it could be grown in temperate climates. In the 1890s some European nations began to subsidize internal production of beet sugar. Called bounty sugar, it caused the St Kitts cane sugar industry to move from crisis to catastrophe. At best, sugar produced in St Kitts sold on the world market at the cost of production and usually for around £2 per hogshead less than production cost. Only the financially strongest planters could continue to operate under these conditions and the way they reduced costs was to lower wages of the workers in the industry.

Wages began to fall in 1894 on some estates and did so on more the following year. By 1896 the situation had become intolerable for the workers and trouble started. A Dispatch sent to the Assistant Secretary of State of the United States 24 February 1896 by Leopold Moore, Commercial Agent of the United States in Basseterre, describes the situation so succinctly that it is worth quoting it in full:

I have the honor to make the following report in reference to labor trouble now going on in this island.

At the beginning of the harvesting of the sugar crop about 6 months ago, the labourers on the various estates struck for an increase of wages, their wage having been reduced last year owing to the low price and the short crop in the island.

In some instances the wages were advanced but where they were not the men began to set fire to the canes and night after night cane fields were destroyed by fire, the authorities doing nothing to prevent these fires claiming they were powerless to do so.

The managers of the various estates increased the men's wages with very little beneficial result, as the spirit of disaffection continued to prevail among the laborers and they continued to demand a still further increase and when it was not at once granted, they burned the cane fields and struck work.

Things went from bad to worse when last Monday (Feby 17) when the boat men struck and refused to permit any small boat to go off to any vessel in the harbor. They behaved in a most disorderly manner all day continually blowing the 'shell' (a sort of horn made from a shell which means open defiance to the law) and acted in a riotous manner generally. They were joined from time to time during the day by gangs of labourers from the estates marching in on the town from the country armed with sticks and stones to the tunes of their own native music. Fortunately earlier in the day H.M.S. *Cordelia* arrived in the harbor on tour of inspection and remained intending to leave the following day.

Toward 3:00 in the afternoon reports came in to the effect that rioting was going on at Old Road (a place about 6 miles from town) and at 5:00 the administrator sent off an official notice to the War vessel to land 40 Marines and blue jackets down at Old Road which was immediately done.

About 7:00 in the evening the mob began to march through the streets throwing stones and smashing windows of the houses and stores as they went along and later on broke all the street lamps leaving the town in almost total darkness. Toward 9:00 they broke into the provisions stores and saloons and a general looting took place, the *Cordelia* then landed a few more men and the row at Old Road not being as bad as it was represented, the Marines were quickly ordered up to town and after some skirmishing in which 3 black rioters were killed and several wounded partial order was restored.

Fourteen (14) stores in all were looted and four destroyed and taken by the mob and the loss is estimated at about $5000.00.

Several attempts were made to fire the town but the Marines quickly extinguished the flames. The Governor was telegraphed for and arrived the following day from Antigua, and it was decided that the War Ship should remain for the present as the island will certainly not be safe without some protection, for the blacks are still going around making threats to burn the town and murder the white people at the first opportunity.

The island is now under martial law and no one is allowed out after sunset.

It is the unanimous opinion of both whites and blacks had not the *Cordelia* been in the harbor or had the rioting began a day sooner or been deferred a day later the town must have been destroyed and that few of the white people would have escaped with their lives.

My own opinion is that the worst is now over'.[19]

The term 'Portuguese Riots' probably derived from the fact that the disturbances immediately preceding the night of rioting occurred on an estate belonging to a planter of Portuguese descent. A telegraph had been installed in Basseterre in 1872 by the West India and Panama Telegraph Company and it was available to send word to Antigua, enabling the Governor to arrive and keep the situation under control.

Cordelia had actually landed 66 bluejackets rather than 40, and led by their officers and F. S. Wigley of St Kitts, they commandeered the steamer *Greenwood* and travelled to Old Road to relieve two constables confronted by angry workers. Upon arrival of the marines, the crowd dispersed without incident.

Cordelia departed after HMS *Tartar* arrived in Basseterre carrying more British troops and *Tartar* remained for some time. Sixty prisoners were sent to Antigua as there were not sufficient cells in St Kitts to house them. Nevis was also placed under martial law and a few marines were landed in Charlestown, as disorder had spread across to there and angry workers were burning cane fields.

The Council granted £1000 relief to storekeepers who had been looted and passed a special expenditure of £750 for maintaining protective forces in both St Kitts and Nevis. The cost of replacing and repairing damaged street lamps in Basseterre amounted to £117 14 shillings and 11 pence.

Subsidized European beet sugar took its toll in St Kitts. Another dispatch to the United States Department of State dated 13 February 1897 declared:

> … cane cultivation on the following nine estates (plantations) will cease directly the present crop has been harvested, viz. Cranstouns, Caines, Cunningham, Lavington's, Fountain, Saddlers, Harris's, Pinneys in Nevis and Clarkes. What this must mean to the labouring class, depending for daily bread on the only industry of consequence which the Island affords, can be better imagined than described.[20]

A lawyer in St Kitts commented wryly in 1897 that 'It appears when one is going down a hill every neighbour gives him a push'.[21] It was a desperate battle for estates to stay in operation and some owners and merchants gave no quarter to others when failures and bankruptcies threatened. A visiting American writer observed the same year: 'Yet there is only a shadow of the old prosperity throughout the island ... There is here, as in all the West Indies, a certain pathos due to a sense of time long past'.[22]

Another American in the late 1890s commented that 'The financial condition of St Kitts is indeed deplorable, far worse then any of the other islands. We were almost mobbed when we landed [by beggars]'.[23] This observation is of considerable interest as St Kitts was the richest of the Leewards, and it was confirmed by others over the next half century.

In far less prosperous Nevis, the average person lived in better housing and Charlestown had a better appearance than did Basseterre. As late as 1942 a survey of housing was made in the two islands to try and determine what effect war-caused shortages would have on the population and the results were printed in the local press. The quality of housing in the country in St Kitts was noted as being poor, and in Basseterre very poor. In Nevis, Charlestown housing was rated as being good, and in the country, relatively good. The explanation seemed to be that Nevis had developed a peasant class of farmers and workers who were not directly tied to the plantation system, while in St Kitts that had not occurred.

Although economic conditions remained poor overall, money was found for Queen Victoria's Diamond Jubilee celebration in St Kitts. The President of the Council gave an address in which he declared:

> We cannot forget, on the occurrence of this glorious episode in the annals of the Anglo-Saxon race, that little St Kitts was, with the possible exception, perhaps, of Barbados, the first corner stone of the almost limitless Colonial Empire that now joyfully and thankfully owns your Majesty's sway.
> Nor can we help remembering that the cruel curse of slavery was fully and for ever removed from St Kitts and Nevis and the other British West Indian Islands at the very beginning of the Victorian Era.[24]

Following the Spanish-American War in 1898, American eyes turned towards the Caribbean. Proposals were actually made within the State Department that the United States buy St Kitts and Nevis from Great Britain in the event that the purchase of the Virgin Islands from Denmark did not take place until 1902.

The United States Navy had sent a fleet into the Caribbean in 1901 and for a few days it anchored in Basseterre harbour. The commander, Admiral Higginson, observed that 50 modern ships could anchor there and it would make a good coaling station for the Navy. This was of special interest to the Navy as the United States was beginning construction of the Panama Canal and would need to have warships in the Caribbean to protect it.

Some local people brought up the subject favourably with the visitors as well. There was considerable good will between the United States and Britain at the time, and both sides played on it. An American correspondent wrote in 1903, 'The islands of St Kitts and Nevis are English and only English is spoken while the people are loyal to their mother country, their eyes at present are turned to the United States, like Mohammedans to Mecca, in prayer'.[25]

Sale to the United States for use as a coaling station would certainly have brought a needed economic boost but the prospective purchaser worried about political instability caused by bad economic conditions. The Virgin Islands purchase was voted down by Denmark in 1902, but by 1916 Denmark reconsidered and made the sale to the United States for 25 million dollars. At that time American interest in the purchase of St Kitts and Nevis ceased.

The financial strains of a huge empire were beginning to show in Great Britain. British naval worldwide superiority had its beginnings in the Caribbean, fuelled by profits from sugar and slaves, but by 1900 Britain was willing to cede primary naval power in the western hemisphere to the United States. The two nations had begun the nineteenth century at war with each other but by its end were firm allies. Britain could not maintain naval superiority over all the seven seas and other European countries, especially Germany, were building up powerful navies and envied Britain her empire. Bound to the United States by language and history, the two nations were comfortable with one another and remain so to this day.

Britain was not comfortable enough, however, to sell the United States even a tiny part of her empire. St Kitts and Nevis would remain in the British Empire for another 83 years. It is sad to contemplate the fact that Britain had allowed her once important Caribbean possessions to deteriorate into what was called an 'imperial slum' in spite of her great wealth.

12

The Twentieth Century

The 1896 riots in St Kitts prompted the British parliament to appoint a Royal Commission under Sir Henry Norman in 1897 to look into the situation of the sugar industry in the Caribbean islands. The Commission concluded that bounty beet sugar production was the major cause of the ' ... present great depression in the Sugar Industry throughout the West Indies, but in this island in particular [St Kitts]'.[1]

The report of the Commission resulted in the Brussels Convention of 1902 and the consequent ending of bounties for beet sugar production. Other recommendations were made for the Leewards and St Kitts, especially the use of large central factories for sugar refining as opposed to individual estate production. This means of production was used in Cuba, the Dominican Republic and Puerto Rico and had resulted in considerably lower costs. In 1912 the St Kitts Sugar Producers Association built the central factory and started a railway to transport sugar to it from distant parts of the island. It came on stream just in time for the increased demand for sugar brought on by the Great War in 1914.

The one great issue which lurked beneath the surface and was not directly addressed by the Royal Commission was the long-standing racial problem of black workers being held at the bottom of the economic and social ladder and the deep resentment generated by that situation. It was written about emancipation 'There would be no social revolution; or at least not yet; for the surgery of emancipation had removed the infection which might have violently disrupted the body politic'.[2] However, the job was left only half done by emancipation. The permanent solution would not come until self-government arrived in the 1960s.

In the early years of the twentieth century, further conflicts arose between St Kitts and Nevis, as well as Anguilla. The Federated Leeward Islands Colony had placed governing authority in the St Kitts Legislative Council and included two members from Nevis and one from Anguilla in the total number of ten legislators. This arrangement had unhappy consequences then which continue to the present day. The crux of the problem was, and is, that the Federation government was the local government of St Kitts as well as being in charge overall of the other two islands. With the legislature constituted in that fashion, local St Kitts interests were bound to prevail over those of the two smaller islands.

Thomas Liburd, one of the Nevis members, became angry over the fact that the Nevis hospital, destroyed in the 1899 hurricane, had not been rebuilt by 1904 and patients had to be housed in the Nevis jail. He declared conditions there were unacceptable because of crowding and bad odours from a nearby tannery. He stated that money for non-essential matters was being spent in St Kitts while Nevis's fundamental needs were being ignored.

Since 1872 St Kitts had an international telegraph system but never connected Nevis to it. Nevis therefore had no advance warning of the 1899 hurricane and this fact rankled Liburd as well. In a prepared speech he declared ' ... the Island of Nevis has been shut out from any further benefit, snubbed, and her interests utterly disregarded by the local Government'.[3]

Charles T. Cox (later Sir Charles), Acting Governor of St Kitts, called Liburd 'puerile' and responded angrily ' ... my colleagues in the Legislative Council who I regret to say regard Nevis and Anguilla as a drag on St Kitts and would willingly see a separation'.[4]

Liburd did not give up and sent a letter of complaint to the West India Committee at the Colonial Office in London. In a dispatch to the Federation government dated 14 July 1904, the Committee agreed with Liburd that the people of Nevis had a genuine cause for complaint and action should be taken promptly to rebuild the Nevis hospital. Nothing was done until 1907, however.

The Legislative Council President, Sir Robert Bromley, appointed in 1905, was a man with a strong social conscience and directly addressed some of the problems in St Kitts and called for action. Conditions were very bad for the workers in the island.

> The majority dwell herded together in small wooden shanties with practically no sanitary arrangements of any kind. They have apparently no desire to improve their surroundings, and this cannot be wondered at where there is no real family life, and where there are frequent changes of husband and wife, and therefore no family interest and no community of property ... These conditions in themselves would demoralize any race but they have been aggravated very considerably by the depression that for so long has overshadowed these islands, and the consequent impoverishment of the estates which has led to the doing away with of estate villages and so driven many of the labouring population into the towns ...[5]

Bromley's solution was to improve sanitary conditions, which had not kept pace with the movement of people from villages, education of the people, and a public dole to stop the begging which had become so prevalent in the previous decade. By 1906, the government had moved into a budget surplus but internal economic conditions had scarcely improved. Unfortunately, Bromley died in 1907 and his efforts towards social improvement were not followed by subsequent administrations with great zeal.

Economically, however, advances were being made. In 1911 the construction of the central sugar factory commenced along with the railway designed to transport sugar to it. The company formed to build the railway was given the right to the compulsory acquisition of land for that purpose. At the same time remittances from Kittians working overseas in Canada, the United States and the Panama Canal Zone were helping to improve the local economy. The telephone system built in St Kitts in 1896 was at last expanded to include Nevis in 1913.

Modern conveniences were becoming more evident. In 1912 an Act was passed requiring bicycles and motor bicycles using '… pneumatic or silent tyres …' to have a bell or other device mounted on it and sound it before passing '… any other such vehicle or bicycle, horse, mule, ass or other beast of burden or such foot passenger …'[6] In 1914, regulations were passed governing the importation and use of motor cars.

The Great War and its Consequences

The commencement of the war in Europe had little immediate impact on St Kitts. After a review of its defences, it was decided that should an enemy warship appear, there was nothing to be done to prevent it from shelling Basseterre if it decided to do so, as all the heavy guns in the forts were antiquated smooth-bores and useless against modern iron ships. Practically, it was believed the might of the Royal Navy would not allow such a thing to happen and this proved to be a correct assumption. However, £39 was spent to purchase a Maxim machine gun and build a mounting for it at the harbour and two men were dispatched to Barbados for instruction on how to operate it.

Sugar prices rebounded as the war stopped the export of European beet sugar to Britain. Export taxes were quickly placed on sugar to augment government revenue. This economic benefit was soon offset by increasing prices of imports as German U-boats began sinking British ships on the high seas. Expenditures for defence increased in the island in spite of its remoteness from the conflict, and the call-up of soldiers for the West India Regiment increased. It was necessary to pay for their training, upkeep and uniforms. By 1916 50 men had been called up in St Kitts and 25 more were promised.

That same year, it was noted by the Legislative Council that some people were stirring up 'class hatred' among St Kitts sugar workers, and a 10 per cent bonus was paid to government employees because of rising prices. The war was beginning to have an effect locally.

The President of the Legislative Council cautioned that it was possible that German U-boats could appear and shell the town, and a plan for evacuation to the countryside should be prepared. The government surplus of £30,000 in 1914 had been reduced to half that figure by 1916. In 1918 an aeroplane was purchased for £2000 granted by the Assembly and given to the Royal Air Force. It was named 'St Christopher'.

In 1918 when the war ended, £560 was spent in St Kitts for a victory celebration. The expenditure was justified to point out to the population in general how important and complete the victory was, and how the British Empire had once again vanquished its foes. The West India Regiment returned in triumph to St Kitts on 24 July 1919 and all officers and men were granted a demobilization bonus of £5.

In 1916, Theodore Roosevelt, formerly President of the United States, visited St Kitts with Mrs Roosevelt. No longer occupying the White House, no provisions had been made for an official greeting by the President of the Legislative Council. However, he was unexpectedly met at the harbour in Basseterre by an old friend.

This man was the remarkable James Derrick Cardin. Well known throughout the Caribbean, his character and achievements were so notable that later in life he would be awarded an OBE in recognition of them. Cardin had been born in St Kitts, one of 11 children, to a widowed mother who was unable to look after him properly. He was cared for and educated by the three spinster Auld sisters of Basseterre, who recognized his ability early on. As a young man he migrated to the United States and after some time obtained a job as head porter of the Wagner Palace Car Company, which operated luxury railway carriages between New York and Washington DC for the rich and famous of America. He held the job for 18 years and when he resigned and returned to St Kitts in 1910, he had been earning US$162 per month, a princely sum at that time.

Cardin had met the then Governor of New York, Theodore Roosevelt, while serving as head porter. The two had become firm friends and visited together on Roosevelt's many railway journeys. Cardin told Roosevelt that he was resigning to return home to look after the Auld sisters in their old age. The Governor urged him to remain in the United States as he had a good future there, but Cardin explained he felt an obligation to assist them, as they had looked after him as a child.

When the Roosevelts arrived in St Kitts, Cardin heard they were there and that there was no greeting party to meet them. Cardin commandeered the services of two police constables in full white dress uniform, obtained a boat, decorated it with red, white and blue bunting, and sailed out to meet the former American head of state. Roosevelt was dumbfounded to meet his old friend whom he had not seen for six years. In his exuberant style, Roosevelt reached over the ship's rail and pumped Cardin's hand vigorously. Cardin took them ashore and led them on a tour of the island. Mrs Roosevelt commented that she was descended from the Cooper family of St Kitts, many of whom were buried on the island, and some of her ancestors had participated in the siege of Brimstone Hill in 1782.

The Roosevelts were very moved when they heard from other persons the facts of Cardin's life during the six years he had been in St Kitts. The Auld sisters had fallen on difficult times financially and were unable to pay him a salary. He never asked for money, but invested his savings in a stationery and book shop in Basseterre, and supported himself from the income of the shop. Two of the Auld sisters had died in his arms, thanking him tearfully for giving up his good life and future in America to return and care for them in St Kitts in their old age. He inherited their little remaining property, which was all the compensation he ever received for his selfless generosity.[8]

The Beginning of the Labour Movement

In 1916 a suggestion was made before the Legislative Council that a Labour Union and a Planters Union be established ' ... under competent leadership'.[7] This was probably in response to the 'class hatred' which had been stirred up among workers in the cane fields earlier that same year. This suggestion was not accepted, however, and because of the war organizing any labour union was forbidden for the duration. However, the fledgling union changed its name to the St Kitts Benevolent Society and continued to exist under close watch from the authorities. 1916 was also the year in which Robert Llewellyn Bradshaw was born. He would become active in the St Kitts labour movement and ultimately lead the island as its first elected Premier.

The attempted establishment of a union unsettled the wealthier people of the island and many feared it. The police department added men and the Legislative Council discussed using police intervention to close down the Benevolent Society, but the majority believed that use of the police in such a manner would cause a crisis. It was decided that for one month no action would be taken and if at the end of that time use of the police was considered necessary, it would be done. It proved to be unnecessary.

The union imported a printing press from the United States in 1918 and it was feared by the Legislative Council that they would violate the Newspaper Surety Ordinance of 1909. A paper called the *Union Messenger* was put out. No note is made in the Legislative Council Minutes that the Act was violated by the union.

In 1920 there was labour unrest in St Kitts but not of a serious nature. The Central Factory continued to operate but there were strikes at Ponds, Needsmust and La Vallée estates. What further complicated matters was that there had been a break in the telegraph lines and word could not be sent to the Colonial Governor in Antigua. The Legislative Council wanted to request a warship to be sent to keep the peace, but the strike was settled peacefully and outside intervention was not required.

The labour situation was further complicated by the fact that following the war, sugar prices fell when European beet sugar factories returned to production in the 1920s. In addition to sugar, cotton production in St Kitts and especially Nevis had become significant after 1900 and the war demand for cotton was so considerable that in 1918 the entire crop from St Kitts, Nevis and Anguilla was purchased by law by the British government and private sales were forbidden.

A considerable amount of cotton and sugar had been sold to Canada in the early twentieth century under Imperial Trade Preferences, but that would soon decline after the war ceased. Cotton production in the 1920s further increased in St Kitts and Nevis, but demand for it fell after the war and the annual crops were very difficult to sell. Later in that decade the boll weevil (or boll worm) appeared first in Nevis and then St Kitts. Both yield and quality of the crop declined and cotton became only marginally profitable and once more labourers suffered.

Life went on in St Kitts, and local matters had to be dealt with regardless of world economic conditions. In 1917 the London Electric Theatre was opened and for the first time the public could view films, which soon became immensely popular. The electric current required to operate it was produced by a steam powered electric generator. The theatre operators had to pay the government £10 a year for the water supplied to the generator, and they could not show films on Sundays. However, the public clamoured for Sunday viewings and a compromise was reached with the Legislative Council. Films could be shown Sunday afternoons provided that 10 per cent of the box office receipts were given to charity.

Begging and vagrancy continued and became a greater problem as employment opportunities decreased. Some measures were taken to relieve poverty through a modest public dole, but it did not solve the core problems. Beggars and prostitutes frequented the docks and piers to such an extent that loading and unloading cargo and passengers was hampered.

The Legislative Council boldly took action in that regard in 1922. Begging was outlawed on piers, and prostitution was curtailed. The law read in part ' ... except when passengers are embarking or disembarking, no females of notoriously bad character shall be allowed on any pier at any time'.[9] It is not clear from reading the Act whether it recognized that 'females of notoriously bad character' had a right to travel on ships, or it was designed to encourage them to solicit only persons arriving to or departing from St Kitts.

Another reason for that law might have been revealed in a letter from a health inspector dated 12 October 1929. It estimated that 50 per cent of the population was infected with syphilis. As appalling as that statistic was, the same letter noted that in 1900 the percentage probably had been 80 per cent.[10] In the same timespan the population of St Kitts had plummeted by 43 per cent, but Nevis by only nine per cent. As late as 1928, the Governor of the Leeward Islands spoke out against educating the working classes in the islands as it raised their expectations to a level which could not be met. It seemed then the only hope of a good life for most people was to leave, as local conditions appeared hopeless.

Government action on the health front had made some inroads into health problems but they remained acute. An American visitor had this to say about conditions in the poorer parts of Basseterre: 'Filth and vileness are on every hand. Pestilence seems to lurk around every corner and disease to fill the air with germs, while a fresh smell greets at every turn'.[11] The infant mortality rate in St Kitts was the highest in the West Indies as late as 1938, and the average lifespan about 15 years lower than in Britain.

The slow years of the 1920s when bulk sugar prices were 12 US cents per pound (weight) on the world market would look good in the 1930s depression when the price dropped by a half to 6 cents per pound. Although sugar prices move up and down, today the consensus is that the sugar industry in St Kitts has no real long-term future.

In the present, the economy of the island has expanded and diversified to the extent that tourism has replaced sugar as the primary product of the island. In the 1930s, however, there was nothing else but sugar. The crash in its price meant that workers' pay was severely cut and labour trouble was the predictable result.

In 1936, the situation exploded. Leewards Governor Sir Reginald St Johnston happened to be visiting in St Kitts when a riot began which resulted in the loss of three lives. St Johnston wrote the following account:

> On the twenty-ninth of January, while we were giving a big garden party at Government House in St Kitts, where I happened to be on an inspection visit, there suddenly flared up a full-sized riot, in the unexpected way these things happen in the West Indies.
>
> The reaping season for the sugar-cane crop had started the day before, and although there had been the usual annual 'preliminary discussions' among the labourers as to the rate of wages, all had turned out peacefully for work. All, that is, except a few malcontents who still advocated the strike. I drove around the island an hour or two after this to see the state of things for myself. At that time all was apparently quiet. But proceeding in the opposite direction to me a dozen or more of the strikers enlisted a drummer at their head and started to march around the island, calling to their ranks the labourers from each estate as they passed. The mob swelled like a snowball, and finally, taking confidence in their numbers and getting excited, proceeded to excesses. At one estate they severely assaulted an elderly white planter who had always been particu-

larly kind to his labourers, and at another place a planter had to defend himself from a bad fusillade of stones by using a shot-gun.

The mob then became unmanageable, and the magistrate and the head of the police came to Government House and asked me to call out the Defence Force. This was a very serious step to take, but I had to come to a quick decision, and after a few minutes' careful thought and many questions as to possibilities I signed the order. I also sent a wireless message out for a warship, though I knew none could reach us for two days. And I ascertained that guards were being posted on the wireless station and at other vital points. Finally, I issued an order closing all the liquor shops at once ...

It was just as well that I took the decision to call out the armed troops to support the small body of police, as within an hour, and as dusk was approaching, the situation at the entrance to the town became grave.

The Riot Act was twice read, and the mob still refusing to disperse the only thing left to do was to order rifle-fire. Three men were killed and eight wounded, but regrettable as this was it undoubtedly saved the town and thousands of innocent people from the menace of burning to their houses and violence to their lives.[12]

Beginning in St Kitts, wage-driven riots spread throughout the Caribbean and resulted yet again in the appointment of a Royal Commission, this time led by Lord Moyne. The commission report was not completed until December 1939 and it pointed out to the British government, then preoccupied by the war in Europe, that economic and living conditions throughout the Caribbean were wretched and something had to be done by imperial Britain to correct them, otherwise disturbances would continue and probably get worse.

However, the conclusions of the commission were not made public until after the war as it was feared German propaganda would publicize them worldwide to the detriment of the British Empire. This was a correct assessment. On 9 August 1939 the Germans, probably having got wind of the commission report through their intelligence network, issued a statement critical of British administration of the West Indies, declaring 'You decadently leave territories of your huge Empire sterile and undeveloped. We with our Fascist Vigor and our Nazi Energy could make them rich and valuable'.[13] As poor as British administration might have been, one shudders to think what 'Nazi energy' would have done in the Caribbean had they won the war.

Among other things, the report pointed out that education was lacking, public health was a problem (but less in St Kitts than some other islands), and the death rate of both infants and adults was unacceptably high everywhere in the West Indies. If health problems were fewer in St Kitts than elsewhere, the rest of the West Indies must have been very bad indeed.

An article in the London *Times* in 1938 had pointed out clearly the major cause of labour unrest. 'For most inhabitants of the West Indies life means work for a white boss at the subsistence level and has never meant anything else since the first Africans were brought over four hundred years ago'.[14]

It would be left to St Kitts' first Premier, Robert Llewellyn Bradshaw, to finally begin correcting this situation. Looking at conditions prevailing in St Kitts prior to World War II, the progress made in the past 50 years has been little short of miraculous.

The moribund sugar industry did not generate sufficient profit to allow higher wages and there was no alternative employment available in the islands. As late as 1940, an American visitor to St Kitts commented on the large number of beggars in Basseterre and observed that in his opinion it was the least happy of all the islands. By then, shortages caused by World War II were making themselves felt in addition to ongoing local problems.

The fears of the islands of German raids during World War I had not been realized. During World War II, the islands were in the midst of it from the beginning. German U-boats prowled the area, and during the first three years of World War II, 30 per cent of Allied shipping losses occurred in the Caribbean area. U-boats were first sighted in the Caribbean on 6 September 1939, only five days after the war started, when a Dutch freighter steamed at top speed into neutral San Juan harbour in Puerto Rico after sighting a submarine.[15]

The first naval conflict in the area of St Kitts was not fought by a U-boat, but by a disguised German surface raider. On 20 July 1940, two British freighters steaming in the Atlantic off of St Barthélemy were approached by what appeared to be a freighter flying the Swedish flag. When it neared them, the Swedish colours were hauled down and the German swastika flag was hoisted. The supposed freighter was a disguised warship mounting six 6-inch naval guns. The crews of the British freighters, *King John* and *Davasian*, were ordered to abandon ship at once, which they did, and both vessels were then promptly sunk by the German raider.

The crews drifted in lifeboats for over four days until 68 of them were picked up by another ship and carried to French St Barthélemy. From there they were sent by another ship to St Kitts, where they were housed in private homes until they could be repatriated to Great Britain. A local newspaper observed that this was the first naval engagement of any kind fought near St Kitts since the French wars in the early nineteenth century.

In 1942, 182 ships were sunk in the Caribbean area, in 1943, 45, and in 1944, five. During those years when Britain alone stood unconquered in Europe, petroleum products from Venezuela and the Netherlands Antilles and Bauxite ore from Surinam were essential to the British war effort. The Netherlands Antilles stayed in the hands of the Allies after Holland fell to the Germans, but following the conquest of France, Martinique and Guadeloupe were controlled by the pro-German Vichy French government. The Germans used Martinique as a base for refuelling and re-supplying their U-boats in the Caribbean. Allied supply ships bound for Halifax, Nova Scotia, to convoy for the North Atlantic crossing usually passed well out to sea from Martinique.

The strict censorship of newspapers and letters put into effect during the war makes facts about specific ship sinkings in the area difficult to come by, but there were so many survivors of sinkings brought into St Kitts that the Red Cross constructed a shelter to house them before they were repatriated. In 1942 a local boat race was organized for entertainment of ships' crews housed in St Kitts. It proved so successful that it was repeated several times during the war years.

On 20 January 1942 the government gave Great Britain funds towards the purchase of two Spitfires for the Royal Air Force, which were named St Kitts and Nevis I and II.

Disaster hit home to St Kitts when the passenger liner *Lady Hawkins* was sunk by a U-boat 19 January 1942 with the loss of 350 lives. She was one of the 'Lady' steamships, owned by the Canadian National Steamship Line. Named for the wives of British naval heroes, they had been calling in St Kitts since 1912, and were a familiar sight in every major West Indies port. Most of their passengers and crews were West Indian.

As *Lady Hawkins* made her way north to Canada after calling in St Kitts and other ports, without warning two torpedoes slammed into her and the resulting explosions tore the ship apart. She sank so fast that only a few people were able to reach the lifeboats. For ten days they drifted and 71 survivors, under the skilful command of the Captain, were ultimately rescued. Several survivors of the sinking died in the lifeboats. Three Kittians perished in the disaster, E. James, C. Blanchard and D. Blake. The exact location of the sinking is not known because of wartime censorship.[16]

Almost immediately industrial products became scarce in St Kitts. Flour virtually vanished from stores as did many other imported food products. Cassava flour replaced wheat flour in the island diet just as it had served the first settlers of the island in the seventeenth century. Starvation never threatened but food was in short supply and agricultural self-sufficiency sustained the population to a great extent.

An attack in late May 1942 by a submarine in Castries harbour in St Lucia resulted in the sinking of two British ships. Immediately blackout provisions were put into effect in St Kitts, including vehicle headlights, on 5 June 1942. Petroleum products were rationed beginning on 5 August of that year and some food products soon followed.

Sugar was once again in great demand and its price escalated. However, as in World War I, the higher cost of imported goods offset the benefits of the price rise. The squeeze resulted in a seven-week strike in St Kitts in 1940 over wages in the sugar industry which would have an indirect effect on future events on the island.

Britain's resources were strained to the utmost and few warships could be spared from home defence to battle submarines in the Caribbean. In addition, U-boats were ordered to harass the British in every way possible and that included sinking not only Allied shipping to and from Europe, but inter-island shipping as well.

Wooden schooners used extensively for commerce between the islands were often victims of submarines. U-boat crews believed that sinking a sailing ship was bad luck and they hated to do it, but they followed orders. If the British Caribbean islands suffered from shortages, Britain would have to divert shipping and supplies from home to assist them. Rather than waste a torpedo on a wooden ship, the submarine would surface and sink it with the deck gun. Time was usually given to the sailors to abandon the sailing vessel first unless an aircraft or warship threatened the U-boat. A single direct hit to a wooden ship would cause it to sink at once. The U-boat crews could relate to the helpless sailors on those relics of time past and after the war several of them related that it was heartbreaking to watch a wooden sailing ship go down under fire from a modern warship.

When the United States entered the war at the end of 1941, jointly with Britain an anti-submarine base was built in Trinidad and the entire Caribbean area was soon covered by allied aircraft patrols. Steel Bands originated in Trinidad when creative local musicians found that they could 'tune' the tops of the drums in which petrol was carried and play music on them. The World War II hit song 'Rum and Coca-Cola' came from a local calypso song written about that base in Trinidad.

On 20 September 1943, a United States Military Aircraft crashed in St Kitts. It was kept so secret that word of it never even reached the local newspapers. It was a Navy VMS-3 based in St Thomas and the make of the plane was a Vought OS2N-1 Kingfisher. The pilots flew from St Thomas to St Kitts and had lunch at Shorty's Restaurant, where they reportedly had several drinks with their meal. Upon taking off, they were performing acrobatics and lost control of the aircraft, which plunged to earth and burnt near the airport. A large American military transporter came to St Kitts the following day and removed both the wreckage and the bodies of the two airmen, Second Lieutenant Howell Cordell and Sergeant Alfred T. Shickering.[17]

What had been a favourite operational area for U-boats soon grew hazardous. In 1943 the United States put pressure on the French Caribbean Islands where U-boats were supplied by blockading them. Foodstuffs and every other imported commodity were in critically short supply and the population was growing restive. The United States threatened to invade Martinique and destroy the U-boat base. On Bastille Day, 14 July 1943, the local Vichy-run government was dissolved after a rebellion in the army barracks and a Free French Government took control. Admiral Robert, leader of the Vichy Government, fled Martinique for Puerto Rico by agreement with the United States. By 1944 U-boats had ceased to be a major problem in the area and conditions in St Kitts and the other islands improved. Unknown to the Allies, all U-boats were recalled from abroad to defend the home country by mid-1944, as the war was going badly for Germany by then.

The Bradshaw Years – Progress, Conflict and Controversy

In 1939 the Leeward Islands passed a law allowing the formation of Labour unions and in 1940 the Trades and Labour Union was formed in St Kitts with Edgar Challenger as its President. Because of the war a 'no strike' clause was agreed upon in labour contracts; nonetheless, a strike over wages was called on 1 April 1940. At the time the annual inflation rate was 15 per cent because of the war-caused scarcity of goods but no increase in pay was offered to workers until that rate reached 20 per cent, even though sugar prices had risen. The union called a strike which lasted seven weeks and was not a success.

Robert Llewellyn Bradshaw, then an employee in the machine shop of the sugar factory, participated in the strike and because of that, lost his job. He had long been an advocate of unions as a means of obtaining adequate wages for workers in the sugar industry. Losing his job proved to be a significant event in the history of both the labour movement and St Kitts itself. The man who would become first the leader of the union and then the first elected leader in St Kitts devoted himself to working for the union and for improving the lot of black labourers who had never been allowed to participate fully in society or government yet were the vast majority in the island.

Bradshaw came from the humblest surroundings. The illegitimate son of a woman who cleaned the homes of the managers of the sugar factory, he obtained as much of an education as he could before having to leave school to work. As he grew older, he educated himself and listened to the voices of those who advocated independence of the British Caribbean colonies and the assumption of power of the workers who had been deprived of it for the entire history of the island.

Marcus Garvey visited St Kitts in 1937 and emphatically declared that black people should be in charge of their own destinies. Garvey's theories made a great impression on Bradshaw, as did Labour-oriented publications which reached St Kitts from England. He came to believe that strong unions and socialism were the best means of righting the long-standing wrongs of slavery and continuing dominance of the island by the planters and their allies.

The labour movement in St Kitts was powerful and struck a chord with the population of the island. The violent strikes which swept the Caribbean in 1896 and 1935 had both originated first in St Kitts, which was an indication of the depth of the discontent of the population. In addition, visitors from foreign countries to St Kitts from the 1890s to the 1940s all commented on the mobs of beggars and pervasive poverty evident both in Basseterre and the countryside. This was the case even though St Kitts was richest of the Leewards.

In 1943 Edgar Challenger resigned as head of the union under pressure from a faction backing J. Matthew Sebastian, who succeeded him. Following Challenger's departure the 'no strike for the duration of the war' clause was removed from the labour contract unilaterally by the union. Sebastian then called a strike in 1944 which was not successful. Shortly thereafter, he died and Bradshaw took over leadership of the union.

Things then began to happen. Bradshaw was an articulate and forceful speaker and widely admired for standing up to opposition from the planters and against colonialism in general, not just in St Kitts but Nevis and Anguilla as well. More importantly, he became the voice of a long oppressed people who were determined to change the system under which they had lived so long.

In March 1946, after the war had ended, a 'go slow' action was called because a closed-shop clause was not included in the contract offered to the workers. It lasted for two weeks and again was not a success. Even so, Bradshaw impressed the membership by his leadership skills and consolidated his position as head of the union.

In 1948 a strike was called which lasted from 17 January to 19 April, in which 10,000 workers participated and much of the crop was not harvested. For the first time the union was able to show its strength. Even though membership was only about 500, many non-union workers followed its direction.

In Anguilla there had never been a strong plantation system and on Nevis the once strong system had collapsed in the 1930s depression. As a result, these islands were not affected as much by the inequalities and conflicts between planters and workers as was the case in St Kitts. Basically more conservative for this reason, some people in those islands were becoming ill at ease with Bradshaw's leftist political leanings.[18] Even so, they continued to admire him as a spokesman of the people and certainly did not support the planter class in St Kitts in their bitter opposition to Bradshaw at that time.

In 1951 a momentous event occurred. For the first time in history, popular suffrage was granted to the people of the Leewards. At long last islanders were able to vote and control their own destiny. This event would herald the greatest shift of power in St Kitts since Europeans displaced Indians in the early seventeenth century.

It was only natural that the labour movement would give birth to a political party in St Kitts. Bradshaw founded the Workers League and in the 1952 election, candidates were named by them for all seats and every one of them won in St Kitts. The Workers League received 10,528 votes and their opposition, the Democrats, received only 482 votes. The Democrats consisted mainly of the old planter and merchant establishment of the island.

Bradshaw was a candidate and leader of the party and he remained head of the union at the same time. His decision to keep both positions was questioned by some persons prominent in the labour movement, Edgar Challenger being one of the most influential of them. It was thought too much power was concentrated in one man, and there was a possibility of conflicts of interest. In retrospect, this was probably a correct assumption.

All along, Bradshaw pushed for independence from Britain. Looking back, independence, if desired, was then all but a certainty and only the date of its occurrence was in doubt. Bankrupt and exhausted following World War II, the British Empire was sliding into history. Independence was desired by most people in the colony, yet some had reservations. Conservative Anguilla and Nevis preferred to remain colonies rather than become independent under the control of St Kitts and the dominant Labour Party.

It was planned in Britain that a Federation of the West Indies would be established and all the islands of the Caribbean which wished to participate in it would do so. Caribbean intellectuals had been calling for such a federation since the 1920s, which would give the English-speaking Caribbean a single voice in world politics. As long ago as 1743, the French priest Père Labat declared to residents of all the islands of Antilles, 'You are all together, in the same boat, sailing the same uncertain sea ... citizenship and race [are] unimportant'.[19]

Bradshaw was an enthusiastic supporter of this federation and when it was formed in 1958 he was named Minister of Finance and worked tirelessly for its success. The beliefs of Bradshaw and almost all the rest of the leaders were clearly of populist/socialist leanings.

> It was felt the Cuban Socialist model was the answer to the long standing problems of income inequality, health, unemployment and distribution of wealth, but it was not, over the long term. It succeeded in wealth redistribution and health at the cost of human freedom, and proved to be unable to provide self-sustaining economic growth.[20]

Very unfortunately, the federation failed. It could be fairly said that the goals were too ambitious, but for those familiar with Caribbean history, failure could not have come as a great surprise. Rivalries between the individual Leeward Islands had been written about as early as 1862 and federating even these few islands in 1883 had required strict application of British colonial power.

Conflicts began almost at once in 1958 over which of the larger Caribbean islands would be the home of the grandiose new capital city the federation would construct for itself. Jamaica and Trinidad were the chief rivals. An independent group proposed Barbados as a compromise. The compromise did not succeed, and Trinidad got the capital. No small island was even considered as the larger ones believed that smaller islands were no better than parasites. This early failure to work together to reach an agreement was the beginning of the end of the federation.

Armed with an unrealistic agenda and represented by politicians who had little practical experience, the rivalries between the islands prevented anything concrete from being accomplished. Jamaica pulled out first, and the federation began to fragment. Bradshaw, Vere Bird of Antigua, and several others desperately attempted to salvage something from the wreckage and establish a 'small eight' federation of the smaller and at that time poorer islands, but even that did not succeed. In 1962 the federation was dissolved.

Bradshaw felt bitter disappointment with the inglorious end of the experiment. Always a visionary, he had seen the federation as the beginning of independence for the British Caribbean and the assumption by black people in the islands of the power and influence which was rightly theirs. He reflected sadly:

> I verily believe that we are the only people in creation who, having fixed the time for independence, failed to keep our collective date with destiny ... the shameful break-up of the West Indies Federation in 1962 scattered hopes and achievements almost to the depth of the Caribbean Sea.[21]

Bradshaw returned to St Kitts determined that his vision of the Associated State of St Kitts, Nevis and Anguilla would not meet the same fate as the federation had. In order to keep it on track he assumed more and more power personally and would not brook any opposition. His attitude raised doubts about his administration not only in Anguilla and Nevis where he was already regarded with suspicion, but internally in St Kitts as well.

In 1966 elections were called and the Workers League, having changed its name to the Labour Party, won all seven seats in St Kitts but none in Nevis or Anguilla. Bradshaw became Premier of the new government. The St Kitts internal government was not only the local assembly, but was also the government of the entire federation. Nevis had two seats and Anguilla one out of a total of ten.

This system was the one established by Britain in 1883 to govern the Leeward Islands Colony. With authority coming from Britain downwards to the islands, it worked adequately as an administrative unit. However, with the advent of free elections in the islands, it would prove a defective and divisive governing system and remains so today. Local St Kitts politicians felt they had to please their own constituents and as a result, Anguilla and Nevis believed themselves short-changed and effectively powerless. In many cases funds which should have been distributed to Anguilla and Nevis remained in St Kitts for local political reasons.

The Mouse that Roared – the Anguilla Revolution[22]

Anguilla is a flat, relatively infertile island 70 miles distant from St Kitts. Settled by the English in 1650, it was and still is subject to frequent droughts because of low altitude. Sugar cane was grown there and slaves were imported for its cultivation but the sugar was of inferior quality and used almost exclusively for local consumption and the manufacture of rum. By 1967 the population was around 5000.

Early on it was a haven for pirates. In the late seventeenth century Bartholomew Sharpe, the famous pirate discussed earlier in this book, called it home. The people who stayed there were of necessity hardy souls and scratched a marginal living from their own lands by growing vegetables, fishing and raising animals, with occasional ventures into piracy and smuggling between nearby islands. In 1825, it was placed under the Colonial Administration of St Kitts for convenience. For the most part it was forgotten until famine threatened in 1890 because of a severe drought. Over £2000 was spent by the government in St Kitts on food supplies which were dispatched from there to Anguilla. Following that, it remained well out of the Caribbean colonial mainstream until 1960.

As late as the 1960s Anguilla had no electricity, paved streets or telephones. Job opportunities were nil. Young people with ambition migrated to other islands seeking work. One of these was a youth named Ronald Webster. One of 16 children, only eight of whom survived infancy, he left Anguilla to work in Dutch St Martin. For 27 years he worked on a combination dairy farm and factory with such diligence that the childless owner and his wife treated him as a son and upon their deaths left him their entire estate, worth at the time one and a half million US dollars.

This remarkable man would in a short time acutely embarrass the Federation of St Kitts, Nevis and Anguilla, face down Great Britain, and ultimately appear twice before the United Nations in a situation which could not have been concocted by Hollywood in its wildest imaginings.

Having inherited a small fortune in St Martin, he returned home to Anguilla in 1960 and was distressed to see that his isolated island home remained a century behind its neighbours and its people still lived very hard lives. He was determined to use his inherited money to do something to about it.

In September 1966 he contacted Robert Bradshaw in St Kitts and proposed to personally fund development of an electricity generating plant and road improvements in eastern Anguilla, which with labour donated by the people of Anguilla, in five years would cover the whole island. He was granted a licence to operate a power plant but on two subsequent trips to St Kitts, Bradshaw would not see him and he was shunted off to low-level government functionaries and his visits accomplished nothing. Webster deeply resented this dismissive treatment.

In connection with the 1966 elections, Bradshaw visited Anguilla and informed the islanders that associated statehood would commence on 27 February 1967. He told them that the council proposed for Anguilla would have no real power to govern locally and that he, Bradshaw, would be their contact with the new state government and all decisions would come from him. Anguillans were told they had no alternative to obeying the new government and that Britain could not help them. Webster refused to accept this ultimatum and with others of like mind, disturbed meetings called to prepare for statehood by blowing conch shells and disrupting them. When a British representative appeared to explain how the new government would function, Webster's allies disrupted the meeting and stormed the court house where it was being held and broke it up.

It is difficult to imagine that the new government under Bradshaw could have been any less responsive to Anguilla's needs than Britain had been for over three centuries. However, if the old system was to be changed, Webster was determined that Anguilla would have a voice in determining its own destiny. Britain was a known quantity but the Bradshaw Labour government was not and Webster did not trust it.

The first real confrontation came at a beauty pageant organized on 4 February 1967 to celebrate statehood. Webster organized a group of 15 people who determined to break up the Queen Show. Held at night in the secondary school, Webster and the group outside the building threw stones through the windows and onto the galvanized roof of the building during the show, causing the pageant to break up in confusion and people to run from the building. As the Warden hastily left the show his car was stoned.

Armed police recently sent from St Kitts responded by firing tear gas bombs at Webster and his group, and then opened fire on them with rifles. Two men were slightly wounded and the rest fled into the bush. Bradshaw claimed the disruption was caused by a few whites and mulattos who wished to take over the island. This was incorrect. Almost everyone in Anguilla was of mixed race or black, including Webster himself, and internal racism hardly existed there.

On 6 February 1967, 40 armed members of the St Kitts defence force were dispatched to Anguilla by air. Upon arrival they were confronted at the airport by a hostile armed crowd led by Webster and departed for the police station in such a hurry that they left their ammunition behind in the aeroplane. It was seized at once by the rebels. Immediately after the arrival of the police, the rebels drove vehicles onto the dirt airstrip to prevent further landings and over the next few days replaced the vehicles with oil drums.

Bradshaw acted at once. He requested the British government to dispatch the frigate HMS *Salisbury* from Basseterre to Anguilla carrying 500 members of the St Kitts defence force to put down the riot. It arrived 14 February in Anguilla where its crew were greeted by a crowd carrying home made Union Jacks and singing 'God Save the Queen'. Seeing no riot to suppress, *Salisbury* returned to St Kitts the same day carrying the members of the defence force who never even disembarked.

On Statehood Day, 27 February 1967, Anguillans tore down the new flag and held a procession carrying an empty coffin, symbolizing the death of associated statehood. Events remained at a quiet but uneasy level until 8 March, when Warden Vincent Byron's house burnt down and he and his wife fled the island for St Kitts. It is very likely the fire was caused deliberately, but Webster denied it and declared the fire originated from an electrical fault.

On 29 May a crowd surrounded the police station to protest the policemen's shooting of automatic weapons to intimidate the people although there had been no casualties. On 30 May the 40 police officers departed Anguilla for St Kitts. They were disarmed at the Anguilla airport by the rebels who took 30 automatic rifles, 500 grenades and 5000 rounds of ammunition.

A team of negotiators then went to St Kitts to try and resolve matters but their efforts failed. Webster decided to attack St Kitts on 10 June 1967 rather than wait for troops from St Kitts to invade Anguilla. Ronald Webster was Minister of Defence in the *ad hoc* Anguilla government. Three American citizens and 15 Anguillans, carrying a quantity of military ordnance, boarded a 35-foot boat which set out for St Kitts. Webster would later insist the Americans, from the US Virgin Islands, were volunteers rather than paid mercenaries as the St Kitts government claimed.

Weapons carried by the men were two machine guns, two sub-machine guns, four M-1 automatic rifles, four carbines, six 0.25 calibre automatic pistols, three 0.32 calibre pistols, three 30.6 hunting rifles, six 0.303 rifles, explosives, and a supply of tear gas and gas masks.[23] Their numbers were few but they were certainly well armed.

Webster had held secret discussions with the Kittian Dr William V. Herbert of the opposition Peoples Action Movement (PAM) party. Herbert told him that if the invasion took place, opposition to Bradshaw was so strong that many Kittians would join them, overthrow Bradshaw, and let Anguilla go its own way after Bradshaw's opposition took over the government. Some say that they donated funds towards arming the invaders, but that has never been proved or disproved.

Against the advice of some other leading Anguillans, Webster decided to proceed with the invasion. He intended to capture Bradshaw and Paul Southwell and take them back to Anguilla as hostages. In the process, the Police Station, the Defence Force Headquarters and the power station were to be blown up.[24]

The actual invasion was a comedy of errors. First, the boat got lost between Anguilla and St Kitts at night and instead of reaching its intended destination, it made landfall on Saba at 11 p.m. The invaders corrected their navigational error and set out from Saba to St Kitts, arrived early in the morning, and landed the offensive force at Half Way Tree. The Kittians waiting there were not the crowds which were expected but only a handful of persons. Following the landing, the boat's engine would not restart for a time and after it did, it departed from St Kitts and proceeded back home to Anguilla. On the way the engine finally died completely and the boat had to be rowed home in bad weather.

Word of the invasion force's landing had leaked out and Bradshaw sent members of the defence and police forces out to round them up. Some were captured but others made their way to Statia and from there back to Anguilla. Before being taken, some invaders set off explosive charges at the Police Station and Defence Force Headquarters, but fortunately they did little damage and only slightly injured two persons.

Bradshaw reacted, or it could be said overreacted, by declaring a national emergency and taking full control of the government. Even some members of the labour unions felt this action was uncalled for and struck in protest, but the strike was not widespread. Press censorship was imposed and Anguillan mail, which passed through St Kitts, was embargoed and held in the post office. Bradshaw frequently dressed in military fatigues at public appearances which provoked some derisive comment, as he used as his personal transport a stately and elegant 30-year-old yellow and black Rolls-Royce. The two seemed incompatible.

In nearby Nevis, public opinion wholeheartedly supported the Anguillans and Nevisians would have joined them in separation had they been able to do so. Armed St Kitts defence forces were assigned to Nevis and in one instance they commandeered a lorry, loaded troops in it, and drove around the island road at night, firing automatic rifles into the air in each village they passed through. Armed troops were placed aboard the ferry between the two islands as well. This military presence kept Nevis in line, but most of its population developed a bitter hatred for and fear of Bradshaw and the Labour Party because of these actions.

The captured Anguillan invaders and local collaborators were tried in St Kitts and released, along with Dr Herbert. The court ruled government had failed to prove its case against them. Several British citizens who opposed Bradshaw and supported Anguillan independence were arrested, imprisoned and then deported. The British Governor, Sir Fred Phillips, who had been selected by Bradshaw to hold the position, fell out with him over these actions. He told Bradshaw that the state of emergency should be lifted and that the persons arrested 'were not an immediate threat to the country' which was a legal requirement.[25] Phillips was ignored.

Negotiations recommenced with a team from Anguilla going to St Kitts. Little progress was made. Bradshaw would not allow separation, declaring Britain had guaranteed that the state government would include Anguilla. An agreement was prepared in St Kitts ending secession which was signed by two of the three Anguilla representatives. Ronald Webster refused to join them.

A referendum was held in Anguilla where the vote was 1813 to five in favour of independence. Independence was then declared and a constitution drawn up and the newly-created government posts filled by Webster and his supporters.

The two sides were at a stand-off. Bradshaw called for a Caribbean force to invade Anguilla and put down the rebellion, but there was not a favourable response as most people in the other islands felt that Anguilla was entitled to self-determination. Anguilla's case was presented to the United Nations. Britain, the colonial power involved, refused to provide the Special Committee on Colonialism with any information, stating that the matter was the concern only of the new state government.

In September 1967 a British delegation was dispatched to Anguilla to try and resolve the conflict. They appeared to act with remarkable incompetence. In July 1968 public elections were held in Anguilla and the delegation's representative refused to recognize the results. It became clear after a year that their purpose was not to allow Anguilla to become an independent entity but to bring it back into the newly created state.

Tony Lee was appointed the British representative and was welcomed upon arrival but after a year, when he departed, his car was stoned and he was booed. Webster and Bradshaw travelled to London for discussions but nothing was resolved and only junior Foreign Office personnel were involved. The British Prime Minister would not meet with Webster or intervene in the proceedings. Webster returned home disheartened.

A second independence referendum was held on 6 February 1969 and the vote in favour was 1739 to four. Britain did not recognize it. Anguilla then declared itself a republic. They issued stamps and coins to generate revenue. People who bought them at the time made a wise investment, as some are worth a considerable amount of money today. Britain and Anguilla were at a stand-off, and the Anguillans were not about to give in.

On 18 March 1969, 300 British paratroopers and 22 London Police invaded the island from two frigates by helicopter. After two years Britain had not been able to resolve the matter peaceably so resorted to force. They had been constantly prodded by Bradshaw to act and finally did. Upon landing there was no active opposition and no injuries. British troops searched the island for arms and recovered some, but by no means all, of those which had been brought in and hidden.

Ronald Webster fled the island. Tony Lee, the representative who had left under a cloud the year before, returned and was appointed Commissioner and assumed power over the island. His return was celebrated by a mock funeral and was attended by a sullen and angry crowd.

Worldwide hoots of derision were directed at the British when news of the invasion reached the media. An American humorist wrote that the successful invasion of Anguilla would rank alongside such great British victories as Agincourt, Waterloo and El Alamein in military annals, and that the British army had proved it could rout a force of 400 sheep and suffer no casualties.[26]

Embarrassed, the British immediately tried to gain the friendship and cooperation of the Anguillans but met with little success. Webster travelled to New York and addressed the General Assembly of the United Nations and declared he had nothing against the British but believed with all his heart that Anguilla should have the right of self-determination. Even the Soviet Union's delegate agreed with him. Following his well-received speech, Lord Caradon, the senior British United Nations delegate, travelled from New York to Anguilla.

At last a capable man entered the picture. He told the British delegation in Anguilla to use common sense in resolving the problem and dismissed Tony Lee. At Caradon's request, Webster returned to Anguilla from the United States where he was given a tumultuous welcome and carried from the airport on the shoulders of the crowd.

Caradon and Webster drew up a document called the Seven Point Declaration. Bradshaw refused to accept it, and he called Anguilla ' ... my Biafra', referring to a civil war then going on in Nigeria.[27] After further talks between Webster and Lord Caradon, and another appearance by Webster before the United Nations, Anguilla ultimately got what it wanted. The Anguillans never backed down, even in the face of near bankruptcy and a British invasion.

It took some years to complete the transition from the old to the new situation but Anguilla, led by Ronald Webster, ultimately became a self-governing

British colony on 19 December 1980 and has since prospered. The mouse had roared and the whole world heard it.

Many Kittians declare that this incident changed Bradshaw and caused his leadership to harden. His personal shortcomings became more evident and the contradictions in his character more pronounced. His lack of a formal education seemed to work against him and any criticisms of his policies, even well meant, seemed to him to indicate personal opposition even when it was unintended. In short, he had become an elected dictator.

He affected an English accent and placed great importance on proper dress and punctuality, and seemed often to be more of an Englishman than a Kittian. He frequently told associates never to trust a white man, but he married a white woman. He dressed as a military officer in fatigues but rode in a Rolls-Royce with a driver. He declared he was not a Communist but was a close associate of the Marxist dictator of Guyana, Forbes Burnham, and admired many of the policies of Fidel Castro.

From his utterances it seemed Bradshaw had little use for the United States, and there was mutual reciprocation of those feelings. An American visitor wrote in 1968 that:

> St Kitts is now in the grip of wily Trade Unionists who come as close to practicing the doctrine of Black Power as does any government in the Caribbean ... From sources of varying color, at the bar and behind it, we were beginning to piece together an impression of the Bradshaw government and its role in St Kitts' dilemma; the once richest island in the Leewards now the poorest, the island with everything to offer tourists and not a single operating tourist hotel in sight.[28]

The Labour Party's practice at that time of addressing one another as 'comrade', and use of other socialist buzz-words, did nothing to encourage foreigners, especially North Americans, to invest in developing St Kitts and Nevis, not that they were wanted in any case.

Catastrophe – the Sinking of the *Christena*

On 1 August 1970, a disaster occurred when the ferry between St Kitts and Nevis went down in the Narrows. On its way from Basseterre to Charlestown, *Christena* was badly overloaded, carrying about 100 more persons than she had been designed to carry. The best available figures put the death toll at 233, with 91 saved.

The vessel had been undergoing repair work on her engine shafts in Basseterre. Although the work was not completed, Captain James Ponteen ordered the workmen off the vessel and she was loaded with passengers and departed on schedule. However, it seemed the workmen had not closed the watertight doors below decks and she was taking on water unbeknown to the captain and crew. When *Christena* reached the Narrows and its rougher waters, she only had a few inches of freeboard remaining and her handling was notably sluggish. Captain Ponteen came about, heading back towards the shore of the southeast peninsula where he hoped to beach her. He never made it.

Christena was going down by the stern and as water poured across the deck, she first listed to port and then capsized and sank. The unanchored chairs slid across the deck and blocked the exits and terror reigned as panicked passengers attempted to save themselves. There was time for only a few to escape, let alone get life jackets on, before she sank. *Christena* took most of her passengers and crew down with her.

Of those who were able to escape from the ferry, many could not swim and unless they were lucky enough to lay hold on floating objects, they drowned. The sinking was witnessed by Winston Skeete, a fisherman from Nevis. Skeete raced his small boat at top speed towards the scene of the disaster and was the first to arrive. He picked up as many people from the water as his boat could safely hold and carried them to shore on St Kitts. He returned as many more times as possible.

In spite of heroic efforts by Skeete and Michael King of St Kitts, among others, the few little boats able to reach the scene could rescue only small numbers of people struggling in the water. However, lacking their presence, the death toll would have been far higher.

Most of the passengers were from Nevis and scarcely a family on the island was spared the loss of a loved one or a friend. Both St Kitts and Nevis were grief-stricken over the catastrophe. An investigation was undertaken and the results did little to ease the pain and loss.

Shortly before the accident a prominent Nevisian, Cecil Byron, had written a letter to the government in St Kitts complaining of frequent overloading of *Christena* and her resulting lack of balance at sea. His letter had been ignored. The investigation indicated that in spite of the sale of tickets being restricted to a set number of passengers, it was customary to allow additional persons to board. The implication was that these persons paid cash and the Captain and crew pocketed the extra money. This allegation could never be proved or disproved, as the persons allegedly involved had drowned.

The political implications were that the laxity of government supervision of the operation of the ferry was the major cause of the sinking and the high number of casualties. The effects in Nevis were substantial. The Labour government was blamed and Nevis became even more determined to separate from the federation.

Shortly after the sinking in 1970 another election was called. When the vote occurred in 1971, Labour once again won all the seats in St Kitts, but none in Nevis. In the next few years under Bradshaw changes were made in St Kitts which would effectively bring down and remake the social system which had been in place for centuries. These alterations would not be accomplished without conflict and opposition.

About 15 white or mixed-race families controlled the St Kitts economy owning not only most of the sugar estates, but the factory and some mercantile enterprises. In 1972 Bradshaw decided that the sugar estates had to be brought under government control. By doing so he believed, correctly, that the back of what was termed the 'plantocracy' which had run the island for centuries, would at last be broken. It was something which had to be done to give working people the economic and social rights they deserved.

In 1972 the government took over the administration of the sugar lands, and in 1974 owners of the lands offered them to the government for purchase. The sticking point was the price and the sum could not be agreed upon. The government insisted the maximum it would pay would be US$10 million but the owners held out for 25 million.

In February 1975 the Sugar Estate Lands Acquisition Act was passed by the Assembly and the price to be given for the lands was set at 10 million dollars. The owners immediately brought suit and challenged the constitutionality of the Act. The High Court agreed with the owners and it was ruled unconstitutional. The result was challenged by the government and the Court of Appeals upheld the High Court. Government and the owners then released a statement that: first, the lands would not be returned to the owners under any circumstances; second, the fundamental question was price; and third, both parties would negotiate regarding the price.

Negotiations commenced and government held to its offer of US$10 million for the estates. The owners contended that they were worth US$25 million, but they were willing to reduce the amount slightly. The two groups talked but government would not budge from the 10 million figure and the owners also remained firm in their demand for more.[29]

The discussions continued five years until Premier Bradshaw's death in 1978 with neither side budging from its respective position. In the election held in February 1980, Labour lost for the first time when PAM and the NRP party of Nevis formed a coalition and held a majority of seats in the Assembly. Dr Kennedy Simmonds, leader of PAM, became Premier.

PAM believed the negotiations had dragged on long enough and for the good of the country the matter had to be settled promptly. Ultimately a figure of US$20 million was agreed upon by the parties in 1981. However, the matter still has not been settled completely. Evidently there was a side agreement that some owners would be allowed to sell their lands privately in order to raise cash as the government did not have sufficient funds available for outright purchase. This became a political matter and what exactly has taken place in regard to the sugar lands since 1981 is not entirely clear. In addition, on 11 June 1987, Camps and West Farm Estates were seized when two resolutions were passed in the Assembly. It would be worthwhile for someone to make a full study of the change of ownership of the sugar estates when all documentation becomes available.

The nationalization of the sugar factory followed in 1976 and setting a price was much less difficult than for land. By these two actions, as well as the nationalization of the cement factory and property at Frigate Bay, the power of the plantocracy was effectively broken. However, the law of unintended consequences applied.

Nationalization of the sugar industry accomplished more or less what was expected of it, which was to bring the working people of the island higher pay. However, the old plantation system was locked in place, with the government now acting in the position of the planters. Like their predecessors, they had to deal with falling world sugar prices and wage demands of the workers.

This has proven difficult over time. Fortunately for all concerned the economy of St Kitts has expanded in the intervening years with tourism edging sugar out of its historically predominant position in the economy. Alternatives to working in the sugar economy now exist. Sugar production frequently makes an annual loss but this no longer causes the economic disruption it did half a century ago. As the price of sugar on the world market continues to fall, the value of the estates nationalized falls with it and will continue to do so until more a profitable utilization can be made of them.

Because the sugar industry was not allowed to die a natural death, the creation of an independent peasantry did not fully take place in St Kitts as it had in Nevis in the 1930s. The Moyne Commission had urged such a development as early as 1939 to increase the self-reliance of the population. As was noted, living conditions were better in islands where such an event had occurred even though the overall economic situation was poorer in those places. For this reason, development and advancement in St Kitts has been hindered.[30]

As Kittians raised themselves economically, it became necessary to import workers from poorer places to do the hard work of cutting the cane. Not enough locals would do it when better employment existed. In 1999 a group of workers from Guyana who had contracted to work at a set price struck for higher wages after arrival in St Kitts. When they refused to return to work at the contract price, they were promptly sent back to Guyana by the Labour government. Most sugar workers come from there and St Vincent on a temporary basis today.

Robert L. Bradshaw died on 23 May 1978 after a long battle with cancer. His plan for a comprehensive social security system was in place, although his dream of independence for St Kitts and Nevis would not occur for five more years. Significant expansion of the educational system also occurred during his administration in both St Kitts and Nevis with free secondary education made available to all without selection. The federation was the first place in the Caribbean where this was done. A literacy rate of over 96 per cent indicates how successful these actions were.

Upon Bradshaw's death Deputy Premier C. A. Paul Southwell, Bradshaw's long-term partner both in the union and the Labour Party, assumed the Premiership. At the time he took office Southwell was in poor health and died almost a year to the day after Bradshaw. Allegations were made that his passing in St Lucia was not of natural causes but there is no question that it was entirely natural.

Southwell worked hard for years to develop the Organization of Eastern Caribbean States (OECS), which in many ways has acted as successor to the short-lived Federation of the West Indies. He had worked with Bradshaw in the federation and was as unhappy as Bradshaw was at its failure. Here was an opportunity at last for the Caribbean to speak with a single voice and Southwell was instrumental in its organization.

Lee Moore QC, took over leadership of the party but when a by-election was held on 25 January 1979 to fill Bradshaw's seat. Labour lost in a very close vote, the results of which were decided in a court of law. Dr Kennedy Simmonds, leader of PAM, took the seat. Labour was shocked to the core. Yet, leadership of the party had been a one man show and Bradshaw's firm control did not allow the party to develop strong alternative internal leadership. Upon succeeding to office, Simmonds was treated harshly by Labour and many Kittians disapproved.

As a result, when Labour called an election for 18 February 1980, PAM took three seats and Labour four. However, the two Assembly seats from Nevis went to the Nevis Reform Party led by Dr Simeon Daniel. St Kitts was stunned by the results of the election. PAM and NRP reached an agreement and a coalition government resulted. Kennedy Simmonds became Premier, and for the first time since universal suffrage, control of the government of St Kitts and Nevis was no longer in the hands of the Labour Party.

This political realignment had a significant effect on the new constitution then in the process of being drafted. At the insistence of Dr Daniel it contained a provision allowing Nevis to secede from the federation upon a two-thirds majority of all votes cast in a referendum in Nevis alone. Nevis had not wished to join the Labour Party-controlled federation and preferred to remain a self-governing colony as Anguilla was. A local, non-binding referendum was held in Nevis and the result was a vote of over 90 per cent in favour of independence from the federation. Britain said no to that, but the constitutional provision for secession was the next best thing to independence as far as most Nevisians were concerned.

Independence

Robert Bradshaw, always the visionary, had worked hard for independence throughout his political career. It would be achieved after Bradshaw's death under the leadership of Kennedy Simmonds on 19 September 1983. Bradshaw travelled to London four times regarding a new constitution and independence and Simmonds, his successor, twice.

At the Independence celebration, Princess Margaret represented the British Crown and the handover of power occurred amid general rejoicing in St Kitts in spite of a movement by Labour to boycott some of the festivities. The Federation of St Kitts and Nevis remained in the British Commonwealth but for the first time in their history the islands had self-government and full democracy.

In the next election held 21 June 1984 the Labour Party under the leadership of Lee Moore challenged the PAM government under Simmonds. PAM won six of eight seats and had a full majority. Nevis's two seats were no longer required for a coalition government with PAM although they remained in the hands of the NRP.

As long as the Nevis delegates were required for a coalition, their leaders believed that Nevis should remain part of the federation as it would be able to benefit from its pivotal position. Yet, Nevis gained little. Its infrastructure remained marginal, with roads, harbours, the airport, electricity and telephone systems all remaining far behind those in St Kitts.

Many expected that Nevis would hold an independence referendum following the election in St Kitts but it did not come about. The Nevis delegation in the Federation Assembly more or less went its own way and relations between PAM and the NRP in Nevis remained good. Each island had local self government and there was little interference by the federation in Nevis's local affairs.

Development in St Kitts continued to proceed. Healthcare and education continued to progress and by the 1980s the average lifespan of a person in the federation had increased so greatly that it is today more or less equal to that of Europe and North America. In the 1930s it was well below those places. Tourism gradually replaced sugar as the major source of income for St Kitts. It should also be noted that money remitted home from Kittians working abroad remained a major source of funds. As it was not part of government receipts it was not counted in revenues and the exact amounts were unknown.

Calculations have been made of the amount by using banking records to determine approximate amounts and the figure remains considerable to this day.

An election was held on 29 November 1993 and the situation changed considerably. PAM and Labour split the St Kitts seats four and four. Once again, Nevis became pivotal in the Assembly and a coalition with one of the other parties became a necessity. In 1992 the Concerned Citizens Movement (CCM) had won a majority in Nevis over the NRP. Labour hoped to form a coalition with them and return to power, as the NRP had historically favoured PAM.

A Labour-CCM coalition was not to be. Premier Amory found himself in a political hot seat. The Labour Party was unpopular in Nevis and he dared not form an alliance with them so he proclaimed a policy of 'neutrality' and declared CCM would not ally with either party in St Kitts. He stated that the St Kitts Assembly was its local government and Nevis should not interfere in it. The Labour party under its new leader, Dr Denzil Douglas, was bitterly disappointed at missing the opportunity to assume power once more.

The NRP under its new leader Joseph Parry held only a single seat in Nevis but Parry was also one of Nevis' two representatives in the Federation Assembly. He was contacted by PAM and agreed to form a coalition government with them. Because of this PAM and Dr Simmonds would remain in power in St Kitts until 1995.

Problems were beginning to surface in St Kitts. Allegations of corruption were being made against PAM by Labour often through the party newspaper *The Labour Spokesman. The Democrat* was PAM's voice and charges flew back and forth. Independent journalism was and is lacking in both newspapers and the charges and counter-charges were believed or disbelieved for the most part only by the party faithful.

Some of the allegations were that payoffs were flowing into Labour Party coffers through three of their local supporters wanted on drug related charges in the United States. These payments were alleged to have been made to preserve the three from extradition to the United States for trial. Similar charges were made by Labour against PAM.

1994 proved to be one of the most volatile and violent years in the history of St Kitts and its events shook the island to its core. On 19 June at 6 a.m. Dr William V. Herbert took his wife and four friends on what was to be a Sunday morning boat ride. They would never be seen again. Herbert was a founder of PAM and a man of great influence in St Kitts. In spite of a diligent search by the St Kitts and Nevis coastguard, later assisted by the United States and French coastguards and Venezuelan authorities, not a trace of the Herberts, their friends or the boat has ever been found. A reward of US$0,000 was offered as well but to no avail.

It had been alleged by the FBI that Herbert had been involved with laundering money obtained by the Irish Republican Army (IRA) from drug sales in the United States through a bank in Anguilla. The proceeds were supposedly used by the IRA to purchase arms. The vessel carrying them had been stopped at sea by the British Royal Navy and the contraband seized. Some believed that Herbert's disappearance was retribution by the IRA, but this has never been proved or disproved. Herbert had earlier won a libel suit against a UK newspaper which stated he had laundered the money involved and he was awarded compensation of EC$125,000.

Labour declared that this disappearance was a crime related murder while PAM insisted it was a tragic accident. Scotland Yard was called in to investigate the matter but they turned up nothing significant. It is likely the truth will never be known.

On 1 October 1994 Vincent Morris and his female companion Joan Walsh vanished. They were last seen in Basseterre at 11 p.m. in a rental car. In spite of a diligent search they could not be located. He was the son of Sidney Morris, Minister of Education in the PAM government. It was assumed that they had met with foul play and the crime was drug related, as Vincent Morris's two brothers had been arrested on drug charges. A police investigation led to charges of conspiracy to commit murder against six local men, all of whom were alleged to be involved in drug shipments passing through St Kitts from South America to the United States.

Superintendent Jude Matthew headed the Special Branch of the Police Force which had investigated the disappearances and brought the six men up on charges. On his way to work on 15 October an assassin fired into his vehicle from the kerb with a shotgun and murdered him. The nation was stunned at this blatant act of terrorism and the government immediately called in Scotland Yard for the second time that year to investigate Matthew's murder. One David Lawrence was charged with the murder but was later found innocent.

As if Matthew's murder was not enough, on 12 November the bodies of Vincent Morris and Joan Walsh were discovered in the boot of their burnt-out rental car in a cane field. They had been shot gangland style probably on 1 October but the vehicle and their bodies remained undiscovered until 12 November. On 15 November Sidney Morris resigned from his government post on the basis of what was almost certainly a drug related murder and the arrest of his two other sons on drug charges.

Newspapers around the world reported on this series of grisly killings and unexplained disappearances and concluded that St Kitts was in effect controlled by drug interests and was not only unsafe to visit but thoroughly corrupted by drug money. These conclusions were bolstered by the fact that all persons accused of the murders of Morris, Walsh and Matthew were found innocent of the charges. Tourist visits plummeted in both St Kitts and Nevis and even the Nevis offshore financial sector was adversely affected by this negative publicity.

It is possible that drug money was and still may be flowing to both parties. This is a very serious matter which threatens the future of the federation. It has been inflicted on the islands by the dangerous and misguided drugs policy of the United States.

The incredible profits made from drugs flowing from South America into the United States enables the South American drug barons to buy off island governments. The small islands themselves have had until recently no real local hard drug problem, but influential people are sometimes bribed to look the other way when drugs pass through the area. The island drug problem seems to have arisen when some local criminals who assisted the South American producers were paid off not just in dollars but in hard drugs as well, which are now sold locally.

In the United States internal drug consumption evidently cannot be controlled so authorities are attempting to stop the flow of drugs into the country. More recently, the war on drugs has targeted alleged money laundering operations in Caribbean offshore financial centres. The sovereign rights of small and relatively powerless countries such as St Kitts and Nevis are under attack by American authorities in the name of law enforcement.

Following these scandals it became evident that PAM was losing much of its authority. Labour did not help itself when protests against the PAM government were held and turned violent. The disorder was not really serious and did not hasten the election, but did result in more tourist holiday cancellations and additional loss of business to the offshore financial sector.

The election was held 3 July 1995 and Labour predictably won, taking seven of eight seats and returning to power for the first time in 15 years.

St Kitts and Nevis – Together or Apart?

The Labour victory in St Kitts stirred up apprehensive memories in Nevis of the turbulent Bradshaw years, where St Kitts under Labour leadership ruled Nevis with an iron fist. The idea of secession re-emerged but in talk more than action. Wiser heads said that the Labour Party had changed a great deal from the old days and that its leadership was more responsible than it had been. Nevis adopted a wait-and-see attitude.

The economic relationship between the two islands had changed considerably since independence. Once rich and powerful, Nevis had collapsed economically in the early years of the eighteenth century and remained by far the poorer of the two islands until growing tourism and the new offshore financial industry combined to create local economic prosperity which had been absent for almost three centuries.

Ever since the two governments had combined in 1883, their joint income had been divided at year end by the 80 per cent (St Kitts) to 20 per cent (Nevis) formula devised at that time. Nevis had been on the receiving end of the income division until 1991, when it was unexpectedly called upon to contribute five million dollars into the pool. The economic growth rate in Nevis had begun to exceed that of St Kitts with the opening of the Four Seasons Resort and growth in the offshore financial sector. It is almost impossible to make the necessary calculations to prove this as the accounts of both islands are kept jointly in many cases.

The offshore financial business in Nevis commenced in 1984 with the passage of the Nevis Corporation Ordinance 1984 which allowed quick formation of companies not taxed in the federation. The federation government, then under PAM, had opined that Nevis could operate an offshore programme independent of St Kitts and given it their blessing. Precedent for this was that each Canadian province and state in the United States had its own corporate and trust laws rather than a single federal law. After a slow start the offshore business in Nevis began to produce substantial income for the Nevis Island Administration by 1991.

In 1993 St Kitts became aware of the income potential of this activity and updated their own laws to take advantage of it. The 1993 St Kitts Act specifically exempted corporations formed in Nevis from the coverage of their Act after discussions between Dr Simeon Daniel and the Attorney General of St Kitts. However, the results of these new Acts in St Kitts did not meet expectations and little business resulted.

Following Labour's victory in 1996 the new administration decided to overhaul thoroughly the offshore laws of St Kitts and the federation once more in an attempt to increase business. The government of Nevis continued to pursue the policy of neutrality and participated only marginally in the federation government in St Kitts. Nevis was unaware of the proposed new Acts until a few weeks before they were scheduled to them in the Assembly, which was a foregone conclusion with Labour's majority. The proposed new Acts were a new corporation ordinance, a new trust Act, a banking Act, and finally the creation of a financial services committee which would oversee the administration of the offshore service communities both in St Kitts and Nevis.

The Nevis offshore sector was not exempted from the coverage of these Acts. When asked by the Nevis Island Administration for an exemption, it was refused and the St Kitts government implied that the administration of the offshore sector in Nevis was lax and to protect the reputation of the federation they had to step in and take control of it.

The Nevis Island administration was extremely upset. They believed that these several acts represented an attempt by St Kitts to take overall control of the offshore business in Nevis. It was pointed out that in 14 years of operation of its programme there had been no major problems or scandals arising from it and Nevis was capable of continuing to administer the programme on its own.

Early attempts at a compromise failed and as a result, Premier Amory of Nevis called for a secession referendum pursuant to the constitution. Feelings ran very high in Nevis. All the slights, real or imagined, which Nevis had suffered through the years under the administration of St Kitts were recalled in detail. For over two centuries there had been disagreements between the two, including but not limited to the payments Nevis was called upon to make in 1782 to the victorious French, the failure to rebuild the Nevis hospital after the 1899 hurricane, the Bradshaw years, and finally what Nevis called an unwarranted intrusion into its local affairs in connection with its successful offshore business. Additionally, it had been felt for years that St Kitts retained development money for itself when some of it should have gone to Nevis.

Local opposition to secession argued that Nevis standing alone as an independent country was ludicrous with a population of only 9000, and that even though it was prospering, by itself it could not afford independence. When the referendum was held on 10 August 1998, 62 per cent of the Nevis vote was in favour of secession. However, the constitutional requirement was 67 per cent, so secession failed – at least temporarily. Many other Caribbean island states breathed a sigh of relief, as some were also twin-island states and feared the possibility of an internal break-up if Nevis set a precedent.

The 1962 failure of the West Indian Federation had left a void in the Caribbean. The problem of Nevis's secession could well have been solved had an overall government of all the islands existed with the real or apparent power to deal with the situation. Indeed, it is very likely that the 1983 St Kitts and Nevis constitution would not have contained a secession provision at all if the West Indies Federation had come about.

Ironically, Premier Amory's CCM party had originally opposed secession and the rival NRP, now headed by Joseph Parry, had supported it. The parties both did a complete reversal of their earlier stands. Following the vote a constitution committee was appointed by the federation to prepare a new constitution which would address the concerns of both Nevis and St Kitts.

Headed by the able Sir Fred Phillips, the governor of St Kitts and Nevis during the Bradshaw years, after considerable study sensible proposals have been made for resolution of the constitutional conflicts between the islands. They must, however, be approved, put into place, and tested before they become final. Under the existing constitution Nevis can call for another secession referendum at any time.

The most important proposal is that the administrations of both islands should be independent of one another and have a small joint overall federation government to handle international and local affairs affecting both islands. If agreed to, this will at last put an end to the cumbersome colonial administrative system of the local St Kitts government being at the same time the government of the entire federation. Had this matter been dealt with when self-government was instituted in the 1960s, and the West Indies Federation been in existence, the Anguilla revolt probably would never have occurred.

If one could hope for the best of all possible worlds for the Federation of St Kitts and Nevis in the new millennium, it would begin with a final resolution of the constitutional and political problems between the two islands. In St Kitts, the people would profit by the calming of bitter conflicts between political parties. Each should recognize the good things done by the other and eliminate the all-or-nothing requirement of party loyalty. This would allow the island to move forward in cooperation rather than conflict. The elimination of the evil of drug money flowing into the island would more than anything else help eliminate the potential corruption which clouds future progress so severely.

The federation of St Kitts and Nevis is one of the smallest countries in the western hemisphere in terms of both size and population. As such, it is extremely vulnerable to economic, political and natural difficulties which would hardly be noticed in a larger nation. The Caribbean itself is badly fragmented in terms of nationality and language and as long as that remains the case, dealing with local problems is much more difficult than it should be.

Yet, steady progress is being made. Since the St Kitts population was enfranchised 50 years ago and subsequently became self-governing and independent, living conditions have improved at a rate surpassed only by few nations. From an 'imperial slum' a century ago, it has become a largely middle-class nation. The government has now decided that sugar production will be phased out from 2002. Eliminating subsidies for it will be economically positive for the country, but cutting the ties with the commodity which for 350 years has largely dictated the economic and social direction of the country will not be easy. However, there is no difficulty in believing that St Kitts will face and overcome this problem as it has done with countless others in the past.

Notes

Chapter 1: Natural History

1. Blome, Richard, *The Present State of His Majesty's Isles and Territories in America*, London, 1687, p. 99. It should be noted that this book, like many others of the era before copyright law existed, plagiarizes other works considerably.
2. *Ibid.*
3. Oldmixon, John, *History of the British Empire in America*, London, 1708. Of early historians, Oldmixon is one of the most respected and accurate although his work contains recognizable passages borrowed from others, especially Cesar Rochefort.
4. Rochefort, Cesar, *The History of the Caribbee Islands*, English translation by Davies, London, 1666. An invaluable early source, especially for naturalists. Written in 1649, it was later translated into English with its illustrations of animal and plant life intact.
5. Wynne, John Huddleston, *A General History of the British Empire in America*, London, 1770.
6. Rochefort; *Supra*.
7. *Ibid.*
8. Anonymous, *An Account of the late Dreadful Earthquake in the Islands of Nevis and St Christopher*, British Library, London, 1690.
9. Blome, *Ibid.*, p. 102. This was taken from Rochefort's description verbatim.
10. Millas, José Carlos: *Hurricanes of the Caribbean and Adjacent Regions, 1492–1800*, Miami, 1968. This superb scholarly work was a lifetime effort by Dr Millas who left Cuba following Fidel Castro's seizure of power. He used English, Spanish, French and Dutch records, numbered each hurricane and followed its track. Anyone interested in the topic should read the book, now out of print.
11. *Ibid.*, p. 113, quoting the French Priest Father Jean Baptist du Tertre, *Histoire générale des Antilles habitées par les Français, 1667*.
12. *Ibid.*, p. 131, quoting Lieutenant 'Stormy Jack' Evans, RN, Nautical Magazine, London, 1837.
13. *Ibid.*, p. 133, again quoting Evans.
14. *Ibid.*, p. 144, quoting Christopher Jeaffreson of St Kitts.
15. Marx, Robert F., *Shipwrecks in the Americas*, Florida, 1992.
16. Robertson, Revd Robert, *A Short Account of the Hurricane, that pass'd thro' the English Leeward Caribee Islands, on Saturday the 30th of June 1733*, London, 1733 (Nevis Archives). This is one of five books written by the Revd Robert Robertson who served St Paul's church, Charleston. Extremely rare, only one copy each of four books is known to exist, and the fifth, dealing with the disposition of French lands in St Kitts after the 1713 treaty, has never been found.
17. Millas; *Supra*, p. 235, quoting *The Gentleman's Magazine*, London, (1772, XLII, 590). 1772 was the most active year ever for Caribbean hurricanes, with at least nine reported, some very powerful.
18. *Ibid.*, pp. 253–259. This monster 1780 storm tore the Caribbean apart as none other has before or since. Especially graphic is the account of the destruction of

the octagonal stone Governor's Mansion in Barbados with walls two-and-a-half feet thick, which left the Governor and his staff standing in the wine cellar in rubble and waist-deep water holding children on their shoulders to keep them from drowning. All miraculously survived.
19. St Christopher Legislative Council Records, 1899–1908, St Kitts Archives.

Chapter 2: Indians

1. The author wishes to thank Dr Samuel Wilson of the University of Texas for his observations regarding Amerindian settlement of the Antilles, based on his studies and archaeological excavations in several islands.
2. Oldmixon, *Supra*, p. 262.
3. *Ibid*.
4. Raynal, Abbé *History of the Settlements and Trade of the Europeans in the East and West Indies*, (English translation), London, 1783, Vol. VI, pp. 28–33.
5. Oldmixon, *Supra*, p. 230. His account of Amerindians in the region of Apalachicola, Florida, speaking the Carib language in my opinion is very significant for the study of migration of tribes in the pre-Columbian era.
6. Hilton, John, *Revelation of the First Settlement of St Christopher and Nevis by John Hilton, Storekeeper and First Gunner of Nevis*, Egerton MSS, British Library, London, 1656 (reprinted by the Hakluyt Society, London, 1925).
7. Labat, Père Jeane Baptiste, *Memoirs 1693–1705*, (translation) Frank Cass & Co. Ltd, London 1970, p. 76.

Chapter 3: European Settlement

1. Merrill, Gordon C., *The Historical Geography of St Kitts and Nevis, The West Indies*, Mexico City, 1958.
2. Calendar of State Papers, 1620, Public Record Office, Kew.
3. Southey, Captain Thomas, *A Chronological History of the West Indies*, London, 1827, p. 252.
4. Watts, David, *The West Indies: Patterns of Development, Culture and Environment Change since 1492*, Cambridge University Press, 1987, p. 164. Of all current works discussing the West Indies, I believe this is among the very best in its scope, breadth and readability.
5. Williams, Eric, *Documents of West Indian History, Trinidad*, 1963, p. 297.
6. Southey, *Supra*, p. 262.
7. Hilton, *Supra*.

Chapter 4: The Spanish Attack

1. Crouse, Nellis, *The French Struggle for the West Indies*, Columbia University Press, 1940. This book and Crouse's *French Pioneers in the West Indies* together give well researched and written accounts of French activities in the area. Both are in English.
2. Williams, *Supra*, p. 178.

Chapter 5: The Coming of King Sugar

1. Baker, Philip, *From Contact to Creole and Beyond*, University of Westminster Press, 1995, p. 53.
2. Burns, Sir Alan, *History of the West Indies*, London, 1965, quoting CSP 1701 no. 34.

3. Robertson, Revd Robert, *Letter to the Lord Bishop of London*, 1732, p. 28 (Nevis Archives).
4. Oakley, Amy, *Behold the West Indies*, Longman, Green & Co., New York, 1951, p. 228, quoting Christopher Jeaffreson.
5. *Ibid.*
6. Merrill, *Supra*, p. 72, quoting CSP 1701, no. 1132, 30 Dec. 1701.
7. Robertson, *Supra*.
8. Rochefort, *Supra*.
9. *Ibid.*
10. Letter from Christopher Jeaffreson, 1641, Bienecke Collection, Hamilton College, Clinton, New York.
11. This story was related to the author by Dr Marcos Troncoso of Santo Domingo, Dominican Republic, ten years ago. In addition to being a senior partner of the law firm of Troncoso and Cáceres, he is an active member of several historical organizations there.
12. Burns, *Supra*, p. 101.
13. Benford, Timothy, *The Eighteenth Century Countermarked Coins of St Kitts and Nevis*, draft of text, 1991.

Chapter 6: The Birth of the French Caribbean Empire

1. Oldmixon, *Supra*, p. 225.
2. See Crouse's works for details of this most interesting and capable French governor.
3. Labat, Père Jean Baptiste, *New Journey to the Islands of America*, 1742.

Chapter 7: The Birth of the British Caribbean Empire

1. Merrill, *Supra*.
2. Pitman, Frank Wesley, *The Development of the British West Indies 1700–1763*, Yale University Press, New Haven, 1967 (reprint), p. 194, quoting CSP 1706–1708 no. 1273.

Chapter 8: Important Conflicts

1. Crouse, *Supra*, *(French Struggle*, etc.) quoting du Tertre.
2. Crouse; *Ibid.*, gives details of this engagement from the French side.
3. Raynal, *Supra*, Vol. VI, p. 306.
4. Berry, Captain John. *Letter to the Right Honourable Governor Henry, Lord Willoughby and Captain Henry Hawley*, April 1667, Bodleian Library, Oxford University.
5. Crouse, *Supra*, (French Struggle, etc.), p. 155.
6. Labat, *Supra*, *(Memoirs)* p. 218.
7. *Ibid.* p. 57.
8. *Ibid.*
9. Crouse, *Supra*, p. 255, quoting letter of the Comte de Ponchartrain.
10. Public Record Office, Kew, *Claims from Nevis and St Christopher for damage done in French Attacks*, 1705–1706.
11. Oldmixon, *Supra*, p. 254.
12. Crouse, *Supra*, p. 302.
13. Anonymous, *A letter from Mrs Smith's*, Public Records Office, Kew, detailing the French attack on Nevis, 1706.

14. Assembly Acts of St Christopher, 1722.
15. Raynal, *Supra*, Vol. VI, p. 78.
16. French, George, *The History of Colonel Parke's Administration*, London, 1717.

Chapter 9: Pirates and Privateers

1. Burns, *Supra*, p. 367.
2. Alleyne, Warren, *Caribbean Pirates*, Macmillan, London, 1967.
3. Esquemeling, John, *Bucaniers of America*, London, 1684, p. 68.
4. *Ibid.*, p. 83.
5. Marx, Jennifer, *Pirates and Privateers of the Caribbean*, Malabar, Florida, 1992. Of all the modern books about pirates, this one seems to contain more facts than most.
6. Alleyne, *Supra*.
7. Marx, *Supra*.
8. Labat, *Supra*, (Memoirs), p. 230.
9. Raynal, *Supra*, Vol. VI., p. 52.
10. Oliver, William Vere, *Caribbeana* and Walker, Canon George P. G. *The Story of the Pirates Executed at St Christopher in the Year 1828* (Manuscript), circa 1990. Both give details of this macabre incident. The Walker manuscript mentions the discovery of the bodies near Basseterre in the 1980s, gives more details, and is available locally from The Heritage Society of St Christopher.
11. Walker, Canon George P. G. *The Story of the Pirates Executed at St Christopher in the Year 1828*.

Chapter 10: The Eighteenth Century – the Best of Times and the Worst of Times

1. Pitman, *Supra*, p. 57.
2. *Ibid.*, p. 390, quoting Charles Leslie.
3. *Ibid.*, p. 386.
4. Jeaffreson Letters, Bienecke Collection, Hamilton College. This 'rum clause' in the lease caused bad feelings between General Christopher Jeaffreson and the Earl of Romney, who rented his estate. Jeaffreson complained that the amount sent was constantly in arrears and the quality was inferior. Ultimately, that disagreement was a major factor in Jeaffreson not renewing Romney's lease in 1819 after Romney's family had rented the estate since 1713.
5. Walker, Canon George P. G., *Account of a Duel*, Manuscript, circa 1990.
6. *Ibid.*
7. Beake, Thomas, *Petition to the Royal Navy for Ordnance for St Kitts*, 1731, Bienecke Collection, Hamilton College.
8. Williams, Eric, *Documents of West Indian History*, p. 21.
9. Angier, F. W. and Gordon, S. C., *Sources of West Indian History*, Longman Caribbean, Trinidad, p. 12.
10. Acts of the Assembly of St Christopher, 12 September 1776.
11. *Ibid.*, 1769.
12. Anonymous, *The West India Sketch Book*, London, 1830, p. 39.
13. Calendar of State Papers, 1757.
14. Pitman, *Supra*, p. 350, quoting letter of 20 February 1760.
15. Original Grant to Major John Jeaffreson from the Earl of Carlisle, 9 July 1628, Bienecke Collection, Hamilton College.
16. Letter to the owner from his agent in St Kitts, Bienecke Collection, Hamilton College.

17. Letter from Sir Patrick Blake to General Jeaffreson, Bienecke Collection, Hamilton College.
18. Innis, Sir Probyn, *Historic Basseterre*, 1985, p. 26, quoting a contemporary report. This excellent small book gives the history of Basseterre as a town and I highly recommend it for anyone interested in its history from its establishment to today.
19. Minutes of the St Christopher Assembly, 4 May 1837.
20. Raynal, *Supra*.
21. Schaw, Janet, *Journal of a Lady of Quality (1774–1776)*, ed. E. W. Andrews, New Haven, 1939, p. 92.
22. *Ibid.*, p. 124.
23. *Ibid.*, p. 127.
24. CSP 25 November 1778, Public Record Office, Kew.
25. CSP 25 October 1780, Public Record Office, Kew.
26. Pares, Richard, *A West India Fortune*, 1936.
27. Pitman, *Supra*, p. 99.
28. Tuchman, Barbara W., *The First Salute*, Alfred A. Knopf, New York, 1988.
29. Shyllon, Folarin, *James Ramsay, The Unknown Abolitionist*, Canongate Press, Edinburgh, 1977, p. 50, quoting Rodney's journal.
30. Southey, *Supra*, Vol. II, p. 88.
31. Chartrand René, and Chappell, Paul, *British Forces in the West Indies 1793–1815*, Men-at-Arms Series, Osprey Military Messenger, Northants, UK, 1996.
32. Minutes of the St Christopher Assembly, 22 December 1781.
33. Chauvenet, William Marc, *A Winter Trip to St Kitts*, Cosmopolitan Magazine, March 1897, p. 549.
34. *Ibid.*
35. Governor Herbert's Account, Nevis Archives.
36. Tyson, George F., *Revista Mexicana del Caribe*, 1975–76, Vol. V, No. 4, p. 652.
37. Minutes of the St Christopher Assembly, 22 December 1782.
38. *Ibid.*
39. Innis, *Supra*, p. 27, quoting Rodney's journal.
40. Howarth, David and Stephen, *Lord Nelson*, 1988.
41. *The Economist*, Caribbean Review, April 1990, and subsequent letters to the editor.
42. Kelly, Thomas, *The History and Origins of the Missionary Societies*, London, 1828.
43. Coke, Reverend Thomas, *Extracts of the Journals of Rev. Thomas Coke*, Dublin, 1816, p. 86.
44. *Ibid.*, p. 116.
45. *Ibid.*, p. 198.
46. *Ibid.*
47. Southey, *Supra*.
48. Letter of 22 December 1830, Lord Combermere to Viscount Goderich, Public Record Office, Kew.
49. Morgan, Michael, Men of the Constellation, *A History of the Naval War with France*, Navy Department Library, Washington 1969.

Chapter 11: The Nineteenth Century – the Decline Sets In

1. *A Complete Historical, Chronological and Geographical Atlas*, Cay & Lea, London, 1822.
2. Young, Sir Thomas, *The West India Commission Book*, London, 1807.
3. Coleridge, Bishop Henry Nelson, *Six Months in the West Indies*, London, 1825.

4. Anonymous, *The West India Sketch Book*, Vol. II, p. 69.
5. *Ibid.*, p. 88.
6. Minutes of the St Christopher Assembly, 1832, St Kitts Archives.
7. *Ibid.*
8. Shyllon, *Supra*, p. 4.
9. Merrill, *Supra*, p. 70.
10. St Christopher Legislative Council Minutes, 1862.
11. Candler, John, *Visit of John Candler to St Kitts*, 1845, Heritage Society, St Kitts.
12. Davy, John, *The West Indies Before and After Emancipation*, p. 85.
13. St Christopher Legislative Council Minutes, May 1853.
14. Hall Douglas, *Five of the Leewards 1834–1870*, Caribbean University Press, 1971, pp. 169–170. For the years mentioned this excellent book is probably the most complete, factual and readable one about the Leewards.
15. *Ibid.*
16. Burns, *Supra*, p. 80.
17. St Christopher Legislative Council Minutes, 1863.
18. Ober, Frederick, A., *Our West Indian Neighbors*, New York, 1916.
19. García Muniz, Humberto and Borges, José Lee, *United States Consular Activism in the Caribbean*, Revista Mexicana del Caribe, Vol. 5, 1998.
20. *Ibid.*
21. *Ibid.*
22. *Ibid.*
23. Chauvenet, *Supra*, p. 547.
24. Garretson, F. A., *A Snap-Shot of the West Indies*, Newport, RI, 1902, p. 186.
25. St Christopher Legislative Council Minutes, 19 January 1897.
25. Muniz, *Supra*.

Chapter 12: The Twentieth Century

1. García and Borges; *Supra*.
2. Hall, *Supra*, p. 146.
3. St Christopher Legislative Council Minutes, June 1904.
4. *Ibid.*
5. *Ibid.*, 14 February 1905.
6. *Ibid.*, June 1912.
7. *Ibid.*, April 1916.
8. St Christopher Legislative Council Minutes, October 1922.
9. Davis, Robert H., *The Caribbean Islands*, New York, 1926, pp 181–185.
10. Letter from Terence Macnaughten, 12 October 1929, Heritage Society Archives, St Kitts.
11. Day, Susan, *Cruise of the Sythian*, p. 88.
12. St Johnston, Sir Reginald, *A Colonial Governor's Note Book*, London, 1936.
13. *Union Messenger*, 9 August 1939.
14. Waugh, Alex, *The Sugar Islands*, Farrar, Strauss & Co., New York, 1949, p. 52, quoting Harold Stannard in the London *Times*, 1938.
15. *Union Messenger*, 6 September 1939.
16. *Ibid.*, 22 January 1942.
17. Letters in Government Archives, St Kitts. The crash was being investigated by private persons in the United States who inquired whether there was any mention of it in the local press, and when told no, sent the information they had found elsewhere.

18. Murrain, Dennison T., *Let's Look Back, Nevis*, 1992, quoting correspondence between Premier Simeon Daniel of Nevis and Robert Bradshaw concerning appointments of officials in Nevis and armed guards on the ferry. Daniel termed Bradshaw's government 'Communistic', and Bradshaw accused Daniel's NRP Party of planning to steal the ferry.
19. Knight, Franklin, W., *The Caribbean*, Oxford Press, New York, 1990, p. 307, quoting Labat.
20. *Ibid.*, p. 324.
21. Browne, Whitman T., *From Commoner to King, Robert L. Bradshaw – Crusader for Dignity and Justice in the Caribbean*, University Press of America, Inc., Lanham, MD, p. 209.
22. My apologies to Sir Fred Phillips for using the same metaphor for the Anguilla disturbance that he did in his most interesting book *Caribbean Life and Culture*, in 1991. I had thought of it as most appropriate before reading his informative work, so I plead innocent to plagiarism. Perhaps he is as fond of the late Peter Sellers's comedies as I am.
23. Petty, Colville L. and Hodge, N., *Anguilla's Battle for Freedom, 1967*, Petnat Publishing Company Ltd, 1987, p. 63.
24. Webster, Ronald, *Scrap Book of Anguilla's Revolution*, Seabreakers (Anguilla), 1987, p. 21.
25. Phillips, Sir Fred, *Caribbean Life and Culture*, Heinemann Publishers (Caribbean) Limited, Kingston, Jamaica, 1991, p. 85.
26. Webster, *Supra*, p. 126, quoting Art Buchwald in the *New York Times*.
27. *Ibid.*
28. Rodman, Selden, *The Caribbean, New York*, 1968, pp. 44–46.
29. *The Labour Spokesman*, 12 August 1982.
30. In this regard, note the conclusions of Glen Richards of the University of the West Indies in his several works listed in the Bibliography and others in the St Kitts Archives. For a thorough analysis of the good and bad effects of nationalization locally, there are no better references available.

Bibliography

Acts of Assembly Passed in the Island of St Kitts 1711–1769.

Alleyene, W. *Caribbean Pirates.* Macmillan, London (1967).

Anonymous. *A General Survey of that Part of the Island of St Christophers, Which Formerly Belonged to France, etc.* London (1722).

Anonymous. *An Account of the late Dreadful Earthquake in the Islands of Nevis and St Christopher.* London (1690).

Anonymous. *A Brief and Perfect Journal of the late Proceedings and Successes of the English Army in the West Indies.* London (1665).

Anonymous. *The West India Sketch Book*, Vol. 11, London (1830).

Archibald, W. *Reflections on an Epic Journey.* St Kitts (1993).

Aspinall, A. *The Pocket Guide to the West Indies.* New York (1927).

Auguier, F. R. and Gordon, S. C. *Sources of West Indian History.* Trinidad (1962).

Baker, P. *From Contact to Creole and Beyond.* London (1995).

Beake, T. 'Petition of Thomas Beake to Royal Navy Ordnance (to replace military ordnance in St Kitts following the explosion of Brimstone Hill Magazine)', 1731, Bienecke Collection, Hamilton College, Clinton, NY.

Bellin, Map of St Christopher, 1758.

Benford, T. *The Eighteenth-Century Countermarked Coins of St Kitts and Nevis,* (manuscript) (1991).

Blome, R. *The Present State of His Majesty's Isles and Territories in America.* London (1687).

Bridenbaugh, C. and R. *No Peace Beyond the Line, The English in the Caribbean 1624–1690.* New York (1972).

Brown, J. 'Leewards', *The Advocate Ltd.* Barbados (1961).

Browne, W. T. *From Commoner to King, Robert L. Bradshaw – Crusader for Dignity and Justice in the Caribbean.* Lanham, MD (1992).

Browne, W. T. *The* Christena *Disaster in Retrospect,* St Thomas (1985).

Burdon, K. J. *A Handbook of St Kitts-Nevis,* London (1920).

Buckley, R. N. *The British Army in the West Indies.* Gainesville, FL (1998).

Burns, A. *History of the West Indies.* London (1965).

Calendar of State Papers (British Colonial Office Public Records).

Candler, J. *Visit of John Candler to St Kitts, 1845.* St Kitts.

Chartrand, R. and Chappell, P. 'British Forces in the West Indies 1793–1815', Men-at-Arms Series, *Osprey Military Messenger.* Northants (1996).

Chauvenet, W. M. 'A Winter Trip to St Kitts', *Cosmopolitan Magazine,* March 1897, Bienecke Collection, Hamilton College, Clinton, NY.

Coke, Bishop T. *A History of the West Indies, containing the Natural and Ecclesiastical History of each Island.* London (1811).
Coke, Bishop T. *Extracts From The Journals of Thomas Coke.* Dublin (1816).
Coleridge, H. N. *Six Months in the West Indies in 1825.* London (1825).
Colliber, S. *History of Naval Battles in the Anglo-Dutch Wars.* London (1727).
Colt, H. 'The Voyage of Sr Henry Colt to ye Illands of ye Antilles', MS Cambridge University Library, 1631 (reprint) *The Hakluyt Society.* London (1925).
Crouch, N. *The English Empire in America.* London (1685).
Crouse, N. M. *French Pioneers in the West Indies 1624–1664.* New York (1940).
Crouse, N. M. *The French Struggle for the West Indies 1625–1715.* New York (1940).
Davis, Robert H. *The Caribbean Islands,* New York (1926).
Davy, J. *The West Indies Before and After Emancipation.* London (1854).
Day, S. De F. *The Cruise of the Sythian.* New York (1899).
De Baecque, J. and C. 'St Kitts The Mother Colony', *IMAGES* 4, Neuilly S/Seine, France (c. 1996).
Dyde, B. *St Kitts, Cradle of the Caribbean.* London (1993).
Edwards, B. *The History, Civil and Commercial of the British Colonies in North America.* London (1817) (reprint Philadelphia 1905).
Esquemeling, J. *Bucaniers of America.* London (1684).
French, G. *The History of Colonel Parke's Administration.* London (1717).
García, M. and Borges, H. 'United States Consular Activism in the Caribbean', *Revista Mexicana del Caribe,* Vol. 5, 1988.
Garretson, S. P. *A Snap-Shot of the West Indies.* Newport, RI (1902).
Gooding, S. J. *Introduction to British Artillery in North America.* New York (1972).
Goss, P. *The History of Piracy.* London (1932).
Green, W. A. *British Slave Emancipation.* Oxford (1976).
Hall, D. *Five of the Leewards 1834–1870.* Caribbean University Press (1971).
Harlow, V. T. (ed.). *Colonising Expeditions to the West Indies and Guiana 1632–1667.* London (1925).
Hart, R. *From Occupation to Independence.* London (1998).
Higham, C. S. S. *The Development of the Leeward Islands Under the Restoration, 1660–1688.* Cambridge (1921).
Hilton, J. 'Revelation of the First Settlement of St Christopher and Nevis by John Hilton, Storekeeper and First Gunner of Nevis', Egerton MSS, British Library, London, 1675 (reprint by The Hakluyt Society, London, 1925).
Inniss, P. *Historic Basseterre.* Antigua (1985).
Inniss, P. *Whither Bound St Kitts-Nevis.* Antigua (1983).
Jeaffreson, J. C. *A Young Squire of the 17th Century.* London (1878).
Jeaffreson Papers, Bienecke Collection, Hamilton College, Clinton, NY.
Jeffreys, T. *A General Description of the West Indies, etc.* London (1780).
Johnson, C. *A General History of the Pyrates.* London (1726).
Jones, S. B. *Annals of Anguilla.* Belfast (1976).

Kelly, T. *The History and Origins of the Missionary Societies.* London (1828).
Knight, F. W. *The Caribbean.* New York (1990).
Labat, J.-B. *Memoirs 1693–1705* (translation). London (1970).
Labat, J.-B. *New Journey to the Isles of America, 1742.* Martinique (1972).
Lamb, J. B. *Comte de Grasse's Sea Chest.* London (c. 1980).
'Lease of a plantation in St Peter's parish, Basseterre' (John Hart Cotton's estate), 1810, Bienecke Collection, Hamilton College, Clinton, NY.
Lewis, G. K. *The Growth of the Modern West Indies.* London (1968).
Long, G., Porter, G. and Tucker, G. *America and the West Indies.* London (1845).
Low, C. R. *The Great Battles of the British Navy.* London (1872).
Mars, P. *Ideology and Change, The Transformation of the Caribbean Left.* Detroit (1998).
Marx, J. *Pirates and Privateers of the Caribbean.* Malabar, FL (1992).
Marx, R. F. *Shipwrecks in the Americas.* New York (1987).
McConnell, D. *British Smooth-Bore Artillery; A Technological Study.* Canadian National Park Service.
Merrill, G. C. *The Historical Geography of St Kitts and Nevis The West Indies.* Mexico City (1958).
Millas, J. C. *Hurricanes of the Caribbean and Adjacent Regions, 1492–1800.* Miami (1968).
Miller, H. H. *Colonel Parke of Virginia.* Chapel Hill, NC (1989).
Mordecai, J. *The West Indies, the Federal Negotiations.* Northwestern University Press (1968).
Morgan, M. *Men of the Constellation. A History of the Naval War with France.* Washington DC (1969).
Murrain, D. T. *Let's Look Back.* Nevis (1992).
Newton, A. P. *The European Nations in the West Indies 1493–1688.* London (1933).
Oakley, A. *Behold the West Indies.* New York (1957).
Ober, F. *Our West Indian Neighbors.* New York (1916).
Oldmixon, J. *History of the British Empire.* London (1708).
Oliver, W. V. *Caribbeana,* 6 vols. London (1908–1919).
Pares, R. *A West Indian Fortune.* London (1940).
Pares, R. *War and Trade in the West Indies 1739–1763.* London (1936).
Petty, C. L. and Hodge, N. *Anguilla's Battle for Freedom, 1967.* Petnat Publishing Company Ltd. (1987).
Phillips, F. *Caribbean Life and Culture.* Kingston, Jamaica (1991).
Pitman, F. W. *The Development of the British West Indies 1700–1763.* New Haven, CT (1967 (reprint)).
Lewis, G. K. *The Growth of the Modern West Indies.* London (1968).
Raynal, Abbé. *History of the Settlements and Trade of the Europeans in the East and West Indies* (translated by J. O. Justamond) London (1783).
Renwick, J. D. B. 'Report on the sinking of the *M. V. Christena*', 1 October 1970.
Richards, G. 'Friendly societies and labour organization in the Leeward Islands' (In Turner, M. *From Chattel Slaves to Wage Slaves.* London (1995)).

Bibliography

Richards, G. 'Masters and servants: the growth of the labour movement in St Kitts-Nevis 1896–1956', unpublished Cambridge University PhD thesis, May 1989.

Richards, G. 'The pursuit of higher wages and perfect personal freedom – St Kitts-Nevis 1836–1956' (*In Before and After 1865*, Moore *et al.* (eds) Kingston, Jamaica (1998).

Robertson, Revd R. *A Short Account of the Hurricane, that pass'd thro' the English Leeward Islands the 30th of June 1733*, London, 1733. (Nevis Archives).

Robertson, Revd R. *Letter to the Lord Bishop of London*, London. (1732 (Nevis Archives)).

Rochefort, C. *The History of the Caribbee Islands* (translation) London (1666).

Rodman, S. *The Caribbean.* New York (1968).

St Christopher Legislative Council Minutes, St Kitts Archives.

St Johnston, R. *The French Invasions of St Kitts-Nevis.* St Kitts (1933).

St Johnston, R. *A Governor's Handbook.* London (1940).

Schaw, J. *Journal of a Lady of Quality 1774–1776*, ed. E. W. Andrews, New Haven, CT (1939).

Sebastian, C. M. *The Life and Work of the late Hon. Robert L. Bradshaw.* St Kitts (1995).

Shyllon, F. *James Ramsay, The Unknown Abolitionist.* Edinburgh (1977).

Sloane, H. *A Voyage to the Islands of Madeira, Barbados, Nieves, St Christopher and Jamaica.* London (1707).

Smith, Revd T. *The History and Origin of the Missionary Societies.* London (1828).

Smith, Revd T. *The History and Origin of the Missionary Societies*, London (1828).

Southey, Captain T. *A Chronological History of the West Indies*, London (1827).

Southey, T. *A Chronological History of the West Indies.* London (1827).

Sutton, J. W. *Our Love Prevailed.* Scarborough, Ontario (1990).

Sutton, James W. *Our Love Prevailed*, Sutton Publishing, Scarborough, Ontario (1990).

The *Daily Bulletin*, (newspaper) St Kitts Archives.

The Democrat, (newspaper) St Kitts Archives.

The Economist, Caribbean Review, and subsequent letters to the editor, April 1990.

The Labour Spokesman (newspaper) St Kitts Archives.

The Union Messenger (newspaper) St Kitts Archives.

Thomas, D. *An Historical Account of the West India Colonies.* London (1690).

Walker, Canon G. P. G. 'Account of a duel in St Kitts in 1752' (manuscript). St Kitts (*c.* 1990).

Walker, Canon G. P. G. *The Story of the Pirates Executed at St. Christopher in the Year 1828*, (manuscript), St. Kitts, *c.* 1990.

Watkins, F. H. Handbook of the Leeward Islands, London (1924).

Watts, D. *The West Indies: Patterns of Development, Culture and Environmental Change Since 1492.* Cambridge (1987).

Waugh, A. *The Sugar Islands.* New York (1949).

Webster, R. *Scrap Book of Anguilla's Revolution.* Anguilla (1987).

Williams, A. M. *Under the Trade Winds.* New York (1896).

Williams, W. E. *Documents of West Indian History*. Trinidad (1961).
Williams, W. E. *The Caribbean from Columbus to Castro*. New York (1971).
Williamson, J. A. *The Caribee Islands under the Proprietary Patents*. London (1926).
Willoughby, H. 'Letter to the Right Honourable Edward, Earl of Clarendon, Lord High Chancellor of England, regarding the Battle of Nevis and the capture of Suriname', Bodleian Library, Oxford University, May 1667.
Wynne, J. H. *A General History of the British Empire in America*. London (1770).
Young, W. *The West India Committee Hand Book*. London (1807).

Index

Figures in bold type indicate illustrations.

22 London Police 148
Abbott, Colonel Thomas 58
Act for Better Government of Negroes (1722) 60–61
'An Act to provide for the Compulsory Manumission of Slaves' 113
Adams, John 82
Admirality (British) 92, 93
Alexander, Captain 8
Amelioration Act (1792) 106
America
    British naval embargo 91
    independence movement 40
    see also United States
American Civil War 121
American Revolution 28, 63, 80, 82, 88–92
Amethyste (a ship) 85
Amory, Premier 155, 159
Anglican Church 112
    see also Church of England
Anguilla 53, 128, 129
    cotton production 133
    declares itself a republic 147–8
    described 143
    elections 147
    funding not distributed 143
    independence issue 141, 147, 153
    and the Labour Party 142
    and piracy 143
    Presidency (1883) 123
    Revolution 143–9, 160
    Seven Point Declaration 148
animal life 2–3
animal mills 25, 118
Anne, Queen 57, 61, 62, 80
Antigua 9, 18, 20, 21, 53, 88, 96
    and the Anglican Church 112
    apprenticeship period waived 116
    cathedral 62
    Council 17
    duelling 77
    English retake 49
    fortifications 94
    France takes (1666) 44
    Government House pillaged 62
    Irish disarmed 52
    labour disorders (1858) 120
    naval base 100
    Parke in 61
    and the Portuguese Riots 124, 125
    Rodney commands the British fleet 101
    Royal Governor of the Leeward Islands 123
    settled (1632) 32, 38
    sugar yield 110
Antigua (ship) 66
Aplon, Sergeant 15
Arawak Indians 10, 12
Armes d'Angleterre (warship) 45, 46–47
Arundel (a slaver) 114, 115
Assembly Act (1711) 60
Assistance, HMS 54
Atlantic Ocean 7, 24, 136
Auld sisters 131, 132

Bachelor, Marmaduke 61
'Barbador' 14, 15
Barbados 5, 6, 15, 24, 43, 67, 126
    and Federation of the West Indies 142
    fortifications 94
    French plan to attack 95, 96
    Leeward Islands separated from 51
    loss of Willoughby and militiamen 44
    settled 32
    Sharpe and 67
    sugar production 26, 28, 80, 117
Barbe (an Indian woman) 17
Barbot, John 76, 77
Barbuda 15, 52
Barclay's Bank 113
Barfleur (ship) 101
barter system 86–87
Basseterre **8**, 35, 37, 45, 49, 99, 112, 156
    begging 136, 140
    College Street 7, 8, 35, 53
    courthouse 112–13, 122
    De Gennes' men 57
    duelling trial 77
    English take (1690) 53–54
    fires 41, 122
    floods 7–8
    health problems 134
    housing 126
    hurricanes 4–5, 6
    Irish Town 103, 122
    Jesuit College 35, 53
    Moravian church 5
    New Town 122
    and the Portuguese Riots 125
    in the Seven Years' War 84
    Spanish take the fort 20
Basseterre Harbour **9**, 20, 21, 48, 51, 54, 66, 68, 85, 108, 111, 116, 121, 126, 131
Basseterre Volunteers 120
Beake, Thomas 77

begging 133, 136, 140
Bel-tache 6
Benefield, Mr 15
Berkeley, Hon. Thomas Berkeley Hardtman 122
Berkly (a frigate) 85
Berry, Captain (later Admiral Sir John) 48–49
Bills of Attainder 60
Binns, Robert 15
Bird, Vere 142
'black dogs' 87
Black, W. 105
Blake, D. 137
Blanchard, C. 137
Blenac, Count de 51
Blessed William (a privateer) 52, 66
Bloody Point 18
Bloody River 18
boll weevil (boll worm) 133
Bonaparte, Jerome 109
Bond, Mr 15
Booby Island 123
Boreas (a frigate) 102
Boston, Massachusetts 82
Bouille, Marquis de 90, 95–9
Boulogne, Father 42
Bourdet, Captain 45, 46
Bradshaw, Robert Llewellyn **11**, 136, 157
  background 139
  contradictions 149
  and Federation of the West Indies 141, 142
  first elected Premier of St Kitts 132, 142
  founds the Workers League 141
  government control over sugar estates 151
  leadership skills 140
  pushes for independence from Britain 141
  response to the Anguilla Revolution 145–8
  self-educated 139, 149
  and the social system 151, 153
  and Webster 144, 146
  works hard for independence 154
  death in 1978 151, 153
Brazil 13, 25, 117
Breda, Treaty of 50
'Brethren of the Coast' 65
Brigs, Mr 11
Brimstone Hill **7**, 11, 31, 32, 51, 54, 78, 80, 86, 93–7, 102, 109
  British garrison withdrawn 120
  fall of 99, 100, 102
  siege of (1782) 98–100, 132
Bristol Cathedral 43
Britain
  depression (1848) 119
  French quarter given up to the British 32
  world's leading military and economic power 119
  see also England
British Army 91, 93–4, 110
British Caribbean Empire 33
  birth of 38–40
British Empire 15, 28, 40, 85, 110, 111, 127, 131, 135
British fleet
  the battle of Frigate Bay 96–7
  engaged in North America 95, 96
  escapes from de Grasse 100
  Great Hurricane (1780) 6
British Intelligence 96
British parliament 59, 62, 90, 110, 115, 119, 128
Bromley, Sir Robert 129, 130
buccaneers 14, 36, 42, 43, 54, 65, 67
Buchan, tenth earl of 89
Buenos Aires 71
Buisson 35
Bull, Dr Zachariah 105
Burgoyne, General John 91
Burke, Jordan 106
Burke, William 80
Burnham, Forbes 149
Burt, Governor 89–90
Butler, Gregory 30
Buysan, Captain José Lazaro 71, 72, 73
Byron, Cecil 150
Byron, Vincent 145

Cabasson, Father 37
Caesar, Julius 58
Canada 49, 85, 88, 101, 102, 111, 122, 137
Canadian National Steamship Line 137
Cape Horn 67
Capisterre 20
Captain Wright (ship) 6
Capuchin monks 34–35
Caradon, Lord 148
Cardin, James Derrick 131, 132
Carib Indians 13, 16
  and Arawaks 10, 12
  and cannibalism 11–12
  in Dominica 18
  fierce fighters 12
  and the French 41, 44, 47
  plan to kill Europeans foiled 17–18
  raids by 14
  removed from St Kitts, Nevis and Antigua 18
Caribbean
  effect of emancipation on sugar production 117
  English in full naval command of 49
  fragmented in terms of nationality and language 160
  Spanish claims 13, 19
  success of Methodism 104
  in World War II 136, 137, 138
Cariola, Province of *see* Leeward Islands
Carlisle, Earl of 14, 15, 38
Carlisle (ship) 19, 20
Carraboo (a brigantine) 71, 72
Cartagena (Colombia) 14, 54
cassava (manioc) 1–2, 5, 16, 137
Casse, Jean de 66
Castelo, Felix **1**
Castries harbour, St Lucia 137
Castro, Fidel 149
Cayenne (French Guiana) 33, 57, 87
Cayman Islands 16
Cayon, St Mary's parish 104, 105, 112
Central America 53, 119
Challenger, Edgar 139, 140, 141
Charles I, King 26–27, 29

Charlestown 59, 102, 105, 106, 112, 125, 126
Chateau La Fontaine 2, 3–4, 35
Chavagnac, Admiral Count Louis-Henri de 58, 59
Child's Play, HMS 6
Chile 67
Christena ferry disaster (1970) 149–50
Christmas Guard 79, 80
Christopher, St 13
Church of England 103
   see also Anglican Church
Cleverley Point Fort *see* Fort Charles
Codrington, Governor Sir Christopher 27–28, 52–56, 86
Codrington, Sir Christopher, the younger 56, 57, 61–62, 66, 68
coinage 31, 86–88, 113
Coke, Bishop Thomas 104, 105
Colbert, Jean-Baptiste 5, 35–36, 37
Coleridge, Bishop Henry Nelson 112
Coleridge, Samuel Taylor 112
Collingwood, Captain 85
Colombia 54
Colonial Bank 87, 113
Colonial Office 100, 121
   West India Committee 129
Colt, Sir Henry 2
Columbus, Christopher 4, 10, 11, 13, 66, 88
Columbus, Don Diego 79
Combermere, Lord 106, 107, 122
Compagnie de Saint-Christophe 21, 22, 35
Company of Adventurers 38
Company of Merchants Trading with Africa 15
Company of the Isles of America 35
Concerned Citizens Movement (CCM) 155, 159
Congo, Johnny 61
Constellation (a frigate) 108
Continental Army 91
convicts 64
Cooper, Alfred 73
Cooper family 132
Cordelia, HMS 124, 125
Cordell, Second Lieutenant Howell 138
Cornwallis, General Lord 95
Coronation (ship) 48
Corromante slaves 27–28
cotton 133
Court of Appeals 151
Coventry, HMS 5, 45
Crescent (a frigate) 85
Cromwell, Oliver 24, 29, 30, 53
Crynsens, Admiral Abraham de 47, 48, 49
Cuba 1, 19, 117, 119, 128
Curaçao 36

D'Albert de Rions (of the *Pluton*) 97
Las Damas Argentinas (pirate schooner) 71, 72
Daniel, Captain 70
Daniel, Dr Simeon 153, 158
Dasent, Mrs 76
Dasent's estate, Nevis 76
Davasian (a freighter) 136
Davis, Reverend Daniel Gateward 72
de la Barré, Antoine Le Febvre 36, 44–9
de las Casas, Bartolomé 10–11, 12

death rate 135
The Democrat newspaper 155
Democrats 141
Denmark 126, 127
Dennistoun of Glasgow 84
Department of Public Works 122
La Desirade 33
d'Esnambuc, Pierre Belain, Sieur 16, 17, 32, 33, 34
d'Estaing, Admiral Count 94
Devil's Island 33
Diamond Jubilee celebration 126
d'Iberville, Pierre LeMoyne 58, 59
Dieppe Bay 15
Dillon, Count 100
Discovery, HMS 30
d'Olive, Lienard 32, 33, 89
Dominica 12, 13, 17, 18
Dominican Republic 10, 109, 128
Douglas, Dr Denzil **15**, 155
Drake, Sir Francis 13
Drew, Thomas 113
drug trade 65, 156–57, 160
du Casse, Jean 51, 52, 53, 54
Duckworth, Admiral Sir John 109
Dutch
   freebooters 14, 65
   French defeat (1678) 37
   and the Indians 11
   and merchant shipping 36
   and plantation colonies 36
   and St Eustatius 51, 91
   slave trade 39
   and trade 21, 26, 29, 35, 36, 37, 38, 39–40, 91
   see also Holland
Dutch navy 36, 41, 49
duties 37, 39, 40

earthquakes ix, **2**, 3–4, 117
The Economist 103
education 135, 153, 154
elections 114, 143, 147, 151, 153, 155, 157
Emancipation Act 115–16
Emulous (a packet) 72
Enabling Act (1795) 80
England
   Anglo-French treaty (1627) 16, 31, 32, 41
   Anglo-French treaty (1686) 51
   calendar 58
   defeated by the Spanish at St Kitts (1629) 20
   duties on goods 37
   English settlers' arrival in 1623 4, 11
   incursions into the Caribbean 13
   joint British-Portuguese invasion of Cayenne (1809) 87
   joint venture companies 15
   merchant fleet 38, 39
   Nine Years' War 51–54
   settlers sent to Nevis (1689) 52
   in the Seven Years' War 84, 91
   slave trade 39
   Spanish Armadas fail (1588–1604) 14
   see also Britain
English West India Company 38

epidemics ix, 75, 76, 120
Esmit, Governor 65
European settlers
    arrival in 1623 ix, 4, 11
    Indian attacks 12
    in the Leewards 10
Evertson, Admiral Cornelius 51

Far East 111
FBI (Federal Bureau of Investigation) 156
Federated Leeward Islands Colony 128, 153
Federation of the Leeward Islands 121
Federation of the West Indies 141–42
Fig Tree, Battle of (1635) 34
First Anglo-Dutch War (1650) ('Herring War') 38, 41
floods 7–8, 35
Florida 1, 11, 91, 102
Flota Nueva España 14
flowers 2
flutes 45
Foreign Office 147
Fort Charles 51, 54, 59, 78, 93, 98
Fort Thomas 20, 54, 121–22
Fort Thomas Hotel 1
Fountain Estate 4
Four Seasons Resort, Nevis 158
France
    allied with the Carib Indians 41
    Anglo-French treaty (1627) 16, 31, 32, 41
    Anglo-French treaty (1686) 51
    Antigua occupied 44
    arrival of French settlers in St Kitts (1625) 11
    buccaneers 14, 65
    calendar 58
    captures St Kitts 5
    coastguards 155
    decision to give up Canada 85
    defeated by the Spanish at St Kitts (1629) 20
    defeats Dutch (1678) 37
    duties on goods 36
    French quarter given up to the British 32
    German conquest of 136
    incursions into the Caribbean 13
    merchant fleet 38, 39
    Montserrat captured 44–45
    Nine Years' War 51–54
    no longer a military rival in the Caribbean 119–20
    peace treaty with Indians after firing cannon 33
    in the Seven Years' War 84, 91
    slave trade 21–22
    takes St Eustatius 51
    trading companies 21, 22–23, 29, 35, 36, 37
    as a world power 119
Francis (frigate) 64–65
Fraser, General 98
Free French Government 139
free trade 119
freebooters 14, 65
French and Indian War 85
French Antilles 90
French army 59, 85, 94, 98
French Caribbean Empire 4, 33, 36, 37, 39, 81, 82, 119

French fleet
    and the American Revolution 95
    battle of Frigate Bay 96–97, 98
    battle of Nevis 48–49
    de Crynsens withdraws his ships 49
    defeated at Martinique (1667) 49
    first major appearance in the West Indies 94–95
    Great Hurricane (1780) 6
French Guiana (Cayenne) 33, 57, 87
French navy 41
French Revolution 81, 107, 108
French West Indies Company 22–23, 29, 35, 36
Fresnouvelle 18
Frigate Bay 53, 59
    battle of (1782) 4, 96–98, 101, 103
    duelling at 76–77

Garvey, Marcus 139
Gates, General Horatio 91
Gennes, Count Jean-Baptiste de 56–58
geology 1
George I, King 62
Germany, Nazi 135
ghauts (ravines) 7, 49
Gillard, George 115
ginger 8, 24, 29, 36
Glanville, John 92–93
Le Glorieux (ship) 98
Goderich, Viscount 107
Grasscocke, Rowland 15, 16
Grasse, Admiral Count de 95–102
Graves, Admiral Thomas 95
Great Hurricane (1780) 6–7
Great War *see* World War I (1914–18)
Greenwood (a steamer) 125
Gregorian calendar 58
Gregory XIII, Pope 58
Grenada 33, 36, 94–95, 112
Guadeloupe, Windward Islands 5, 14, 19, 32–33, 34, 36, 44, 45, 47, 54, 70, 85, 89, 101, 107, 136–37
Guinea 69
Gulf Stream 88
Guyana 152

Haiti 36, 66, 103, 107, 109
Half Way Tree 146
'Half-Arse' 70
Halifax, Nova Scotia 137
Hamilton, Governor 119, 121
Hamilton, Lady Isabelle 89, 90
Hamilton, Colonel Walter 57, 58
Hamilton, William Leslie 89, 90
Hamilton River 42
Hamlin, Captain Jean 65
Hammett, Mr (missionary) 104
Harman, Admiral Sir John 49
Harper, John 105
Harper, Lieutenant Colonel Thomas 72
Hart, Governor John 69, 75
Hawley, Captain Henry 15, 19–20
health 133–34, 135, 154
Herbert, John 100, 103
Herbert, William 106
Herbert, Dr William V. 145–46, 147, 155, 156

Index

'Herring War' (1650) 38
Hewetson, Captain Thomas 52–53, 66, 67
Heyn, Piet 19
Higginson, Admiral 126
Hill, Governor Thomas 51–52
Hispaniola 21, 30, 79
Holland
    becomes a world power 19
    calendar 58
    falls to Germany 136
    imports 39
    incursions into the Caribbean 13
    Nine Years' War 51
    too small to be a significant power 119
    war with England (1781) 91, 92
    see also Dutch
Hood, Rear Admiral Sir Samuel 96–7, 99, 100, 101, 103
Hopewell (ship) 15, 82
House of Commons 91
Huggins, Edward 94, 106
Huguenots 15, 56
Hunrakan (Carib Indian God) 4
hurricanes ix, 4–7, 15, 44, 45, 95, 111

iguanas 2–3, 16
immigration 75, 78, 118
Imperial Trade Preferences 133
indentured servants 20, 24, 27, 64, 74, 118
India 85, 111
Indian Castle, Nevis 108
Indians 10–12, 13, 16, 70, 140
    British and French fight together 32
    and cassava 1
    killing of iguanas 2–3
    in North America 85
    peace treaty after French cannon fire 32–33
    population of the Caribbean 10–11
    removed from St Kitts, Nevis and Antigua 18
    Spanish treatment of 11, 14
    and sugar 1, 26
indigo 24, 67, 82
Industrial Revolution 119
infant mortality rate 134, 135
Inquisition 25
L'Insurgent (ship) 108
Irish
    community in Irish Town, Basseterre 103
    disarmed 52
    indentured servants 20
    pro-American sentiments 102
    sold into slavery in the West Indies 24
    turncoats 44, 45, 51, 52, 53, 56
Irish Republican Army (IRA) 156
Islands of the Saintes 5, 45, 101
isthmus of Panama 67

Jackson, Captain 38
Jamaica
    becomes England's richest sugar colony 30
    ex-slaves begin farming 117
    and Federation of the West Indies 142
    French prepare to attack 101
    Maroons 30
    Morant Bay rebellion (1865) 121
    pasture land 91
    Spanish surrender 30
    sugar production 28
James, E. 137
James I, King 25
    Royal Patent 14, 38
Jamestown: earthquake of 1690 3
Jeaffreson, Christopher 5–6, 15–16, 24–25, 27, 29, 76, 82–83
Jeaffreson, Lieutenant General Christopher 83–84
Jeaffreson, Frances (née Russell) 27
Jeaffreson, Major John 82
Jeaffreson family 15–16, 82, 83
Jefferson, Thomas 16
Jenkins, Captain 78
Jesuits 35
Jews 25, 92
John Hart Cotton Plantation, St Peter's Parish 110
joint venture companies 15
Jones, Sergeant 15
Josephine, Empress of France 107
Julian calendar 58

Kidd, Captain William 52, 66–67
King, Michael 150
King John (a freighter) 136
Knights of Malta 34, 35

Labat, Père 56, 141
labour movement 132–41
Labour Party/government 14, 15, 141, 142, 144, 147, 149–58
The Labour Spokesman newspaper 155
Lady Hawkins (passenger liner) 137
Langley, Mr 15
Lawrence, David 156
lead poisoning 76
Lebanese 119
Lee, Tony 147, 148
Leeward Islands ix, 3, 45, 55
    crown colony status (1871) 121, 123
    Crown takes over administration (1664) 15
    European settlement 10
    formed into a new colony (1671) 51
    French capture all the Leewards except Nevis 5
    French conquest stopped in its tracks 48
    government 90–91
    inefficient governments 120–21
    Nelson in 102–3
    prosperity 74
    Royal Governor of the Leeward Islands 123
    Royal Patent to begin a colony (1620) 14, 15, 38
    sugar production 9, 28, 111, 128
    under Warner's control 38
Lesser Antilles 28
Liamuiga 13
Liburd, Thomas 129
life expectancy 134, 154
Lion, HMS 52, 66
London Electric Theatre 133
London *Times* 136
Londonderry Fort 78, 122
Lowe, Edward 69–70
Lys Couronne (flagship) 48

McDowall, William 61
Machault de Bellemont, Governor General de 57
Madeira 119
Madingo Tom 110
Madrid, Treaty of (1670) 51
Majorca 71
Majors Bay 55
map, French *c.* 1650 **3**
Maracaibo, Venezuela 38
Marcus ('King of the Woods') 116–17
Margaret, HRH The Princess 154
Mariegalante 33, 36, 52, 66, 70
Marines (British) 116, 124
Maroon Bay 55
Maroon Hill, near Zetland, Nevis 60
Maroon Quarter 55
Martinique 36, 54, 85, 90, 96, 97
    British administration of 107
    and de la Barré 46, 47
    De Thoisy captured 34
    Evertson attacks 51
    French prepare to attack Jamaica 101
    German conquest of 136–7
    Harman attacks the French fleet 49
    hurricanes 6–7
    Lowe tried and hanged 70
    molasses 82
    seat of the French Caribbean Empire 4, 50
    settled (1635) 33
    women and children ordered to 56
    in World War II 138, 139
Massacre, Dominica 17
Mathew, Hon. Lieutenant General 61, 75
Matthew, Superintendent Jude 156
mauby 16
Maxwell, William Charles 107
mercantilism 119
Merifield, Ralph 14, 21
Merry Christmas (pirate ship) 69
Merwars Hope 14–15
Methodists 104–105
Mexico: silver mines 59
Middle Passage 75
migration 117
Mills, Matthew 76, 77
Missiessy, Admiral Edouard 109
missionaries 79, 103–104, 105
molasses 26, 40, 80, 81, 82, 85, 98, 122
Molasses Acts (1730 and 1733) 82, 86
Montcalm, General 85
Montpelier Plantation 103
Montserrat 1, 14, 29
    and the battle of Frigate Bay 97–98
    coinage 87
    English retake 49
    French capture 44–45
    Irish settlers 53
    returned to Britain by the French 102
    settled (1632) 32, 38
Moore, Hon. Lee, QC **14**, 153, 154
Moore, Sir John 80
Moore, Leopold 123–25
Moravian Church 103–24, 105
Moravian church, Basseterre 5, 8, 104

Morant Bay rebellion (1865) 121
Morgan, Colonel 42, 43
Morgan, Henry 67
Morris, Sidney 156
Morris, Vincent 156
Moyne, Lord 135
Mt Misery (later Mount Liamuiga) 11, 60

Nags Head 55, 60, 74, 96
Napoleon Bonaparte, Emperor of France 107, 119
Napoleonic Wars 83, 93, 94, 109
Narrows 20, 149, 150
Nau, Jean-David (L'Olonnais) 70
Navigation Acts 38–39, 61, 86, 102
Needsmust estate 132
Nelson, Lord 100, 102, 109
Netherlands *see* Holland
Netherlands Antilles 136
Nevis 1, **4**, 41, 50, 140
    abduction of de Poincy's nephews 34
    animosity towards St Kitts 121, 128, 129, 159
    Assembly 106
    and the battle of Frigate Bay 97–98
    and Captain Kidd 66
    and the Church 104, 105
    British surrender (1782) 99–100
    coinage 87
    cotton production 133
    Council 98, 100, 103
    court system 123
    de Crynsens fails to take (1667) 47–49
    de Grasse a generous victor (1782) 98
    earthquake of 1690 3
    economic growth rate 158
    emigration to St Kitts 119
    English build-up in (1667) 45, 46
    English garrison 5
    English settle 32
    Evertson attacks 51
    fortifications 58–59, 98
    French attack of 1706 59–60, 74
    French attack fails (1705) 58
    French invasion repulsed (1666) 43
    funding not distributed 143
    hospital 129, 159
    housing 126
    hurricanes 6, 7
    indentured servants 20
    independence issue 141, 153–54
    Indians removed 18
    and the Labour Party 142, 147, 151
    militia 44, 58, 59, 98
    and the Portuguese Riots 125
    Presidency (1883) 123, 158
    prosperity 27, 28
    returned to Britain by the French 102
    seat of a new colony (1671) 51
    secession referendum fails (1998) 159
    settled (1628) 19, 32, 38
    Sharpe and 67
    slavery 36, 75, 79, 98
    Spanish invasion (1629) 19–21, 34
    and the Stamp Act 86
    sugar production 9, 26, 28, 80

supports the Anguilla Revolution 146
  US's proposed purchase of St Kitts and Nevis 126–27
Nevis, Battle of (1667) 47–49
Nevis Corporation Ordinance (1984) 158
Nevis Island Administration 158
Nevis Point (Nags Head) 96
Nevis Reformation Party (NRP) 151, 153, 154, 159
New Amsterdam 47
New France 49
New London, Connecticut 40
'New Spain' fleet 14
New York 47, 50, 66, 95
Newcastle, Duke of 78, 119, 120, 121
Newfoundland 101
Newspaper Surety Ordinance (1909) 132
nicknobby 16
Nieves 13
Nile, Battle of the 103
Nine Years' War 51–54, 55, 66, 83
Nisbet, Frances Woolward (later Nelson) 100, 102, 103
Nixon, Deputy Governor 116
Norman, Sir Henry 128
North America 1, 21, 27, 40, 74, 75, 80
  British fleet engaged in 95, 96
  molasses sold in 82
  purchase of foodstuffs from 91
  rebellion 79, 88–92
  success of Methodism 104
North Atlantic 137
North Carolina 88, 89
Nova Scotia 50
NRP *see* Nevis Reformation Party

Ocean Terrace 1
Ocean Terrace Inn 20
offshore financial sector 157–58, 159
Old Fort Point 54
Old Road 16, 31, 32, 43, 54
  floods 8
  hurricanes 6
  Portuguese Riots 124
Old Road Harbour 21, 68
Organization of Eastern Caribbean States (OECS) 153
Orinoco River 10
Osborne, Governor 44

Palmetto Point 6, 41, 49
PAM *see* People's Action Movement
Panama 14, 67
Panama Canal 9, 126
Panama City 67
Paris, Treaty of 102
Parke, Governor Daniel, II 61–62
Parquet, Captain du 20
Parry, Joseph 159
Pattison, Robert 105
Payne, Governor 80
Pelican Point, Nevis 19, 20
Penn, Admiral 30
Pentecost River 41

People's Action Movement (PAM) 12, 145, 151, 153, 154, 155, 156, 157
Peru 10
petroglyphs 18
Philip II, King of Spain 12
Philip IV, King of Spain 19
Philippines 119
Phillips, Sir Fred 147, 159
Piggott, Captain 62
Piguenit, James George 72–73, 113–14
Pinneys Beach, Nevis 43
piracy ix, 13, 14, 21, 30, 39, 51, 52, 53, 59, 60, 64–73, 143
Pitt, William, Earl of Chatham 95
Plains of Abraham, Quebec City 85
plant life 1–2
Pluton (ship) 97
Plymouth 58
Poincy, Governor Philippe de Lonvilliers de 2, 3, 4, 22, 34, 35
Point Palenque, Battle of 109
Ponchartrain, Count de 57
Ponds estate 132
Ponds Pasture, near Basseterre 73
Ponteen, Captain James 149, 150
population 9, 10–11, 24, 75, 110, 119, 134, 143
Porcupine (a slaver) 68–69
Port Royal, Jamaica 67
Portugal 13, 25
  joint British-Portuguese invasion of Cayenne (1809) 87
Portuguese Riots (1896) 123–25, 128
Powell, Captain 15
Prescott, General 99
privateers 64, 65, 68, 70, 74, 83, 84
Privy Council 107
prostitution 133
Puerto Rico 10, 33, 78, 119, 128, 136

Quamina, Antego 61
Quary, Robert 40
Queen Anne's War 6

Ramsay, Reverend James 92, 114–15
Rawlins, Governor Stedman 72
Red Cross 137
Redonda 12
religion, and slavery 103–55
remittances 154–5
Rhode Island 69
Rhodes, John 15
Richelieu, Cardinal 21, 35
Ringrose, Basil 67, 68
Riot Act 135
Robert, Admiral 139
Roberts, Bartholomew 68–69
Robertson, Reverend Robert 6
Rochambeau, General 95
Rochefort, Cesar 2, 3
Rodney, Admiral George Brydges 92, 96, 97, 101, 102
Roman Catholic Church/Roman Catholics 103, 114
Romney, Lord 76, 83, 84, 116

Romney Manor 116
Roosevelt, Mrs 131–32
Roosevelt, Theodore 131, 132
Rossey, Captain du 20, 21
Rothschild, Baron 116
Royal African Company 15, 86
Royal Air Force 131, 137
Royal Commission (Moyne Commission; 1939) 135, 152
Royal Commission (Norman Commission; 1897) 128
Royal Engineers 8
Royal Navy 39, 41, 49, 68, 74, 77, 84, 85, 92, 111, 114, 118, 156
royal poinciana (flame or flamboyant tree) 4
rum 26, 40, 76, 82, 83, 94, 122, 143
Russell, Governor Sir James 27, 43–44
Ruyter, Admiral Michiel de 4
Ryle, William 15
Ryswick, Treaty of (1697) 54

Saba 1, 36, 51, 146
St Barthélemy 33, 36, 52, 136
St Christopher Corps of Embodied Slaves, The 80, 99
St Christopher Yeomanry Cavalry 120
St Croix, Virgin Islands 14, 33, 34, 36
Saint Domingue (later Haiti) 66
St Eustatius (Statia) 1, 7, 8, 36, 39, 47, 51, 71–72, 91, 92, 93, 97, 104, 110
St George's church, Basseterre 29, 35, 117, 122
St John's Capisterre church, St Kitts 92
St John's church 115
St John's harbour, Antigua 44
St Johnston, Sir Reginald 134–35
St Kitts
  Anglo-French co-operation 33–34, 36, 50–51
  Anglo-French treaty (1627) 16, 31, 32, 41
  Anglo-French treaty (1686) 51
  animal life 2–3
  animosity towards Nevis 121, 128, 129, 159
  apprenticeship period 116
  Assembly 58, 60, 78, 80, 86–89, 91, 105, 113, 114, 117, 121, 123, 131, 151, 152, 154, 155
  British surrender (1782) 99–100
  central sugar factory 130, 132, 152
  cholera epidemic (1853 and 1854) 120
  and the Church 104, 105
  coinage 86–8
  cotton production 133
  Council 61, 89, 118, 120, 121, 122, 125, 126
  court system 123
  Cromwell gathers volunteers to fight Spain 29–30
  decline in the sugar industry 84, 103, 111, 112–13, 123, 125–26, 134, 136
  Defence Force 135, 145, 146
  elections 114
  English quarter 3, 16, 29, 32, 36, 41, 50, 51, 54, 55, 59, 103
  European settlement 13–18
  Evertson attacks 51
  failed English attempt to retake (1667) 49–50
  Federal Government 128–29
  first French settlement in the Caribbean 32
  former French estates 61–63
  former seat of the French Caribbean Empire 4
  fortifications 58, 59, 77, 78, 86, 93, 99
  in French hands 44, 49, 51–52
  French quarter 3, 16, 22, 29, 32, 34, 36, 42, 54, 55–56, 60, 62, 103
  geology 1
  government 113–14, 120–21, 142–43
  housing 126
  independence 153
  Indians 10–12
  Legislative Council 128–33
  mass hanging of pirates 71–73
  militia 51, 75, 78, 79, 99, 116, 120
  natural disasters 3–8
  plant life 1–2
  Presidency (1883) 123, 158
  prosperity 28, 33, 50, 63, 86, 123
  rebellion (1637) 22
  returned to Britain by the French 102
  riots of 1936 134–35
  runaway slaves and Assembly Act 60
  silver mine 3, 29, 31, 32
  slavery 21–22, 27–28, 36, 56, 59, 74, 93
  the Spanish attack (1629) 1, 19–21, 32, 33
  and the Stamp Act 86
  sugar production 8–9, 24–31, 63, 130
  sugar yield 110
  under French control (1666) 43
  US's proposed purchase of St Kitts and Nevis 126–27
St Kitts Act (1993) 158
St Kitts Benevolent Society 132
St Kitts Sugar Producers Association 128
St Lucia 6, 33, 36, 85, 137
St Martin 20, 21, 33, 36, 52, 57, 66, 67, 143
St Mary's church, Cayon 112
St Michel, Maurice de 16
St Pierre, Martinique 6–7, 33, 57
St Thomas, Virgin Islands 10, 36, 57, 65, 138
St Thomas's church, Middle Island 59
St Vincent 152
Saint-Laurent, Governor Charles de 5, 41, 42, 49
The Saintes 33
Saintes, Battle of the 101–2, 103
Sales, Governor de 35, 41, 42
Salisbury, HMS 145
Salnave, Governor de 51
salt pans 32, 33, 34
San Cristóbal 13
San Jorge 13
San Juan harbour, Puerto Rico 136
San Martín 13
San Rosario (a galleon) 67
Sandy Point 6, 34, 41, 93, 96, 97, 104
  Battle of 42–43
  De Gennes' men 57
Sandy Point Harbour 68
Santa Maria (ship) 66
Santo Domingo 30, 36, 54
Saratoga, Battle of (1778) 91
Schaw, Janet 88, 89, 90

Schneller, G.C. 8
Scottish agriculture 88
Sebastian, J. Matthew 140
Second Anglo-Dutch War (1665–67) 5, 37, 41–51
Senegalese slaves 21, 22
Servants' Acts 75
'Setting and Regulating the Trial of Criminal Slaves' 113
Seven Years' War 39, 84–85, 91
Sharpe, Captain Bartholomew 53, 67–68, 143
Shelburne, Lord 100
Shickering, Sergeant Alfred T. 138
Shirley, General 98
Shorty's Restaurant 138
Siboney Indians 10
Sierra Leone 94
silver mines **3**, 29, 31, 32, 59
Simmonds, Dr Kennedy A. **12**, **14**, 151, 153, 155
Skeete, Winston 150
Skerrit, George 105
slavery
    abolished in the British Empire 15
    abolition of 87, 107, 110, 114–17, 119
    Act for Better Government of Negroes (1722) 60–61
    African 15, 21–22, 26, 36, 39, 110
    apprenticeship period 116
    and Assembly Act 60
    and barter system 86–87
    Battle of Fig Tree 34
    deaths 75–76
    Indians 11, 12, 18, 22
    labour 93, 99, 105, 111
    in Mexican silver mines 59
    and the militia 80
    pirates 64–65
    profits from the slave trade 39, 127
    prosecution of mistreaters 106–7
    punishment of slaves 94, 106
    recruitment for military service 94
    religion and 103–5
    resistance of Nevis slaves 59–60
    Roberts' treatment of slaves 68–69
    Second Anglo-Dutch War 41, 42
    slave corps 80
    slaves' produce 88–89
    and sugar production ix, 27, 28, 89
    troops 54, 59
    uprisings 75, 79
    valuing of slaves 110
smuggling 39, 40, 81, 82, 110
Society of Adventurers 15
South America 1, 10, 53, 57, 65, 119, 157
Southey, Captain Thomas: *Chronological History of the West Indies* ix
Southwell, C. A. Paul **13**, **14**, 146, 153
Spain
    Anglo-French treaty against (1627) 16, 31
    Armadas against England fail (1588–1604) 14
    brutal treatment of Indians 11, 14
    claims all of the Americas except Brazil 13
    conquest of the Caribbean 10
    exploration of St Kitts 14

Florida returned to 102
Inquisition 25
loss of the treasure fleet (1628) 19
massacre of French in Santo Domingo 54
and piracy 65
recognizes Caribbean colonies of other European countries 51
Santo Domingo fiasco 30
Spanish invasion (1629) **1**, 19–21, 32, 33
supports the American Revolution 91
War of Jenkins's Ear 78
see also War of the Spanish Succession
Spanish Empire 14, 19, 21, 119
Spanish Navy 71
Spanish Town, Jamaica 38
Spanish-American War (1898) 119, 126
Special Branch of the Police Force 156
Springfield Cemetery, Cayon Street, Basseterre 7
squeaking lizards 2
Stamp Act (1765) 86
Stapleton, Colonel (later Sir) William 49–50
Stapleton, Sir William, the younger 56, 65
Statia *see* St Eustatius
Statia Channel 104
steam engines 118
Strode, Wadham 106
sugar
    absentee ownership 81, 82, 84
    crystallizing 25, 26, 118
    decline of King Sugar 80–82
    duty on 36
    export **6**
    first mention of sugar being grown in the Caribbean (1643) ix
    importance to St Kitts ix, 9
    mills 6, 25, 26, 118
    monopoly 40, 81, 111, 117
    nationalization of the industry 152
    Nevis sugar works destroyed 60
    plantations 2, 8–9, 63, 81, 99, 105–6, 117, 126, 140, 152
    poor sales 122
    Portuguese Riots 123–5
    prices 39, 40, 81, 82, 85, 87, 103, 111, 112, 117, 119, 130, 133, 134, 137, 152
    production 9, 24–31, 40, 63, 74, 80–82, 88, 89, 91, 116–19, 123, 128, 130, 152
    profits ix, 8, 39, 63, 74, 81, 91, 127
    St Kitts' central sugar factory 130, 132, 152
    slavery ix, 27, 28
    and tea 40, 80–81
    wealth 26–27
sugar beet 109–10, 123, 125, 128, 133
sugar cane 1, 26, 29, 80, 83, 86, 89, 98, 109–10, 117, 143, 152
    holing 118
    and Portuguese Riots 124
Sugar Duties Act (1846) 119
Sugar Estate Lands Acquisition Act (1975) 151
Summersal, Mr 104
Surinam 47, 136
    English retake 49
    and the Treaty of Breda 50
Swallow, HMS 69

Tartar, HMS 125
Tasted, William 15
tea 40, 80–81
Tegremond, Chief 15, 17–18
Telford, Joseph 105
Terra Firma fleet 14
Third Anglo-Dutch War (1672–4) 51
Thoisy, Noel de Patrocles de 34
Thomas, Governor 91
Thomson, Charles 113
Thornhill, Sir Timothy 52, 53
Tianos *see* Arawak Indians
Timothy's Beach 53
tobacco 4, 8, 15, 24, 25, 26, 29, 39, 40, 82, 84
Tobago 37
Toledo, Don Fadrique de **1**
  invasion of St Kitts and Nevis 19–21
Tortola, Virgin Islands 71
Tortuga 21, 36
tourism 154, 157
trade 21, 22, 23, 80
  and the American Revolution 91
  and banking 113
  Dutch traders 21, 26, 29, 35, 37, 38
  early trade in St Kitts and Nevis 21
  free trade replaces mercantilism 119
  French companies 21, 22–23, 29, 35, 36
  and piracy 74
Trades and Labour Union 139
Trafalgar, Battle of 103, 109
trees 1, 2
Trinidad 1, 138
  and Federation of the West Indies 142
La Trompeuse (pirate ship) 65
Truxtun, Captain Thomas 108
Tyson, John 83

Union Messenger newspaper 132
United Brethren Church *see* Moravian Church
United Nations 143
  General Assembly 148
  Special Committee on Colonialism 147
United States
  Canadian provinces and states 158
  coastguards 155
  Constitution 60
  Department of State 125, 126
  and drug trade 65
  emerging world power 108
  Panama Canal construction 126
  proposed purchase of St Kitts and Nevis 126–27
  and slavery 28
  sugar sales to 122
  trade 102
  Treaty of Paris 102
  at war with Britain (1812) 111
  in World War II 138, 139
  see also America
United States Meteorological Bureau 7
United States Navy **9**, 107–8, 126
Utrecht, Treaty of (1713) 60

La Vallée estate 132
Vallett, Deputy Governor William 19–20

Venables, General 30
Venezuela 10, 136, 155
Vera Cruz, Mexico 14, 59
Vichy French Government 137, 138–39
Victor (a frigate) 71, 72
Victoria, Queen 126
Ville de Paris (ship) 96, 97, 98, 101
Virgin Islands 57, 65, 126, 127, 145
Virginia 49, 61
Virginia Capes, Battle of the 95
Volery, Captain 5
Vought Kingfisher aircraft 138, **10**

Wagner Palace Car Company 131
Walley, John 106–107
Walsh, Joan 156
War of Jenkins's Ear 78, 91
War of the Spanish Succession 32, 54, 55–60, 68, 74
Ware, Mr 15
Warner, 'Indian' 17
Warner, Philip 17
Warner, Sir Thomas 21, 22, 82
  and the Anglo-French treaty (1627) 32
  Carib mistress and son 17
  division of St Kitts (1627) 16
  and King James' Patent 14
  Leeward Islands under his control 38
  Merwars Hope 14–15
  settles St Kitts (1623) 15
  and the Spanish attack (1629) 20
Warrener, William 105
Washington, General George 95
Washington DC 111
Watts, Governor William 41, 42–43
Weaver, Mr 15
Webster, Ronald 143–8
Wellington, Arthur Wellesley, 1st Duke of 107, 122
West Farm Estates 152
West India and Panama Telegraph Company 125
West India Regiment 130, 131
West Indies Federation 123, 159, 160
West Indies Regiments 94
Wigley, F. S. 125
William III, King 66
William IV, King (as Prince William Henry) 103
Williams, Governor 53
Willoughby, Francis, Lord 5, 43, 44, 45, 49
Willoughby, Henry 49, 50
Willoughby, William, Lord 49, 50
Willoughby family 38
Wilmington, North Carolina 88
Winchester, HMS 6, 45, 46–47
windmills 6, 25, 26, 118
Windward Islands 3
Wingfield Manor 5, 16, 24, 76, 82–84
Withred, Mr 40
Wolfe, General 85
Wood, Reverend Enoch 72
Workers League 141, 142
World War I (1914–18) 128, 130–31, 137
World War II (1939–45) 136–9, 140

Yorktown, Virginia 95